P9-CCO-747

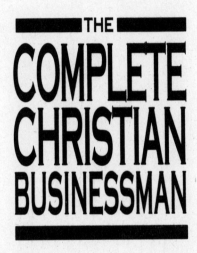

THE
COMPLETE
CHRISTIAN
BUSINESSMAN

THE
COMPLETE CHRISTIAN BUSINESSMAN

ROBERT J. TAMASY
General Editor

*Advice from
Charles Colson,
Larry Burkett, Ron Blue,
Ted DeMoss, Doug Sherman,
Pat Williams, and Other
Leading Experts*

Wolgemuth & Hyatt, Publishers, Inc.
Brentwood, Tennessee

The mission of Wolgemuth & Hyatt, Publishers, Inc. is to publish and distribute books that lead individuals toward:

- A personal faith in the one true God: Father, Son, and Holy Spirit;

- A lifestyle of practical discipleship; and

- A worldview that is consistent with the historic, Christian faith.

Moreover, the Company endeavors to accomplish this mission at a reasonable profit and in a manner which glorifies God and serves His Kingdom.

© 1991 by the Christian Business Men's Committee of USA. All rights reserved.
Published February 1991. First Edition.
Printed in the United States of America.
97 96 95 94 93 92 91   8 7 6 5 4 3 2 1

No part of this publication may be reproduced, stored in a retrieval system, or transmitted in any form by any means, electronic, mechanical, photocopy, recording, or otherwise, without the prior written permission of the publisher, except for brief quotations in critical reviews or articles.

Unless otherwise noted, all Scripture quotations are from the Holy Bible, New International Version. © 1973, 1978, 1984 International Bible Society. Used by permission of Zondervan Bible Publishers.

Wolgemuth & Hyatt, Publishers, Inc.
1749 Mallory Lane, Suite 110
Brentwood, Tennessee 37027

Library of Congress Cataloging-in-Publication Data

Tamasy, Robert.
    The complete Christian businessman / Robert J. Tamasy.
        p. cm.
    ISBN 1-56121-048-X
    1. Business—Religious aspects—Christianity. 2. Business ethics.
I. Title.
HF5388.T36 1991
    650—dc20
                                                    90-24026
                                                    CIP

Dedicated
To the Many Thousands
Of Business and Professional Men
Around the World Who Strive Daily
To Be Faithful Witnesses to Jesus Christ,
Through Their Actions
As Well As Their Words.

CONTENTS

Part Four: His Financial World

INTRODUCTION

T he chasm between the church sanctuary and the corporate board-
     room sometimes appears wider than the Grand Canyon. Platitudes
expressed from the pulpit on Sunday mornings seem of little practical
value for decisions made in the office on Monday. Sermons concerning
"the sweet by and by" fail to transfer to the "nasty now and now" of the
marketplace pressure cooker.

Today, the average Christian professional or businessman has concluded that while his faith is certainly worth having, he dares not put it
to use on the job. Spiritual ideals don't seem to mesh with corporate
realities.

Too often, there is little observable difference between the way the
typical Christian businessman and his non-Christian counterpart transact
business, except perhaps their vocabulary and Sunday activities. In some
cases, declaring oneself to be a Christian in business can become a disadvantage because of "brothers in Christ" who have demonstrated a distinct lack of integrity or have used the term "Christian" merely to capi-
talize on business opportunities.

Does this dismal view of the relationship between business and
Christian convictions have to be? Amid the stresses and strains of today's
ever-changing business environment, is it even possible to inject Biblical
principles into the secular marketplace in a way that is both meaningful
and relevant? The answer, I am convinced, is an unequivocal and re-
sounding *Yes!* This book is intended to explain why — and how.

Most books seeking to relate the Bible and business fail to bridge
the gap from theory to everyday, practical realities. Often they are written by men with impressive credentials in Biblical scholarship who have

spent little time—if any—in the "real world" of the marketplace in the last decade of the twentieth century. This is what makes *The Complete Christian Businessman* different: Most of its authors are war-scarred veterans of the contemporary battleground we call the business world. They have put the Word of God to the test in corporate boardrooms and private offices and have found it sufficient for every need.

Over the past several years, *CONTACT* magazine, published by the Christian Business Men's Committee (CBMC) of USA, has been dedicated to demonstrating how the timeless guidelines of the Bible can and do apply to the secularized, seemingly godless American business environment. Each edition of the magazine has focused on a specific theme—issues and concerns that all business and professional men must face regardless of their spiritual convictions.

Topics have included ethics, stress, goal-setting, the purpose of work, sexual temptation, partnerships, personal financial management, career changes, and even retirement. Some of the articles and interviews have featured "household names"; some are by noted Christian leaders such as financial planners Larry Burkett and Ronald Blue; others spotlighted authors/speakers Joni Eareckson Tada, Gary Smalley, Lois Mowday, and Denis Waitley; some by corporate executives such as Carl H. Lindner III and C. William Pollard. Other articles have been written by "ordinary businessmen," individuals who are not nationally known but understand very well the challenges of seeking to serve and represent Jesus Christ on the job.

The response to these collections of articles in *CONTACT* has surpassed our hopes and expectations. We have received many comments from readers telling us how the stories have ministered in their lives, assisting them in resolving pressing concerns or arriving at critical decisions. For that reason, the time has come to compile this book, an anthology of sorts from the pages of *CONTACT*. Some of the articles were published during the past year, while others appeared a few years ago, but each has an enduring quality and demonstrates that the relevance of the Bible to business remains as great today as when God inspired men to pen His truths thousands of years ago.

In the newspaper business, both as an editor and a publisher, I encountered many struggles and frustrations in trying to put my faith into practice after I became a Christian in 1978. Since joining the staff of

CBMC in 1981, I have talked with hundreds of business and professional men, discussing their faith and how it relates to their personal lives. Almost to a man, they expressed a deep, heartfelt desire to conduct their personal and business lives in a way that makes a difference for eternity, yet they conceded there is often a considerable gap between their "want-to" and the "how-to."

I recall interviewing one prominent corporate executive whose business was widely recognized throughout his community as a "Christian company." I asked him how his firm would be distinguished from that of an equally prestigious, secular-based competitor. The businessman pointed to a Bible lying atop his desk and a plaque featuring a Scripture verse that hung on the wall behind him and stated that once a year, around the Christmas season, he mailed letters to all his clients which contained a spiritual message. But I could see that my question had unsettled him. I could almost hear him asking himself, "How *is* our company different from our ethical, but unbelieving counterparts?"

The company was, in fact, being run according to sound Biblical principles, but it had been a long time since its president had taken "inventory" to see if the firm could pass Scriptural scrutiny. Unintentionally, my question had reminded him that just *being* a Christian does not necessarily guarantee conducting business in a truly Christ-like manner.

While this book does not promise to teach how to be an effective Christian businessman in three easy lessons (or five, or even ten) — because in today's complex society there is no such simple formula — you will find each concise chapter instructive. Some of them suggest specific ideas for implementation, while others communicate the insights a businessman has learned while working through a particular issue in his life.

If you want some procedures on how to manage your time better or how to become accountable to another committed Christian, you will read about them here. If you need assurance that a Christian can run a business ethically without winding up in bankruptcy court, you will receive it in these pages. If you are a Christian struggling to overcome a "besetting sin," such as sexual lust or chemical abuse, the articles will offer help. And if you feel all alone, like you are the only Christian in business and that you are continually fighting a losing battle, you will gain an abundance of encouragement and support.

Although the majority of this book's content relates directly to needs and problems in the world of work, we have also included sections on family relationships and personal financial management, recognizing that today's Christian businessman is multi-dimensional. How effectively he relates his faith to his profession will substantially affect his life as a husband, father, friend, and neighbor.

This book can be read in several ways. It can be read cover to cover, absorbing a wealth of accumulated experience and understanding on more than twenty different topics. If you have a particular area of interest, such as principles for establishing a business partnership that will honor God, you can turn directly to that section. Or you may want to read selected articles at first and then keep *The Complete Christian Businessman* on hand for ready reference whenever you need advice in a particular area—or simply need some inspiration to carry you through the day.

If you are like most business people, you're extremely busy, usually facing more demands than you can find time in which to respond. For that reason, the chapters throughout this book are brief by design. You can read *The Complete Christian Businessman* by setting aside only a few minutes a day, or you can commit an extended amount of time to it whenever an opportunity permits. Regardless of how you read this book, I'm certain that you will find the articles thought-provoking and informative, the interviews intriguing, and the personal experience accounts uplifting and motivating.

ROBERT J. TAMASY
Chattanooga, Tennessee
November, 1990

PART ONE

HIS PROFESSIONAL WORLD

Whatever you do, work at it with all your heart, as
working for the Lord, not for men.

Colossians 3:23

1

WHAT DO YOU DO
FOR A LIVING?

Robert J. Tamasy

R ecently a friend of mind, a financial planner, commented, "I'd
give anything to be able to go full-time for the Lord." I thought
about his statement for a moment and then replied, "What makes you
think you haven't already done that?"

I think many of us labor under a serious misconception: that only
those things performed within the context of a church or Christian organization are "Christian service." Everything else is perceived as activity
designed primarily to pay the bills and fill in the time from one church
service to the next.

It is true that God may call us to *vocational* Christian service, be it
the pulpit ministry, missionary work or perhaps full-time positions with
parachurch organizations like CBMC (Christian Business Men's Committee). I am one of these, at least for the present. But it is wrong to
believe that full-time Christian service means one's salary comes from
an institution whose purpose is explicitly to further the gospel. There is
no such thing as a part-time Christian, and we all are called to serve the
Lord, so we are *all* in full-time Christian service! The only difference is
where the paycheck comes from.

I wish I had understood this years ago. Like many people, although
my Christian convictions influenced how I carried out my responsibili-

ties as a newspaper editor, I never recognized my job as a platform for personal ministry. "Church is church, and work is work, and never the twain shall meet" summarized my attitude at that time. In retrospect, I can remember numerous opportunities that were overlooked, occasions when I could have spoken easily and candidly about Christ with non-Christians who had deep needs in their lives.

Because I failed to see my work as the place where God had put me to serve Him, I rarely took such initiative. When I resigned from the newspaper to move to Chattanooga and CBMC, I did briefly express my faith in an article. At a bank that day, an officer I had worked with on several occasions commented, "I appreciated your article. I knew there was something different about you." Although my life may have reflected my faith, I had never taken the time to articulate what I believed.

In his excellent little book, *Secular Work Is Full-Time Service*, Larry Peabody writes, "The New Testament draws no sacred/secular lines between Christians in *full-time service* and those in other types of work. In fact, the Bible does not contain the phrase 'full-time Christian service.' It teaches that all Christians should serve God full-time, even though our differing vocations display such service in a variety of forms. . . . There is a difference in function between gospel work and ordinary work, but no difference in acceptability before God."

Peabody traces the life of Daniel in the Old Testament as an example, pointing out that although Daniel never attended seminary, pastored a church, or performed a Christian music concert, he had a greater impact for God than any other person of his time. The same is true of Joseph, who triumphed over a series of trials to become Pharoah's chief cabinet member and the intermediary for the people of Israel.

I used to view pastors with awe, as if they had stepped down from the right hand of God. But our reverence — and that exalted position — belong exclusively to our Lord. Our church leaders have a special calling and are uniquely gifted to carry out their responsibilities. But Christians who labor faithfully as CPAs or secretaries, CEOs or salesmen, attorneys or artists, doctors or ditch diggers, engineers or educators, even journalists, have equally special callings. They, too, are divinely equipped to minister in the unique environments where God has placed them.

As Walter A. Henrichsen and William N. Garrison express in their book, *Layman Look Up! God Has a Plan For Your Life*, the first Reformation made the Scriptures available to the layman. A second "Reformation" is occurring today, they claim, in which the *ministry* is getting into the hands of the laity as well. When Jesus chose His disciples, He did not select the cream of the crop among the Pharisees and Saduccees; He called men who would never have been mistaken for religious leaders.

We appreciate the vital role of the clergy, who are called to shepherd us and equip us as saints. But today, when events have brought Christianity under closer scrutiny than ever before, we need Christians in the workplace who understand that they, too, are in full-time Christian service, representing Jesus Christ to groups of people who may never consider approaching a "paid professional" to find answers to their deepest spiritual yearnings.

"For we are God's fellow workers; you are God's field, God's building" (1 Corinthians 3:9).

Whatever you do, work at it with all your heart, as working for the Lord, not for men.

Colossians 3:23

2

DO YOU LIKE YOUR JOB?

Gordon Adams

The alarm sounds relentlessly at 5:30, just as it does every morning, day after day and week after week. Once again, you drag yourself out of bed to face yourself in the mirror and ask the question that always occurs on days when you least feel like going to work: "Why do I do this anyway? What's the purpose of choking myself with this tie and going back to the marketplace 'arena' to get beat up again today? I'd much rather spend my time in *real* Christian work!"

Strangely, men in the marketplace, once converted to personal faith in Jesus Christ, sometimes begin to question their reason for being in business. They contemplate "going into full-time Christian service" as their new faith brings excitement and fulfillment to their lives. Work loses its luster and challenge compared to studying God's Word, meeting with men, and sharing their faith with others. The job atrophies into a meaningless activity endured simply for the sake of earning a living, while real importance is derived from personal ministry to others. A dichotomy is thus created: a secular/sacred distinction between types of work. Eight to five, Monday through Friday, becomes "secular work," while "sacred work" is the work performed by missionaries, pastors, and other vocational Christian workers.

This sacred/secular view of work, however, is not Biblical. The Bible never distinguishes between work performed by "apostles, prophets, evangelists and pastor/teachers" (Ephesians 4:11) and "ordinary fol-

11

lowers" of Jesus Christ who are engaged in other vocational pursuits. In fact, the hierarchy of clergy/laity is never mentioned in the New Testament. Men are urged in the Bible to work and work hard (Colossians 3:23) but are never told that so-called "sacred work" is of more value than "secular work." These are man-made distinctions.

When Jesus Christ gave us the Great Commission to "go and make disciples" (Matthew 28:18–20), He was calling *all* Christians into "full-time, *vocational* Christian service." For one thing, where would the financial support of the ministry come from? If this line of reasoning is pursued, men in the marketplace, once converted, would immediately exchange their "secular" careers for "sacred" ones and begin to perform "holy work" — such as leading Bible studies, evangelizing, and meeting with people to establish them in their faith. Laymen seem to think vocational Christian workers spend every waking moment in direct ministry activities, failing to realize how many administrative and support tasks accompany such ministry.

While God does set apart specially gifted men to spend their time vocationally in ministry, their work is never elevated to a position of more importance than other types of work. The New Testament indicates *all have been called to the ministry*, while the men mentioned in Ephesians 4:11–12 have been given the additional task of *preparing others for this universal work of ministry*. God's plan has always been for the layman to function as the central figure in accomplishing the ministry. While Luther's Great Reformation placed the Bible in the hands of believers, responsibility for the ministry has never been equally entrusted to laymen, largely due to a misunderstanding of precisely whose job the ministry really is!

So if all are called to the ministry, how does work fit into that call? Work is our platform for ministry — our pulpit for a marketplace ministry corresponding to the pulpit occupied by the pastor of a local congregation.

There are only two reasons given in the Bible for going to work:

- It is commanded by God.
- It is where the believer is placed to represent Jesus Christ.

Command to Work

Work existed before the entrance of sin into the world. After the creation of Adam, God put him in the garden and said to him, " . . . till it and keep it" (Genesis 2:15, RSV). Work is an expression of God's grace, not His wrath. Solomon, the wisest man in history, said, "Behold, what I have seen to be good and to be fitting is to eat and drink and find enjoyment in all the toil with which one toils under the sun . . . " (Ecclesiastes 5:18, RSV). Work, then, can be pleasurable.

But work can also be frustrating! In a preceding chapter of Ecclesiastes, Solomon states, "I hated all my toil in which I had toiled under the sun, seeing that I must leave it to the man who will come after me" (Ecclesiastes 2:18, RSV). After sin entered the world with the Fall of Adam in Genesis 2, God pronounced this curse on mankind: " . . . cursed is the ground because of you; in toil you shall eat of it all the days of your life" (Genesis 3:17, RSV). Now, work was no longer pleasant; it became burdensome and tiring.

In spite of the tension created by these seemingly conflicting views of labor, to work and work hard is a command of God, one which remains in effect today. Paul reaffirms God's declaration in 2 Thessalonians 3:10, "If any one will not work, let him not eat. . . ."

Opportunity for Ministry

In the Sermon on the Mount (Matthew 5–7), Jesus spoke these familiar words, "You are the salt of the earth . . . " (5:13); and "You are the light of the world . . . " (5:14). He called on believers to "let their light so shine before men" that unbelievers would see the quality of life they possess and attribute that distinctive to God the Father. The question arises, "Where is this light and salt to function?" The answer, quite obviously, is *in the world,* or *the marketplace.* People in the world who are not yet members of the family of God need to be "seasoned" with the gospel and its transforming power; they need to be "illuminated" by the truth of the gospel and its ability to set them free from bondage to sin.

The marketplace — the world — is where people in need of Christ can be found. Your vocation, when viewed this way, becomes the arena in which to function as an ambassador for Christ (2 Corinthians 5:20). Secular work *is* "full-time service." The man or woman of God who faithfully cultivates this mindset of ministry is a "full-time minister," and he is just as "called to the ministry" as the vocational Christian worker. In fact, if you do not feel as called to the ministry in the context of your job as a professional Christian worker feels called to his job, you should seriously consider changing careers.

A businessman does not need to attend seminary or Bible College to prepare for the ministry. Since God has called all of us to the ministry, the issue revolves simply around spiritual gifting and where God places us in His Body to function. That is, God calls a few to vocational Christian work, based on their special "equipping gifts" enumerated in Ephesians 4. But the remainder are as "called" to the work of evangelism and discipling as these gifted men. God simply places this second group in a different context—on the front lines in the marketplace—and allows them the inexpressible privilege of participating with Him in the work He is doing in the world today. Jesus even "ordained" these laymen to their task in John's gospel, when He said, "Ye have not chosen me, but I have chosen you, and ordained you, that ye should go and bring forth fruit" (John 15:16, KJV).

In over twenty years of vocational Christian work, I have concluded the most effective expressions of the ministry have been carried out not by professionals but by laymen—business and professional men and women who clearly see their call to the ministry and the integral part their vocational platform plays in carrying out that ministry! But what is the key to possessing this proper perspective on life?

Focus of Life

A foreign missionary, dutifully performing "spiritual" work, may do so with an improper focus of life. On the other hand, a person in business or "secular" work may conduct his affairs in the world with a totally different focus. This focus is essential for comprehending work as a platform for fulfilling the Great Commission. Paul, in 2 Corinthians, explains, " . . . for the things which are seen are *temporal*; but the things which are not seen are *eternal*" (4:18, KJV). Either your focus in life is on the eternal, or it is on the temporal; there is no middle ground. Secular work is sacred only when the focus of your life is on the eternal. Therefore, a missionary could have a temporal focus (such as becoming director of the mission), while a businessman can have an eternal focus (working as unto the Lord while seeking opportunities to share his faith). Paul illustrates this temporal/eternal dichotomy in 1 Corinthians:

> For no one can lay any foundation other than the one already laid, which is Jesus Christ. If any man builds on this foundation using gold, silver, costly stones, wood, hay or straw, his work will be shown for what it is, because the Day will bring it to light. (3:11–13)

Here, the apostle describes building materials of two classes: inflammable and flammable, or those which will survive the test of fire and those which will not. We could call this "eternal building materials vs. temporal building materials". On the job, you may either possess an eternal focus of life or a temporal one. Your focus will exhibit itself primarily in your mindset or attitude toward work. Why are you there? To chase dollars and succeed in the same fashion as your unbelieving colleagues, or to work in a manner pleasing to God, trusting Him for opportunities to minister to others? Do you minister to people by meeting their needs, or do you manipulate them to your own ends by using them as a source of financial gain?

Jesus said you are to "seek first his kingdom and his righteousness, and all these things will be given to you . . . " (Matthew 6:23). The workplace is the arena for extending God's Kingdom, but only if it is viewed as a pulpit — as a platform from which to launch your ministry as an ambassador, representing the interests of a sovereign in a foreign land. God plans to populate the earth with His own people, but He has chosen to execute this plan by person-to-person communication of the gospel. By sending out emissaries like you and me, armed with a life-transforming message, God intends to fill the earth with His glory (Ezekiel 43:2).

The world is filled with people needing the Good News of Jesus Christ. God has called all of His children to be witnesses (Acts 1:8), and there is to be no distinction between "professionals" and "laity" in the proclamation of the gospel. The only difference between a vocational Christian worker and a marketplace minister of the gospel is the manner in which God funds their ministries. While the Lord may choose to fund a businessman to do the ministry primarily through his job, He funds the vocational minister primarily through the gifts of His people.

So, when you feel like quitting your job to go into the ministry, remember: *you are already in the ministry!* Change your mind about your job today. Begin to view work with an eternal perspective; you are where people in need of Christ are. You are a key player in God's program — after all, you're a layman!

Whatever you do, work at it with all your heart, as working for the Lord, not for men.

Colossians 3:23

3

RIDING THE WAVES
(Four ways being a Christian makes a difference amid corporate turbulence)

Ken Lutters

S urviving in business today takes more than talent and intelligence. It also demands an ability to "ride the waves." During my more than twenty years with the Sun Company, Inc., a number of waves have swept the oil industry: from diversification to simplification; decentralization to centralization; pure research to applied research; and from self-sufficiency to contracting for as many outside services as possible.

The one constant in modern-day business is change. Once men could "sail" through business; today, the sensation is more like riding the rapids, and the stresses that result are incredible. I have discovered that a strong faith in God provides a resource and perspective that allows me not just to "hang on" but actually to chart a course through the turbulence. As I see it, being a Christian makes at least four major differences in a corporate business environment.

The first difference is that *our goal is to please God, not men.* As it says in Colossians 3:23–24, whatever we do, we are to "work at it with all your heart, as working for the Lord, not for men. . . . It is the Lord Christ you are serving."

In business, the traditional carrot and stick approach to motivation remains popular. Promotions, salaries, bonuses, even physical surroundings (such as a corner office with a view) are geared toward manipulating employees and enhancing productivity. But a person who really believes the Bible will not base his performance on these motivators. Bonuses and promotions are welcomed, but we should work as hard as possible—striving to please God—whether the rewards come or not.

A second difference is one of *true consistency*. Often, business and professional men tend to be chameleons who change their colors depending on the surroundings. Situational ethics and loyalties are the norm as they do whatever they feel is required to protect their best interests.

While such people are controlled by external circumstances, the Christian is internally directed by his understanding of Biblical standards. Jobs and bosses may change, but our behavior can remain the same because our frame of reference is unchanged. The two motivations of "what's in it for me?" versus "what does God expect of me?" produce very different responses in the business environment.

The third difference is *peace of mind* in the midst of turmoil. In 1984, my management consulting department at Sun was eliminated in favor of outside consultants. There is a lot of anxiety at such times; everyone is updating their resumes and inquiring about jobs with other companies.

In spite of the uncertainty, I experienced a high degree of peace and confidence as I faced the future. The Bible teaches that God is in control of *all* things and He will not forsake us at times of need. So I knew that whether I got another job at Sun or went to another company, it would be all right. As it turned out, I was able to stay, although my new position was very different from the consulting work I had been doing for sixteen years.

Fear is a strong motivator—or inhibitor—in business, whether it be the fear of lost security, failure, or even death. As a child, I struggled with a severe stuttering problem. God gave me many opportunities to overcome a fear of speaking to people, whether it was to groups or individuals, and my faith gives me confidence to confront other fears as well.

The fourth difference is *balanced priorities*. The Bible teaches that our priorities should be God, family, and then work. If my relationships with God, my wife, and children are in harmony, I will be a more productive worker, not distracted by family problems.

I've known many people who sold out to the corporation, sacrificing their families to advance their careers. Repeatedly, the result has been divorce and broken homes. Three or four years later, these hard-working corporate types often are laid off for reasons beyond their control. Careers terminated, their private lives are also shattered.

Years ago I decided not to take that course. Even if success in business were worth it — and it's not — there are no guarantees that hard work and dedication will bring the vocational goals we seek.

It's sad to see Christians who ignore the high standards God has set for us. Their attitude seems to be that Christianity works well at church, but it must be put aside at work. Business, they say, is dog-eat-dog, hard-nosed, and too competitive for Biblical ideals.

But Christian principles do work on the job. For instance, "do unto others as you would have them do unto you" translates very well to a customer-oriented approach to service. Just the wisdom of the Book of Proverbs, if applied consistently, offers tremendous guidelines for business success.

A Christian who practices his faith in business? It's almost an unfair advantage.

Whatever you do, work at it with all your heart, as working for the Lord, not for men.

Colossians 3:23

_____ *4*

DOES YOUR WORK MATTER TO GOD?

Doug Sherman and William Hendricks

So often I meet people who tell me their employment is "just a job." They might as well say that their life is "just a life."

I realize that not every job is thrilling or spectacular. Nor must every job be particularly fulfilling. But what I hear these people saying is that their work is boring and insignificant.

This is tragic because God doesn't view your work as insignificant. He regards your job, and you, with great dignity and value. So should you!

Obviously, employers could do far more to remove some of the boredom of many tasks and to convey meaning and worth to their employees. But as a Christian you need to sign in at work as God's coworker and as an employee of Christ.

A business model. One way to gain this perspective is to ask: As God's coworker, how does my work serve other people and their needs?

Let me suggest a model to illustrate this perspective on work. Imagine a triangle with "customer" at the apex, "employees" at one point of the base, and "employer" at the other point.

These are the three human roles involved in most work situations in our culture. And God desires that the needs of *each* should be met. The customer obviously has needs that you and your business are there to serve.

But if you are an employer, you also have a responsibility to serve the needs of your employees. They need adequate, appropriate compensation. But they also need proper, fair management; equitable employment policies; a reasonably safe work environment; appropriate tools, supplies, and equipment; regard for their lives outside of work, especially their families; and much more.

If you are an employee, you have a responsibility to serve the needs of your fellow employees and your employer. Your coworkers need you to do your part with excellence, with a spirit of cooperation, with honesty, and so forth. Likewise, your employer needs a dependable worker who is conscientious, puts forth his best effort, is honest, and gives value in exchange for his wages.

Using the model. Let's use this model in a real-life situation. Suppose that you are a single parent who works for the Department of Defense processing CHAMPUS claims. (CHAMPUS is a sort of medical insurance program for dependents of military personnel.) As God's coworker in the CHAMPUS system, how does your work serve the needs of others? I might suggest a few ways; you can think of others.

First, you directly help those who have filed claims. Any insurance program, military or otherwise, creates a monolithic system. The size is an asset in minimizing risk to the company and those it insures. But it sometimes works to the disadvantage of the individual who needs help from the system.

Now obviously, you cannot be responsible for every aspect of every claim that comes your way. Yet to the extent of your ability and responsibility, you can treat the claims that cross your desk as though they were crossing the desk of Christ.

Why? Because some sixteen-year-old mother of a sick infant whose husband is off on a ship somewhere sits at the other end of that claim. The form is her only way of communicating with the system. When it reaches you, is she dealing with an impersonal "system" or with a conscientious worker representing Christ? It all depends on your attitude at work.

So the mother, her child, and her husband need you to do your best work on their behalf. The same is true for every claim that comes your way.

But your coworkers also need you. This may sound laughable in such a huge enterprise, especially if your boss or others act as though

"No one is indispensable here! There are plenty of other hires where you came from!"

Yet despite the inherent foolishness of this view, your work contributes to the overall objective of supplying health benefits to people. In your own way, you actually help keep the system running. And since the system provides income for you and your coworkers, you serve the needs of your coworkers.

You also serve the interests of American citizens and their government. Your work is part of what it takes to field a reliable defense. It would be difficult if not impossible to recruit qualified people for the service without providing medical benefits for their families. These dependents need such care, and in a small way you make it possible.

Thus, your work ultimately has benefit for me and my family, and for anyone who lives and works under the protection of the United States.

Finally, your work obviously provides an income for you and your family. Since, in our illustration, you are a single parent, your child or children probably need day-care. Certainly you need housing, food, clothing, and transportation. Your work helps to provide for these needs.

Can you see how a Biblical view of work redefines how you think about your job? As God's coworker, you can enter the workplace with a tremendous sense of God's presence and the conviction that God's power is at work in you to accomplish His work on behalf of other people.

Feel His pleasure! Perhaps you saw the movie, *Chariots of Fire.* You'll recall that the film tells the story of Eric Liddell, an Olympic runner from Scotland in the 1930s.

In the film, his sister questions why he intends to run in the Olympics rather than enter the ministry as a missionary. In a very dramatic moment, he turns to her and says, "Jenny, when I run, I feel God's pleasure."

That's an impressive appreciation of the presence of God. Liddell recognizes the fact that God wants to use him in the arena of running. God wants to do the same with you in your sphere of influence. When you do your work, He wants you to feel His pleasure.

Reprinted from *Your Work Matters To God* by Doug Sherman and William Hendricks, ©1987 published by The Navigators. Used by permission of NavPress, Colorado Springs, Colo. All rights reserved.

*He whose walk is upright fears the Lord, but he
whose ways are devious despises him.*

Proverbs 14:2

5

ETHICS AND THE FORTUNE 500: A CEO's PERSPECTIVE

An Interview with C. William Pollard

ServiceMaster, recognized as the top service company in the Fortune 500, generates annual revenues of more than two billion dollars, serving more than one thousand health care facilities, four hundred and eighty colleges, universities, and public school districts, one hundred major industrial plants, and more than two million homeowners.

It is well-known for its commitment to high ethical standards which its forty-five thousand employees across the United States are strongly encouraged to uphold. C. William Pollard, who has served as president and chief executive officer of ServiceMaster since 1983, discusses the company's ethical commitment and strategy for carrying it out.

What's your opinion about ethics in the American business community today?

We are far more open about our mistakes than almost any other culture in the world, so when we read about ethical scandals the perception is that they are more prevalent here than in other places. I'm not sure that is true. It's healthy to be open, because it helps in the correction process. But there is really no frame of reference to tell if ethical problems are better or worse today. There certainly is more discussion now about ethics in the marketplace than there was five or ten years ago, but that may only be because problems weren't known as well before.

ServiceMaster has gained a strong reputation throughout the business world for a high commitment to ethics and integrity. How has that happened?

Today, everyone agrees that ethics is important, but there is wide disagreement about what reference point to use in developing ethical standards. In ServiceMaster, we have four company objectives: to honor God in all we do; to help people develop; to pursue excellence; and to grow profitably. The first two objectives are end goals, while the third and fourth are means goals. These objectives provide us with a reference point for what we do and how we determine that which is right and seek to avoid that which is wrong.

Our first objective is not simply an expression of some religious or denominational belief—be it Jewish, Protestant, or Catholic. Nor is it an attempt to merchandise the free enterprise system or the services we sell, wrapped in a religious blanket. Rather, it is an affirmative statement that the source of our way of doing business begins with God. We reject the notion that man's reason is the final authority or that ethics change according to culture or environment. That reference point helps to shape how we pursue our other three objectives.

For example, we recognize the value of each person as being created in the image of God. Every individual, regardless of intelligence, background, race, or position has great dignity and intrinsic worth. Peter Drucker's classic definition of management is "getting the right things done through others," but at ServiceMaster, we can't stop there. We must take the next step and ask, "What is happening to the person in the process? Is he growing as an individual who can contribute, not only in his work environment, but also in his home and community?"

Marion Wade founded ServiceMaster in 1947, the name representing "servants of the Master," and established the ethical philosophy. But often in business, when new leaders assume control, fondly held values are cast aside. What has ServiceMaster done to remain true to the original standard—and how do you see that

those principles are carried out among more than forty-five thousand employees in fifteen countries in three continents?

We never forget the role God's sovereignty plays in all of this. No matter what standard a company might set, it has to be God who maintains it. I'm ServiceMaster's fourth CEO — Mr. Wade, Ken Hansen, and Ken Wessner preceded me — and we all have shared the same vision and ethical concerns. We don't have a lot of written codes or standards, because they can be filed away and forgotten, or may not directly address issues that change every day.

So we are always in the process of communicating our objectives, beginning with the interviews and training, and carrying on through seminars and retraining. It's important that our people not only understand what ServiceMaster believes in, but also that they buy into it themselves. Most people are not comfortable doing things that they know are not consistent with what the organization believes in, and if there are inconsistencies, they are not likely to remain hidden for long.

You mentioned the men who preceded you as CEO. Each of you has been a Christian. Must the head of ServiceMaster be a Christian to maintain its corporate values?

No, that is not a company policy. We hold to the formula that pay is based on performance and promotion is based on potential. But as I mentioned before, we trust in God's sovereignty and believe He has a strong voice in determining who leads our company.

ServiceMaster has been enormously successful. What's the secret? Do you believe God has blessed the company because of its stand for Him or for your consistent focus on ethical standards?

It depends on how you define "success." If you mean financial success, the answer is an unqualified *no*. Our way of doing things at ServiceMaster starts with the Giver of all truth, but we don't believe that is the reason for our financial success. We don't try and apply it like some simple mathematical formula.

It does help, however, to have an unchanging foundation and reference for evaluating the rights and wrongs in business. With respect to our ability to touch people's lives, enabling them to grow and achieve their potential, then I would say, yes, our commitment to God's principles is largely responsible.

In a competitive environment, the temptation to do anything to gain an edge is great. So what's wrong with bending some rules?

You can't compromise principles and get ahead. Keeping a long-term perspective in a short-term world is not always easy to do. And we're as susceptible to making wrong decisions as others are, but we continually strive to evaluate what we do — and why — always keeping our four objectives in the forefront.

The decision-making process often creates tensions, forcing us to agonize when things can't seem to fit together, but our view is that until we can see how the pieces fit in a way that meets our objectives, we shouldn't move ahead. Creative tension, however, stimulates our thinking and planning, ultimately reconfirming what we believe in.

How do you see the future of ethics in business?

There's still an awful lot of confusion about what ethics really is. It's more than just developing a list of rules that seem good. In a society where there is more concern for the welfare of whales than for unborn children, something is out of whack.

Much is being said and written about ethics, but a recent comment by a young student raises a good point. After observing his minister, professor, doctor, and his father, a businessman, he asked, "Do they walk the talk?" We need to recognize the need for consistency in our behavior, and that can only come from an unwavering source or reference for action. For beliefs to become a reality in the operation of any organization, its leadership must not only state beliefs, but provide an example and maintain a continuing expectation for people in the organization to follow and adhere to those values and beliefs.

*He whose walk is upright fears the Lord, but he
whose ways are devious despises him.*

Proverbs 14:2

6

_____

AN ABSOLUTE SYSTEM OF ETHICS

Robert J. Tamasy and Colonel Nimrod McNair

What American business needs is an absolute system of ethics which maximizes profitability, productivity, and harmony. But where can you find such a system, if indeed one exists?

One suggested source is the twentieth chapter of the book of Exodus, where a list commonly known as the Ten Commandments is found. Some might contend that the Ten Commandments are "religious" and, therefore, cannot be applied in a secular setting. But Colonel Nimrod McNair, chairman of the Executive Leadership Foundation based in Atlanta, disagrees. "The Ten Commandments are no different than the law of gravity. They work. If we violate them, we will pay the price," he asserts.

McNair, who retired from the U.S. Air Force in 1972 after twenty years of service, says that his father taught him to appreciate the Judeo-Christian value system. However, it was not until 1973, while leading a management seminar in Lincoln, Nebraska, that he discovered the Ten Commandments are universally applicable, regardless of religious convictions — or the lack of them.

"We were discussing the decision-making process, and one of the executives inquired, 'How can you know that you're right when you make a decision?' Then he asked me what guidelines I used in reaching my own decisions.

"I explained that basically, I follow the Ten Commandments. Almost immediately someone commented, 'Oh, that's religious,' so I suggested that we take the time to paraphrase the Ten Commandments into contemporary business language. We wrote our conclusions on an easel pad. None of us were theologians, but we came up with some good results which showed that those ancient laws indeed do have relevance in today's business world.

TEN COMMANDMENTS FOR BUSINESS	
I. "I am the Lord your God . . . you shall have no other gods before me."	I. Show proper respect for authority.
II. "You shall not make for yourself an idol."	II. Have a singleness of purpose.
III. "You shall not misuse the name of the Lord your God."	III. Use effective communication in work and deed.
IV. "Remember the Sabbath Day by keeping it holy."	IV. Provide proper rest, recreation, and reflection.
V. "Honor your father and mother, so that you may live long. . . ."	V. Show respect for elders.
VI. "You shall not murder."	VI. Show respect for human life, dignity, and rights.
VII. "You shall not commit adultery."	VII. Maintain a stability of the sexes and the family.
VIII. "You shall not steal."	VIII. Demonstrate the proper allocation of resources.
IX. "You shall not give false testimony."	IX. Demonstrate honesty and integrity.
X. "You shall not covet. . . . "	X. Maintain the right of ownership.

"We started off with the first commandment, 'I am the Lord, your God. . . . you shall have no other gods before me,' and rephrased it to 'Show proper respect for authority.' Then we proceeded through the other nine. Virtually everybody at the seminar responded positively to our discussion.

"When I returned home, I had them typed up as the 'Ten Commandments for Business,' and over the years I have had many opportunities to use them in a variety of business settings."

But how, McNair wondered, could that message be communicated more widely, especially with front-page headlines serving as evidence of such a great need for an absolute ethical standard? The answer came in 1986, when he and eleven other business leaders convened in Dallas to discuss what could be done to point the business world toward a high standard of morality.

"We could have focused on government, education, or religion, but we were all businessmen, and we felt strongly that business institutions are in the forefront of leadership in our society. It used to be the temple and the cathedral, but today it's the corporate headquarters," McNair says. "A revival of sound ethics in the business world could easily have a global impact."

Over the next several months, the group met two more times. The outcome was the formation of the Executive Leadership Foundation, with the purpose of developing a nationwide network of executives who will affect social change as they apply absolute values—based on the Ten Commandments—in their personal and professional lives.

A litmus test of the philosophy was held in Dallas in October of 1987, where an international symposium on absolute ethics was held to see how other business leaders would react. Bill Kanaga, chairman of the advisory board for the Big Eight accounting firm of Arthur Young & Company, served as keynote speaker.

Positive response to the symposium exceeded expectations, and the Executive Leadership Foundation (ELF) was launched. As McNair states it, "We concluded that there is a hot market for ethics." The twelve founders were appointed as the foundation's first board of directors. An advisory council was later added, which included Kanaga. Henry Block of Canada and Hugh Jones of England gave the council an international flavor.

ELF functions in several ways. Its second international symposium was held in Chicago in October of 1988, with others planned for subsequent years. The foundation also sponsors institutes for absolute ethics where business leaders can roll up their sleeves and discuss the why's and how's of operating according to a code of ethics derived from an absolute value source.

To assist business leaders in articulating ethical standards, ELF has drafted a "Model Code of Ethics Based on Absolute Values," a detailed statement on how to apply the Ten Commandments for Business in a corporate setting. In some cases, companies have fully embraced the Model Code, while others have used it as a framework for drafting their own ethical codes.

Rather than keeping its philosophy, training, and publications to itself, a prominent objective of ELF is to "take advantage of the existing distribution systems," according to McNair. For instance, the head of a firm which consults with dentists across the United States has taken the concepts and tools and is adapting them for the dental profession. The Canadian government recently conducted a one-day ethics institute for newly elected representatives. A banking company in Florida and a law firm in Hawaii also have sponsored similar sessions for their staff people.

McNair, who for six years headed Executive Ministries for Campus Crusade for Christ and has spoken frequently at CBMC outreach events, says ELF intentionally does not have a clear-cut evangelistic thrust.

"One time I took a guest to a CBMC meeting who pointed to another man in attendance and asked, 'Is he a member of this outfit?' I replied that he was. My guest responded with disgust, 'He's one of the crookedest men in town.'

"Unfortunately, unethical practices are not uncommon in the Christian community, but at the same time, the guy in the business world— regardless of his religious persuasion—tends to look at the Christian and hope that he has something that works. We want to help business leaders, Christian and non-Christian, discover that God's absolute values, when applied, drive the ethics that yield true success: profitability, productivity, and harmonious relationships. That understanding could become an individual's first step toward a personal relationship with God."

McNair noted that in society, values basically come from three sources:

- Imposed values: A source of values which is dictated from the top or a consensus from a majority, which then is implemented from the top down.

- Situation values: A source of values which has produced the current social situation where every individual is his own final authority.
- Absolute values: A source of values which is absolute and fixed and produces integrity, productivity, profitability, harmony, and societal stability. These values are voluntarily adopted and applied, and leadership-driven.

"The interesting thing about absolute values is that God gives us the freedom to accept or reject them," McNair says. "And if we accept them, they work even if we are not in right relationship with Him. His values apply to Buddhists, Hindus, and Muslims, as well as Christians and Jews. The simple fact is, God's laws on how to deal with people and how to offer a quality product pay off over the long haul. Absolute values have worked for the Japanese, who learned them, ironically, from Americans whose values are now headed in the opposite direction."

He says the ELF leaders don't envision any dramatic changes in America's ethical climate. "As a pilot, I learned that when a plane is off course, you don't try to execute a 90-degree turn. You have to do it more slowly. But let's say, to switch to baseball jargon, that a company is currently batting .200 in proper ethics. It will never bat 1.000, but raising that average to .400 would be a great improvement."

He whose walk is upright fears the Lord, but he
whose ways are devious despises him.

Proverbs 14:2

7

ACTIONS
SPEAK LOUDER THAN WORDS

Ted Sprague

Integrity is such a key quality for a Christian businessman, and yet if you were to ask ten businessmen to define integrity, you likely would get ten very diverse answers. Personally, integrity is not a word I often use in the business world, but that doesn't mean it isn't important. I generally choose words that are more readily understood and agreed upon, such as honesty, faithfulness, and diligence. Those all are attributes God desires for us to demonstrate in our lives.

Integrity is essential if we are to live as consistent, Christian examples in the marketplace. It establishes the standards by which we conduct ourselves daily. Matthew 6:34 says, "Therefore do not be anxious for tomorrow; for tomorrow will care for itself. Each day has enough trouble of its own," (NAS). I have discovered that as I strive to represent God in business, every day becomes an adventure in the routine. It's simply a case of expecting the unexpected.

For example, we as Christians are encouraged to witness to those around us who do not know Jesus Christ. We tend to put such a premium on words, but how we live out each day serves as a greater witness, since that is where we put our faith into action. Colossians 4:2–6 has meant so much to me in this regard, and I believe it speaks directly to this area of integrity. It tells us, "Devote yourselves to prayer, keeping alert in it with an attitude of thanksgiving . . . Conduct yourselves with wisdom toward outsiders, making the most of the opportunity. Let your speech always be with grace, seasoned, as it were, with salt, so that you may know how you should respond to each person," (NAS).

As president of the Atlanta Convention & Visitors Bureau, I don't own this company, I merely manage it. Therefore, my job is not to preach to those I work with each day. My desire is simply to throw seed—to utilize the Word of God in the course of normal conversation and show how relevant it is to everyday circumstances.

One of my favorite verses is Proverbs 14:4, "Where no oxen are, the manger is clean, but much increase comes by the strength of the ox," (NAS). Bible commentator Charles Ryrie puts it this way: "There is no milk without some manure." It's amazing how appropriate that brief passage is to business situations.

I was in a meeting with a group of people who were discussing whether to try to attract a major national convention. As people discussed the advantages and disadvantages of the event, which would bring many thousands into Atlanta, they began to concentrate upon the possible problems. I was starting to get depressed. Then someone asked, "Ted, what do you think?" I hadn't planned to use the verse, but I had prayed asking God for boldness at the meeting, so I said what came to my mind: "Where no oxen are, the stable is clean."

Talk about E. F. Hutton talking and people listening! The entire room became silent. It seemed like an eternity before anyone responded, then one man started laughing. He said, "You're right. If you don't want any mess, just don't do anything." Simply quoting from God's Word turned the course of the meeting around.

On another occasion I was interacting with a top executive. He suggested that I read two books and gave me the names of the authors. I told him of a book I felt he should read. On the back of my business card I wrote, "The Bible—by God." This was not something I would normally do, but we knew each other well, and I felt I had laid the groundwork prior to being so bold. A year later, the executive came to our home for a visit and accepted Christ before he left.

When I have an opportunity to share my faith with others, I try to treat them the way I would want to be treated: boldly but gently, clearly but being sensitive to where I am spiritually.

Of course, integrity for the Christian businessman means much more than evangelism. That has been evident for me since I became a Christian about twenty years ago. I committed my life to Jesus Christ, curiously enough, at Fort Bliss, Texas where I was appealing induction into the Army. I have to admit that today I am not very proud of that episode in my life, but that was a time when I tended to resist authority of any kind.

While I awaited the outcome of my appeal, for the first time in my life, I questioned my strength to withstand uncertain circumstances. Determined to make the best of my time, I decided to start reading the Bible — for its literary content — even though I was a professing atheist. A chaplain at the Army base had given me a New Testament which listed topics of interest in the front. I was particularly interested in the verses on "How to avoid anxiety." That whetted my appetite, and slowly as I read on, I discovered the truth of Psalm 14:1, "The fool has said in his heart, 'There is no God,'" (NAS).

My journey through the Bible over the next three weeks finally brought me to my knees in the base chapel, where I wept openly and uncontrollably. It was hard for me — a "big man on campus" type — to admit I was a sinful person who would not find the answers to life inside himself. When I realized Jesus Christ was the answer to my sin problem, part of me was very sad, but the overwhelming part was ecstatic and joyful.

My military service appeal was upheld, so I returned to the business world. The next nine months were the most confusing period of my life as I sought to find others who shared my faith in Christ. I would approach other people I knew who went to church and tell them about what had happened to me, but they gave me advice such as not to get overzealous about my faith and not to read the Bible except on Sundays. Basically they did their best to put down all the excitement I had gained from reading the Bible.

Then I found a file — tucked among thirty thousand files in our Long Beach, California convention bureau office — about the Christian Business Men's Committee. I got in touch with one of the local CBMCers and he invited me to the next meeting. There a young man talked to the group, telling about his life before and after he came to know Jesus Christ. After nine months of feeling like a man on an island who had found something weird, I discovered there were other men just like me.

I had continued to read the Bible, but I was so starved for Christian fellowship I soon was attending five CBMC meetings a week. Men I met there became my examples in living out Christian principles on a daily basis. One man in particular stood out for me — Ralph Eaton. Ralph was from Phoenix, and when I had an opportunity to head up the Phoenix and Valley of the Sun Convention & Visitors Bureau, I called him for his advice. He encouraged me to take the job. Over my eight years there, I had the privilege of repeatedly hearing of Ralph's reputation as "an honest, religious man," which is how the secular world views him. What a terrific model he has been for me, and what an inspiration to hear how highly he and his company are respected even by people who do not agree with his Christian beliefs.

It's not easy to maintain integrity in the marketplace. Financial, client, employee, and political pressures are great, and it is easy to blow your testimony. We need the support and encouragement of fellow Christians, and dare not forget the reminder from Acts 17:28, "for in Him we live and move and exist. . ." (NAS). The Christian life, in our own strength, is impossible, but we can live it successfully through Christ's strength and power.

Integrity is largely reflected in our attitudes and relationships with others. In the demanding and complex world of business, it is easy to build up negative feelings toward people which are reflected in our actions toward them. I've found the way to maintain integrity and yet not fake feelings is to use Ephesians 4:32 as a guideline: "And be kind to one another, tender-hearted, forgiving each other, just as God in Christ also has forgiven you," (NAS).

That's a verse I have used more than any other in the business world. I certainly did not deserve God's forgiveness, yet through Christ and what He did on my behalf, I have been forgiven. Love like that is supernatural. There are times when I realize it is not in my power to forgive others, but I can do so through Christ's power working in me.

Striving for integrity has never hindered me in business. On the contrary, it has been a tremendous help. People may not agree with my Christianity, but I feel they respect me for how I live and what I stand for. One of the greatest compliments I ever received came fron a non-Christian man who said, "You can always be assured Ted is an honest man."

I'm convinced that integrity and honesty will carry a man further in business. That is not a guarantee against troubles, because those will come, but there is a great need for sincere, straight-forward people both as managers and employees. Those are such rare commodities in the marketplace today. A person of integrity cannot help but be successful.

Do not let this Book of the Law depart from your mouth; meditate on it day and night. . . . Then you will be prosperous and successful.

Joshua 1:8

8

THE PSYCHOLOGY OF SUCCESS

An Interview with Denis Waitley

When it comes to offering expertise in the area of success, no one has succeeded more in recent years than Denis Waitley. Since the release of *The Psychology of Winning*, his popular audio cassette album and book by the same title, Waitley has been in great demand both as a motivational speaker and a productivity consultant.

The Psychology of Winning is the best selling personal enrichment album ever produced, with nearly one million copies sold. Waitley's book, *Seeds of Greatness*, has achieved the rare distinction of appearing on the bestsellers' lists of both the *New York Times* and the Christian Booksellers' Association, with sales over five hundred thousand. He has authored five other books, including *The Double Win* and *Being the Best*, and is completing work on two new videotape series, *The Positive Parent* and *The Winning Generation*. Here he shares some of his insight on success.

Why do you think we have such a preoccupation with succeeding?

The concept of success is bombarded on our senses in all forms. The media has mesmerized society, feeding our fascination with the lives of the rich, the famous, the powerful, and the strong. Unfortunately, the pendulum has swung too far toward a superficial definition of success. Being one of the youngest societies in the world, we are going through the same narcissistic and adolescent stages of self-gratification that other societies have gone through.

It's almost like a cycle in which a society goes through stages of maturity, starting with the childish, adolescent stage which asks, "What can you do for me?" The next stage says, "I want to do it myself," which is almost as bad because you want to do things just for yourself. Finally, the society reaches stages of interdependence, first asking, "What can we do together?" and then, "What can I do for you?"

How does your definition of success differ from the commonly accepted view of success today?

The biggest difference is that I define success as a process, not a status. You never arrive at the point of *being* a success. Most people define success as that financial, physical, or accumulation spot where you have a monument that has been built to your progress and you've arrived.

I've met a number of people, in all walks of life, who are living successfully, but I've never met a "success," because tomorrow brings a set of problems and challenges that are totally different from what we've experienced today. Success is not a resting spot or a place; it's always under construction, like a garden.

Even more importantly, I don't believe you can be a success at the expense of other people. Helping other people succeed gives you success, because success comes with self-respect.

Has your view of success changed since you became nationally known through *The Psychology of Winning* and *Seeds of Greatness* eight years ago?

It's changed tremendously. I've had to be careful not to start believing my own press releases and that I didn't get caught up in a little of what I preach against. The dilemma I've had is that to succeed in the so-called general market, you have to position yourself with strong promotion. The very nature of promoting and positioning is at odds with what I feel and teach. The minute you become an "expert," you start losing your ability to gain expertise.

You have to keep reminding yourself that you are a God-made man, rather than a man-made god, avoiding any form of self-worship. I need to always remember who my Leader is, where my perspective comes from, and that I am changing, growing—and not an expert. I've learned that modesty is serving other people with grace, and arrogance is a sign of shallowness and superficiality. Conceit and arrogance are two of the worst human traits, and yet they seem to be associated with people who are successful. I am constantly striving to subordinate those types of feelings, and yet I teach people to feel special. The dilemma is, how can you feel special and at the same time not flaunt it? I've learned that you can—and you must.

Do you think this is possible for the person who is not a Christian?

No. Without a Christian perspective, you are definitely the do-it-yourself, self-made, self-sustaining individual who takes full responsibility for defining success. The real problem for the non-believer is that he actually begins to believe that the world revolves around him and his opinion. That is very dangerous. We have so many people in history who have gotten that feeling, only to bring themselves and other people down as a result.

You used the word *perspective*. In *Seeds of Greatness*, you state that it is the tenth and most important "seed." Do you still feel this is true?

I feel that way more than ever, and that's what I'm trying to get across to corporate America. They're trying to teach their people to be competitive and individualistic, and it's very difficult to teach perspective to people who are only interested in short-term profit. Most of my work is in the Fortune 500 companies, lecturing an audience of business managers and leaders, trying to get them to teach the "Golden Rule" in corporate life, hoping that they'll also take it home and teach it to their families.

In *Being the Best*, you write, "Perhaps the most important attitude in life is not the view of what success should be, because success differs for each of us. The much more important attitude

to develop is how to face failure and deal with it. . . . I see failure not as a toxic waste but as fertilizer." Can you expand on that?

In the Library of Congress, there are one thousand two hundred books about success, and only sixteen on the subject of failure or losing. Nobody wants to read about disappointment. But the greatest risk in life is doing nothing, since doing nothing ensures failure. I'd rather fail several times in reaching for success than be successful at doing nothing. The very act of experimenting and working will lead to mistakes, disappointments, and failures, because we are imperfect. This is where a Christian perspective comes in again, because if you don't have it, it's much more difficult to justify a mistake.

The greatest fear we have is the fear of rejection. That fear comes very early in life, because normally when you make a mistake and fail, you get labeled, criticized, and pointed out. Children especially tend to identify themselves with their mistakes. The fear of rejection leads to the fear of change or risk, which leads to the fear of success, meaning we won't try anything new or different because we might be rejected or fail. Yet the Lord has already given us the perfect reason for trying; for all of our mistakes and failures, He gave His life in our behalf. He gives us the opportunity to absolve ourselves from our mistakes by trusting and loving Him.

From that perspective, we need to view a mistake as something normal—a learning experience, a temporary inconvenience, and a postponement of success.

It has been said that often we learn more from our failures than from our successes. Would you agree?

The reason more people don't succeed is that when things go right, they attribute it to luck or being at the right place at the right time. We have sort of a lottery mentality. We don't believe we deserve success because we have been rejected, and being so afraid of rejection, then when we do succeed, we tend to discount it, reinforcing a lowered opinion of what was required to get there. When we fail, we either fix the blame on someone else or say that we knew it wouldn't work out anyway with our luck. So most people don't learn from either their successes or their failures. They reinforce their failures, but never their successes.

Is that why you included, in *Winning the Innovation Game,* a section called "Learn to Handle Success"?

Very few people know how to handle success. The minute they get it, they forget everything they learned on how they got there and tend to rest on their laurels. The thing I find most common in business executives or show business people is that, when people believe they are successful, for some reason they develop total amnesia. They forget how and who helped them up the ladder to get there, and they stop being the person that they were in order to be successful.

How do you perceive the link between success and one's relationship with God?

If God created wonders such as the Barrier Reef, the Rockies, a rose, a baby, a tree, a bird—and each of us—why do we continue to knock the product and search for something else? Did not the same loving Creator create great intrinsic value in us—value so great that He was willing to die for us? God has taught me that the value is in the clay, not in the shape that it takes. That also means that there will never be a human being more important, or less important, than another.

As a Christian, I have the Ten Commandments instead of the "Ten Suggestions," and if I live by them and follow God's Word, I'll probably have fewer problems and be able to unfold what God intended for me. I won't have to play the comparison game, since I'm not basing success on the externals, but rather on the internal values of a loving God who created all of us with equal worth, but not necessarily the same uniform.

You have said that you never met a "success," but know of people who are living successfully. Can you give some examples?

I think of Mother Teresa. She may seem too prominent because she has been singled out as somebody who is selfless. But she has taken the talent and energy she was given and has put 100 percent effort into making the world a better place. She loves what she does, and they're not using her for any designer jeans or other product endorsements.

My grandmother was like that. She lived eighty-seven years without a complaint. She would thank God for her blessings, accept things that came her way as "fertilizer" and challenges, and always give more in service than she ever received in reward, because she felt her reward was in the love and respect of the people she helped.

The richest man in America, Sam Walton of Wal-Mart, has several things about him that indicate he is probably living successfully. If you're wealthy, it doesn't necessarily mean that you are corrupt. He still has the regular old car, and he's still living in the same house with the mailbox at the end of the road. He's maintained his humility and modesty, and hasn't become impressed with his position. He still is Sam Walton, rather than the "emperor" among his subjects.

One other man is Roger Rowe, the principal at our local elementary school in Rancho Santa Fe, California. He epitomizes, to me, a person that I know who is living successfully. He remembers the names of parents and characteristics of every student he's had for the past twenty years, and he graduates two hundred a year. He says that his job is to create an atmosphere of loving concern where everyone can develop an "I can, I will" attitude and give everyone the opportunity to reach beyond themselves — and not be surprised when they do. What he does is place great importance, every moment of his life, in bringing out the best in the people he meets.

Years from now, when your time on earth has come to an end and people say you were a successful man, in what ways would you want people to consider Denis Waitley a success?

That he had the love and respect of his wife and children, and that he loved and respected them. And that he devoted his life to planting shade trees under which he knew he would never sit.

"SEEDS OF GREATNESS"

Listed below are Denis Waitley's "10 Seeds of Greatness," as discussed in his best-selling book, *Seeds of Greatness: The 10 Best-Kept Secrets of Total Success.*

1. Self-esteem	6. Communication
2. Creativity	7. Faith
3. Responsibility	8. Adaptability
4. Wisdom	9. Perseverance
5. Purpose	10. Perspective

*Do not let this Book of the Law depart from your
mouth; meditate on it day and night. . . . Then you
will be prosperous and successful.*

Joshua 1:8

9

LIVING AND LEAVING THE AMERICAN DREAM
(Why a hard-driving executive stepped off the fast track at GM)

Thomas S. Fortson, Jr.

I was a black man living the American dream, advancing quickly up the executive ladder with General Motors (GM) in Detroit and enjoying the material rewards that came with it. Friends said I was a role model to other young blacks, living proof that one could achieve in spite of minority status. Why, then, after ten years would I turn my back on GM to move to Atlanta and take a management position with a comparatively small baking company?

Many people asked me that question, including my wife. To be honest, for a while I was not certain of the answer myself, but ultimately it boiled down to my definition for success.

I enjoyed my job as administrator of personnel services at GM's Fisher Body Division—the plush office, the status, the availability of a new car every year, and the ongoing challenge of new and greater responsibilities. After five promotions in six years, I had envisioned myself moving to the top of General Motors. At the same time, however, there was a continual tension in my life. I had committed my life to Jesus Christ as a teenager and understood that I was "God's workmanship, created in Christ Jesus to do good works, which God prepared in advance for us to do" (Ephesians 2:10).

So the pressing question for me was, what did God want me to do? I knew He wanted me to serve Him, but I had a nagging sense that it might not be at GM, where job demands were requiring me to sacrifice more and more time with my wife and children. I also had to resolve another question: What was I trusting in . . . the money and opportunities that a large corporation could provide . . . or God? It was not easy to admit, but I had come to depend on the blessings, rather than the *Source* of the blessings.

As I projected my life into the future, I could see myself always aiming for the next promotion, spending my entire life working to get to the top. Would I become like many men I knew, men who had made lots of money and built successful careers but were unhappy and dissatisfied with it all? Then I thought of my father, who had spent thirty-nine years as a watchman for the Pennsylvania Railroad. His job could not afford us many of the tangible things in life, but there never was a lack of two important intangibles: time and love.

I'd like to say deciding that God and my family had to be my top priorities came easily, but it didn't. The things that come with corporate success were nice. And I knew there was more to come; it was a time when being talented and black afforded more advancement opportunities in large corporations.

But God was breaking me. The material things didn't seem as rewarding, and I was unhappy. Proverbs 1:8 says, "Listen, my son, to your father's instruction and do not forsake your mother's teaching." My father and mother had succeeded in instilling the values and importance of Biblical principles and family life into me, and I recognized that I was not where God wanted me to be.

My internal conflict went on for weeks. I would plead, "But Lord, you've given me an opportunity to be an example for other young executives." And then I would get to a point and pray, "Lord, I give up. What do *You* want me to do?" I shared my dilemma with Crawford Loritz, a good friend whom I had met through Campus Crusade's

Here's Life Black America program. He promised to pray with me, asking that God would make His will for my life clear.

In 1982, I was contacted by Don Patterson, chief financial officer with the Edwards Baking Company in Atlanta. He was calling at the direction of the company president, Joe Edwards, who had gotten my name from . . . Crawford Lorittz. Don told me the company was in the midst of a major expansion, and Mr. Edwards wanted someone to head up the personnel department.

At first, I wasn't interested. The company was small, privately owned, it could not offer many of the benefits I already had at GM, and I didn't relish moving to a new city. But Don was persistent, and finally I agreed to fly down and meet with him and Mr. Edwards.

In Atlanta, Mr. Edwards told me that he had committed his company to the Lord and wanted it to be an example of what a Christian business can be. That turned a light on for me, since I had never encountered a company where such a commitment had been made in terms of policies and products. The more I learned about the Edwards Baking Company, the more it appealed to me. Corporately, it could not compare with GM in any respect, but it did offer me an opportunity to help build something meaningful and be part of a business whose owners were striving to consistently represent God in the marketplace.

Although I was becoming more receptive to a job change, drastic as it was, my wife, Toni, was not. She was six months pregnant with our third child; she loved our home and did not want to leave our many friends. Our children were attending a good school, and we were very active in our church. That was also the year of the child murders in Atlanta, so the city did not seem like an ideal family environment. There were many good reasons for not moving, but God seemed to want us to move to Atlanta anyway. I couldn't help but feel a little bit like Abraham being led into Canaan.

Fortunately, God had given me a wife who was as committed to Him as I was. When I told her I felt God wanted me to take the job in Atlanta, she gave me a blank stare and said, "You can't be serious. God hasn't spoken to *me* about it yet," but she agreed that we would both pray about it. "If God is telling that to you," she said, "He'll tell me, too."

One weekend not long afterward we flew to Atlanta again to continue the job discussions. We were at Don Patterson's home, and Toni was talking with Mrs. Patterson. Suddenly, Toni started crying uncontrollably. "If this is what God wants," she sobbed, "we'll come."

I could understand Toni's tears. In one sense, it was like a funeral and the grieving process that goes with it. We were saying good-bye to a fondly loved part of our life. And my efforts to rise to the top of GM had consumed much of my time and attention. Things would never be the same again.

Arriving at our decision did not resolve all of our problems. Leaving GM, for example, was more difficult than I thought it would be. When I turned in my resignation to my supervisor, he was alarmed. He was afraid I had been offended somehow or that the job was not meeting my needs. Almost immediately I was offered a new position and more money. I tried to explain why I was quitting, but he insisted that I see the corporate vice president of GM personally to explain.

I can remember driving up I-75 to Detroit, with tears trickling from my eyes. My boss had asked me to use his car, a new Cadillac Eldorado, for the trip. Traveling in the comfort of one of the best vehicles my company made, I was driving to the corporate headquarters, the place I had set my career sights to reach. "God, are you asking me to give up all this? Look at all the things I can do for you here." The Lord seemed to answer, "Tom, do you love *Me?* Whom do you love?"

In spite of my misgivings, I clung to my resolve to leave GM. After I had convinced another executive that I was not leaving because of anything the company had done, he said, "Tom, I'm glad you didn't take another position we would offer you. That shows me what you have is real."

Leaving a successful career with a major corporation is not something God asks all Christian businessmen to do. I know a number of Christians who are working and serving the Lord very effectively in huge corporations, but in my situation, He had to get my attention. Psalm 51:17 says, "The sacrifices of God are a broken spirit; a broken and contrite heart, O God, you will not despise." That was what God was doing—breaking me so that I might be more useable for His purposes. I also had the assurance of Psalm 84:11, "No good thing does He withhold from those who walk uprightly," (NAS). We were leaving some cherished things behind but were confident God had even better things planned for us.

The brokenness process did not end with our relocating to Atlanta. Edwards Baking Company, in the midst of a growth plan that would quadruple its production, experienced financial setbacks soon after I arrived. Because I was heading the personnel department, I had the unpleasant job of laying off dozens of people as cash flow failed to keep up with growth projections. I was also struggling personally. We had difficulty selling our house in Detroit, and the combined mortgage and rent payments were taking a financial toll on my family. Did I make the wrong decision? Had I misinterpreted God's intentions? More than once I was tempted to pick up the phone and see if I could get my old job back at GM.

Having never been involved in a situation like that, I was disillusioned. Any day, I feared, my job would cease to exist, along with my ability to provide for my family. But as one Bible scholar has said, "Never doubt in darkness what God shows you in the light."

The continuing problems kept me on my knees before God. He was teaching and building character into me, although it was not a curriculum I would have chosen for myself. You see, as the Lord was building character, He was stripping away my crutches until there was nothing to depend on but Him. I was in the middle of a battle of wills: God's and mine. Being an achiever, I always worked to find options, but the Lord needed to show me that His was the only way. God created me goal-oriented, but He wanted me to be more *eternally* goal-oriented. I needed to understand God's perspective on success: One thousand years from now, is what I'm doing now going to count?

And one thousand years from now, I'll know that I had the time to spend with my wife and family, striving to be the spiritual leader and model that God intended for me to be — so that my children, and their children's children, will know and love God through His Son, Jesus Christ. I will also have had the opportunity to demonstrate to others what it means to take a strong stand for Jesus Christ in the marketplace.

Edwards Baking Company is now growing, expanding, and introducing many new products. But we know there are no guarantees. And

I've learned my lesson. I'm not depending on a corporation or a company; my confidence is not in fringe benefits. My trust must be totally in the Lord.

Colossians 3:23–24 tells us, "Whatever you do, work at it with all your heart, as working for the Lord, not for men, since you know that you will receive an inheritance from the Lord as a reward. It is the Lord Christ you are serving." That, I believe, is what success is about.

THE SUCCESS
OBSESSION

*Do not let this Book of the Law depart from your
mouth; meditate on it day and night. . . . Then you
will be prosperous and successful.*

Joshua 1:8

10

THE DARK SIDE OF SUCCESS

Joe Glover

M any people spend their waking hours in a relentless search for
success. Over the last three or four years, I have stopped trying
to find success — I have been too busy discovering what success is *not*.

Almost from the beginning people said I was destined for success.
In high school at Bossier City, Louisiana, I was class president, head of
the debate club, and was voted "most likely to succeed." I received an
appointment to the U.S. Naval Academy, which everyone seemed to
think was a mark of success in itself.

At the Naval Academy, I became a brigade commander, president of
my class, and graduated with honors. After receiving my commission in
the U.S. Marine Corps, I attended and was graduated with honors from
both the Ranger School and Airborne School. I missed action in Vietnam by two months but had worked earnestly to prepare myself for
combat. I had achieved all the criteria necessary for military commenda-
tion. In fact, in 1975, a dinner was held in Honolulu, Hawaii, in honor
of my selection as the outstanding junior officer in the Pacific Fleet.

I was working eighteen to twenty hours a day, constantly trying to
prove myself, and yet in spite of my "success," the thrill quickly wore
off. So in 1977, after I had completed my tour of duty in Hawaii, I was
psychologically prepared when I unexpectedly received an incredible

opportunity to join a corporation on the West Coast. I had never thought about getting out of the military and going into private business, but being entrepreneurial-minded, I was willing to consider the offer.

Before making my decision, I wrote to three individuals I had served under who had been very influential in my life, asking for their advice. Each supported my feeling that with the Vietnam War over, I could achieve more in the business world. So I began a quest for more and greater success.

Ironically, I declined the West Coast position and instead, accepted an offer to become an executive assistant to H. Ross Perot with Electronic Data Systems (EDS). There, I saw success personified. Almost daily I worked with men whose pictures had appeared on the covers of *Fortune* and *Business Week*. Personally, my financial rewards exceeded anything I had ever anticipated. I moved into management and started a new business division for EDS.

But I began to see that success also has a dark side. In all the literally hundreds of articles about successful men I had been filing away, never was there a mention of their broken marriages or the hardships their "success" had imposed on their families, or the deep sense of uncertainty and insecurity many of these men had. Several of these men candidly told me of their own disillusionment and feelings of being "trapped." I began, at this point, to conceive my "donut lifestyle" theory: although the lifestyles of the business elite look sweet and desirable from a distance, those close to them know that inside there often is really nothing but fluff and air.

Unfortunately, my life was no better. The "donut" still looked pretty good to me. I was working 120–130 hours many weeks and was fortunate that my wife, Lynn, stayed with me. Although I was never unfaithful with another woman, my job was more demanding and consuming than any mistress could have been.

In a very real sense, I was like a puppy dog. I would stay up all night working on an important project and in the morning would display what I had done. I'd get a pat on the head, and I would walk away with my tail wagging. I didn't want to admit it—even to myself—but the money, prestige, and power that a successful business career offered was not nearly as satisfying as I had expected.

The turning point came in 1981 in Dallas, Texas, where I had moved to work at EDS, when I was confronted in a courageous way by the pastor of my church, Bill Bowyer. What he said to me required courage, because I was a heavy contributor to the church, and he knew he was taking the risk of angering me. But, thank God, he cared a lot more for me than the money I was giving to support church programs.

"You think God will use you in a big way, don't you, Joe?" Bill asked me one day while we were driving back from an appointment.

After a brief pause, I replied, "Well, it would seem so, " wondering where the conversation was headed.

"Joe, until God has you in the *little* ways, He'll never use you in big ways." He paused, letting the surprise of his statement sink in, and then added, "I pray that God will show you what I've been telling you."

Bill had been watching me and my family and knew that while my intentions were good, my life was way out of balance. He recognized my total dedication to business would eventually take a tragic toll.

I had been raised in a church-going Christian home and had always been aware of the reality of God, although admittedly, I had practically put Him on a shelf in my life. I had equated a moral life with a Christian life. As I considered what Bill had said, I could see that he was right. After several weeks, I uttered a brief, silent prayer during an evening church service: "God, make me a godly man." How little I understood what I was asking.

About that time, I had decided to go into business on my own, leaving corporate security to exercise my instinct as an entrepreneur. First, I started a computer software business, and then bought three Christian bookstores. My plan was to "McDonaldize" a chain of bookstores from coast to coast. Things went well at first, but over the last several years, I have gone through a series of intense business trials.

We were undercapitalized for rapid growth, and the best of planning could not have anticipated the computer industry slump, the oil price drop, and the real estate crunch we have had in the Southwest. And that is not to mention the stock market and October 19, 1987. There have been days when I didn't know whether we would be facing bankruptcy or succeed in becoming a multi-million-dollar company.

During this time, the truths of the Bible have become more vivid than ever. I can identify with the trials of men like Joseph, David, and

Daniel, and the books of Hebrews and James have served as life rafts for me during some dark times. I have realized that when I asked to be made into a godly man, God began His proven process of breaking and remolding. As far gone as I was, that meant I would have to spend some "prison time"—times of utter helplessness and learning total dependence upon God. Knowing what God did with David's time in the desert and Joseph's prison experiences helped to keep me going.

In the *Living Bible*, the parable of the sower in the Gospel of Mark describes one group as those who hear the Good News of Jesus Christ, "But all too quickly the attractions of this world and the delights of wealth, and the search for success and lure of nice things come in and crowd out God's message. . . ." Only now can I fully accept that that had been a description of me.

One day, while I was in the midst of this growing process, my wife, Lynn, showed her support for this change by giving me a quote from Dr. James Dobson which she had copied in calligraphy and framed. The statement, taken from his *Focus on the Family* film series, has become my creed:

> I have concluded that the accumulation of wealth, even if I could achieve it, is an insufficient reason for living. When I reach the end of my days, a moment or two from now, I must look backward on something more meaningful than the pursuit of houses and land and machines and stocks and bonds. Nor is fame of any lasting benefit. I will consider my earthly existence to have been wasted unless I can recall a loving family, a consistent investment in the lives of people, and an earnest attempt to serve the God who made me. Nothing else makes much sense.

Years ago, at the "height" of my business career, I would have told you that "success" was making the cover of *Fortune* magazine, seeing your earnings double every year, having three thousand people who work for you, and being asked by the President of the Untied States to leave your business for a year to solve some great problem.

Today, I see success as simply becoming all that God intends for me to be and, in business, getting to the point where He is truly "chairman of the board" of my company. I used to be afraid of displeasing men; that concern has been displaced by a greater fear—that of displeasing God.

Have I arrived? Not at all. I'm still a product of the world, a recovering "successaholic" who sometimes falls off the wagon. I have to admit that God can do a miracle in my life at 1 P.M., and by 7 P.M., I still can revert to the old success-oriented, hard-driving, win-at-all-costs Joe again. But I believe that each day I am learning a little more how much I need to test everything I do, everything I say, against what God teaches in the Bible. Daily prayer and Bible study are anchors that I cling to.

I still want to be successful, but not by pleasing men, because that means I have to work according to their criteria. God's view of success is a much higher standard. I can still be a successful businessman, even from a secular point of view, but I've determined that I need to invest my life in other men, helping them to prosper spiritually, rather than in trying to build a bigger company or make more money. Years from now, I would like people to say that Joe Glover was a success because he put his family before himself, and other men came to know something of the reality of God through his life.

*Whatever you do, work at it with all your heart, as
working for the Lord.*

Colossians 3:23

11

BIG BUSINESS: FAMILY STYLE
(The link between United Brands,
Penn Central, and Hanna-Barbera is
stronger than just the Lindner family ties)

An Interview with Carl H. Lindner III

One of the most prominent business families in America is the Carl
Lindner family of Cincinnati, Ohio. The Lindners' American Financial Corporation, with consolidated assets of $11.6 billion and annual
revenues of $6.9 million, is one of the country's largest privately owned
family holding companies.

Among the Lindners' investment interests are United Brands
(Chiquita fruit), John Morrell meats, Penn Central Corp., Great American Communications Corp. (including radio and TV stations, Hanna-Barbera and the Kings Island theme park), and Charter Corp.

Thirty-five-year-old Carl H. Lindner III is one of the key figures in
the family conglomerate. With his father, Carl; Ron Walker, president
and family confidant; and his two younger brothers, Craig and Keith, he
shares responsibilities for directing the diverse corporate holdings. Carl
III is a partner in American Financial Corporation and president of Great
American Holding Corporation, the operating subsidiary which encompasses property and casualty insurance and life insurance businesses.

Through the years, the Lindners have been recognized for their civic-mindedness and philanthropy, but the basis for that generosity is not as widely known. Carl Lindner III discusses the Christian commitment that not only serves as a catalyst for the family's charitable activities, but also influences day-to-day business operations.

In any family business, there is the potential for conflict among people who know each other very well. What's it like being in a family business noted for its aggressive approach to investments and acquisitions?

Without question, there are interesting dynamics working in a large, privately owned company. But we all recognize the dangers of a destructive ego, not only to yourself but also to those around you. Through the years, we have seen how selfishness and greed have brought about the failure of successful entrepreneurs and caused many family businesses to break up. We work hard to avoid such pitfalls.

We share a strong Christian faith and strive to cultivate a servant spirit, following Christ's example. We try to avoid petty jealousies in running our business, instead seeking to "forbear with one another, be patient, encouraging, and edifying," as the Apostle Paul instructed.

Each of us has our own areas of responsibility within American Financial Corporation, but 40 percent of our time is spent serving as an advisory group to one another. One of the benefits of being together in a family business is the built-in accountability. We are able to discuss the many challenges and problems that arise, and then work through them together.

Describe your spiritual pilgrimage to Christian faith.

My father and mother always took us to church, and I received a rich Christian heritage as a child. But it was not until my early twenties that I understood what it meant to have a *personal* relationship with Jesus Christ. Up to that point, my life was out of balance, and I lacked any real sense of love, joy, or peace. That caused me to return to those Christian roots and receive the grace, forgiveness, and unconditional love of God that is only available through Christ.

Now I have a sense of peace that cannot be bought at any price. I try to have a consistent, daily quiet time, reading the Bible and praying. My wife, Martha, is always the first to know when I have missed my quiet time for a couple of days. I'm a different person without it. Those times I spend each morning are very important; they are the crux of my growing relationship with Jesus Christ.

How do you see your commitment to Christ relating to your day-to-day business decisions?

There is no greater area for putting your faith on the line than in running a business, regardless of the size. The pressures are sometimes overwhelming. We recognize that God is really the owner of all we have, and He requires us to be good stewards—not only of the businesses, but also of the people who work for us, our resources, and our time.

In today's business world, we are constantly having to face ethical and moral issues. I'm thankful for God's Word as a point of reference in decision-making. It's also a blessing to have a lot of Christian friends who are business leaders around the country and around the world. It helps to be able to pick up a phone and call them, seeking their advice.

I think my faith also influences my approach to management. For any aggressive business executive, there's always a danger of concentrating on what is wrong, rather than what has been done right. There is a need, as managers, to emphasize the positive—praising, encouraging, and building people up, rather than tearing them down.

For most of us, that's not easy, but as a Christian I'm constantly aware that those around me judge me—and my relationship with God— by how I live, and the example I set.

To be honest, I still have a long way to go in understanding how to effectively apply my faith to my business—I don't profess to be even halfway there yet. The magnitude and complexities of high-level business decisions are so great, but I've learned that as a Christian, I have more resources to draw on.

When American Financial Corporation is in the news, it's usually in connection with plans to buy a new investment property.

How do you see your commitment to Christ relating to corporate buyout strategies?

We prefer a friendly type of situation, viewing ourselves as the "white knight" in a corporate takeover. Generally, we steer clear of so-called hostile takeovers. We recognize that many people's lives are affected — investors, management, employees. American Financial has a track record for negotiating deals on a fair basis, at fair prices, and that's a reputation we want to maintain.

One of our success secrets is that we have a multitude of friendships in business. My father has always said that the business world is a small place. You generally meet the same people on your way up as you do on the way down, so it's a good practice to resolve differences without having to go through litigation.

Takeovers and acquisitions are neither right nor wrong in themselves. What matters is how they are conducted. The free enterprise system is the most efficient and healthy approach to business in the world. But many companies become stagnant and slow to react to problems, or fail to take advantage of opportunities.

Acquisitions — or the threat of them — can be a disciplining and motivating influence on existing managements. The danger arises when poor business judgment causes properties to become overpriced, without sufficient underlying assets. In those situations, a takeover doesn't make sense; it can actually be harmful to investors and employees, the two primary groups of people affected.

Unlike other prominent business leaders, your family has steadfastly maintained a low profile. Why is that?

We have never sought publicity, but we still have plenty of stuff written about us all the time. Generally, our feeling is that you see headlines whenever something is done wrong, but when something is done right, it either gets no coverage or is buried in a back section of the newspaper.

In general, the media tends to focus on atrocities rather than the positive things in life, the things that encourage and edify. As I've pointed out, we operate from a different perpective.

Earlier, in talking about how you came to know Jesus Christ, you stated that your life had been out of balance. Being a member of one of America's prominent business families, how do you avoid the traps that affluence and prestige can present?

I don't always succeed in avoiding the traps, but establishing clear priorities for my life and trying to hold to them has proved extremely helpful to me. The top priority has to be my own relationship with Christ. My daily quiet times are important in keeping that perspective.

My wife and three children (with one on the way) are my second priority. I really want a vibrant God-honoring marriage, and have learned it takes time and commitment. God expects fathers to take a strong leadership role, including spiritually, not turning over the task of raising and teaching to the Sunday school and other people. I enjoy sharing my faith with many people, but I believe God's foremost responsibility for me in evangelism is to my children.

Obviously, our business takes up much of my time. But as I said before, I try to maintain a Christian perspective in whatever I do. I recognize that the Lord has given us the resources, and He expects us to use them to glorify Him in whatever we do. It's important to enjoy your job and have fun in whatever you do for a living—in fact, God requires it. There's nothing wrong with setting aggressive goals for yourself and being a shrewd businessman, as long as it's done in a way that is consistent with God's principles.

Overall, I view the Christian life as one of service to others. I have had great joy in serving as an elder at Mariemont Community Church and in being a founding board member of Cincinnati Hills Christian Academy, which opens this fall. I have also had the privilege of being involved in other evangelical ministries.

One's real personal ministry for Jesus Christ really encompasses the entire realm of life—wife, family, business, church, community. God blesses every believer with a multitude of opportunities to share our faith and disciple those who commit their lives to Christ.

I often think of 1 Peter 3:15, which tells us to "be ready always to give an answer to every man that asketh you a reason of the hope that is in you with meekness and fear," (KJV). From the time I get up until I go to bed, that verse kind of hangs in my heart. Having that perspective really makes being a Christian exciting.

Whatever you do, work at it with all your heart, as working for the Lord.

Colossians 3:23

12

SECOND TO NONE

Jeffrey W. Comment

The first thing the business world identifies with is a person who is committed to his job, his company, other associates, and who wants to be successful. In my experience, I have found outstanding business people who are exciting to be around, dynamic in their nature, and have a strong desire to succeed. Couple these characteristics with knowing the Lord and wanting to fulfill His sovereign plan, and you have the total person that God has called each of us to be.

Unfortunately, too many Christians in the marketplace are either limping along on half of their cylinders or speeding along out of control. From my observations, and excuse me for oversimplifying, I have categorized Christians into three groups: overachievers, underachievers, and God's achievers.

First are the overachievers—the workaholics. They look more like their secular counterparts than like the men and women Jesus Christ wants them to be. Working six or seven days a week, they have no time for family or friends, not to mention their relationship with Christ. The real priorities of life suffer at the hands of "getting ahead."

They look tremendously successful to the world, and most have all the titles and material possessions that go along with secular success. If you were to challenge them, the reply would be something like, "My job demands the time and attention," or "I love what I'm doing." The real question that must be asked—and only they can honestly answer—is, "Am I doing what God would have me do?"

Next come the underachievers—the lazy Christians. These people have no work ethic. They demonstrate no desire to succeed or to see their company be successful. In fact, they think it somehow unspiritual to even mention success, let alone try to achieve it. Legitimate concern about becoming a workaholic deteriorates into failure to put in a good day's work. If their lives were the closest people ever came to seeing Jesus Christ, He might never be seen.

When I see people like this representing Christ in the marketplace, all I can do is lower my head in embarrassment. As Christians, we should be the most sensitive to doing our best, since everything we do is supposed to be "as unto the Lord" (Colossians 3:23). I don't think our performance on the job should be any different. Anything less than our best effort dishonors God.

Writing to the believers in Colosse, the Apostle Paul clearly addressed the issue of responsibility in the performance of our duties. "Let the word of Christ richly dwell within you, with all wisdom teaching and admonishing one another with psalms and hymns and spiritual songs, singing with thankfulness in your hearts to God. *And whatever you do in word or deed, do all in the name of the Lord Jesus,* giving thanks through Him to God the Father" (Colossians 3:16–17, NAS). That passage is all-inclusive regarding our responsibility to give our best performance, regardless of circumstances. No distinctions between secular employment and full-time ministry are mentioned.

The final group of Christian performers, and the one I hope we all strive to be part of, I call God's achievers. They take Romans 12:1–2 seriously: "I urge you therefore, brethren, by the mercies of God, to present your bodies a living and holy sacrifice, acceptable to God, which is your spiritual service of worship. And do not be conformed to this world, but be transformed by the renewing of your mind, that you may prove what the will of God is, that which is good and acceptable and perfect," (NAS).

These people want to be transformed into men and women seeking to honor Christ and serve Him right where they are. They are in the process of developing a lifestyle distinct from the world's model.

God's achievers strive for balance in their lives. They avoid becoming overachievers, but are shocked by underachievers. They blend their commitment to Jesus Christ and everything He stands for with a genuine commitment to their businesses and the people in them. I believe these are the people God has called us to be—models who use His standards, ethical and professional, in our working environment.

God's achiever should demonstrate a work ethic second to none. He must also conduct his business with the highest ethical standards. The kind of success and achievement we see in today's marketplace is often corrupted with immoral business practices and a total lack of integrity. But when men and women achieve success by the world's yardstick, yet maintain high moral and ethical standards in the process, the impact they have on the people around them becomes awesome.

Most Christians, however, don't understand that principle, and consequently, I don't believe we recognize how to be most effective in sharing our faith. We've been taught that witnessing means verbally expressing the gospel message. And then we read Matthew 5 and discover that we are to be "salt and light." We guiltily wonder, "Am I sharing the gospel with my coworkers?" and "Do people understand my faith?"

There are times when we must tell people how to receive Christ, but most of us have a far greater impact with our actions rather than our words. I don't believe evangelism is an either/or proposition. We need to blend our actions with our words to "flesh out" the gospel for the secular world to see.

In my own life as a corporate executive, I have realized that the strongest sharing of my faith results in upholding high business standards linked with the commitment to integrity I can project to people around me. It doesn't take long, especially if you have management responsibility, for the people you direct to understand the basis of your faith. I believe that as Christians, we need to spend less time talking about our faith and more time demonstrating that we are the kind of people God wants us to be.

When you first look around the workplace and see the people you can influence, you quickly find that many of them are not open to the gospel. It would be very difficult to tell them how to place their trust in Christ. But they will watch you. Your work and personal habits will demonstrate who you are. They will soon be able to see if your faith is real.

We should never forget that part of our responsibility before God is to be effective stewards of our time, our wisdom and logic, our physical abilities, and our financial resources. We should exploit our God-given gifts every day.

And being Christians, we should be excited because of who we are. That excitement should spill over into our businesses as we try to be the most outstanding business people in the marketplace. We should demonstrate that our drive for success is not motivated by greed or personal interest, but to honor Christ. When that can be accomplished with integrity and the highest ethical business standards, we have earned the recognition and credibility that will cause other business people to listen to us. The Young Life ministry to high school youths has a motto: "Earning the right to be heard." That concept is just as important in the marketplace.

I'm convinced that when I see Jesus Christ face to face, He's not going to ask me how many times I shared the gospel, how many talks I made, or how many books I wrote. He's going to say, "Jeff, how did you live your life — hour by hour, day by day — so that all of the people I placed around you had an opportunity to see what I look like?"

How do we reflect the personality of Jesus Christ in our day-to-day activities in the marketplace? *That* is the bottom line.

"Whatever you do, work at it with all your heart, as working for the Lord. . . ."

Colossians 3:23

13

THE FATHER OF FRANCHISING

An Interview with William B. Walton

I n 1954, three men in Memphis, Tennessee began discussing a unique venture which would revolutionize the motel industry. The discussions spawned Holiday Inns, which grew during the next twenty years from four motels in Memphis to two thousand company and franchise establishments around the world, hosting 160 million people a year and becoming the fastest-growing hotel and motel chain in America.

One of the key figures in the enterprise was William B. Walton, who served as chief operating officer and is regarded by many as "the father of franchising" as it is known today. He, with Mel Lorentzen, chronicles the Holiday Inns' success story in his recent book, *Inn Keeper* (Tyndale House, 1988). The book is far more than a business biography, however. Walton describes the challenges of applying Christian principles in a corporate setting, his own struggles with ambition and pride, and his discovery at age fifty-two that even though he had strived to follow Biblical guidelines, he had not established a personal relationship with God.

In the following interview, Walton relates some of his conclusions about corporate life and Christian convictions.

The success of Holiday Inns was a classic in the annals of business. From 1963 to 1973, a new Holiday Inn opened somewhere

in the world every two-and-one-half days. How do you account for that phenomenal growth?

Some say that we happened to be in the right place at the right time, or that we were just lucky. But I think it all started when we drew up our constitution and bylaws, in which we determined to build a corporation based on recognizing the dignity of all people and the Christian principle of man's love for his fellow man.

In another book Mel and I wrote, *The New Bottom Line*, we explained that our attitude at Holiday Inns emphasized three principles: Thinking right about *people*, thinking right about *training people*, and thinking right about *leading people*. During the time I was involved in Holiday Inns' daily operations, there were well over one hundred attempts to unionize our employees. But those efforts never succeeded because of our attitude toward our people.

When competitors tried to copy us, it never concerned me. It's no secret how to build a motel room, and corporate marketing plans are all the same, regardless of the industry, but I knew no one could copy our people or the high regard we had for them.

You state in your book that you did not commit your life to Christ until you were fifty-two, yet Christian principles were the centerpiece of Holiday Inns from its founding eighteen years earlier. Why were they so important to you?

For as long as I can remember, I was raised with a strong Christian heritage. My father left us when I was a young boy, but my grandmother and mother had a very positive spiritual influence on me. It always meant a lot to me when my grandmother would say, "Billy, just remember that God loves you and cares about you. Talk to Him as your Father. He is always with you." Even though I didn't yet know Christ personally, it was impressed upon me that our walk with God is the most important thing in life. I also had a reverence for the Bible, believing it was God's Word and that we should live according to its teachings.

How did you come to recognize your need for a personal relationship with God through Christ?

Well, although I had a strong belief in God, I still was determined to accomplish many material things in life. As a boy, we had lost our home to foreclosure, and I had borrowed the line from Scarlett O'Hara in *Gone With the Wind* when she says, "I'll never let that happen again." So early on, I set my sights on either becoming chairman of the board of a large corporation or a U.S. senator. And for along time, it seemed I would reach my goal of heading a big corporation.

But at the same time, I tried to uphold the Ten Commandments and practice the Golden Rule. At Holiday Inns, we started holding an annual prayer breakfast and invited Billy Graham to speak several years in a row. One summer I ran into Billy in Very Beach, Florida, where we both had been sent by our doctors for vacation and rest. We spent quite a bit of time together and became good friends.

In 1972, Billy invited me to sit on the platform at a crusade he was conducting in Lexington, Kentucky. That was the first time I had ever heard God's message of salvation in that form. When Billy invited the people to come forward and commit their lives to Christ, I looked into their faces as they arrived. I realized that was what life was all about — and also understood that I needed to make that decision myself.

Up until that time, I had been absolutely certain that I would one day be at the right hand of God, basing my salvation on my good works. After all, at Holiday Inns we had taken the Bible out of the bottom drawer and opened it on top of the table; we were the first company in the United States to have a chaplain as a corporate officer; we had a chaplain-on-call system for guests; and there was the prayer breakfast at our annual franchise owners meeting. I was certain that God was pleased with all the good things I was doing for Him. It wasn't until that crusade that I realized there was not anything that I could do for God; that He had done it all for me.

Even before you became a Christian, these practices reflected your religious convictions. Were you ever accused of proselytizing?

I didn't view it as such. There was one occasion when that issue came up, and in that instance the complaint was valid. I had become overzealous. In general, we didn't run into a lot of opposition, although times have changed and today we probably would.

But through the early '70s, we enjoyed wonderful cooperation among franchisees of all faiths. There was a sense that our commitment to Biblical principles was at least partially responsible for our success. In fact, one Jewish franchise owner made the motion at one of our annual meetings that every motel contribute one hundred dollars to the Billy Graham Evangelistic Association. Somehow, we all knew that there was a guiding force behind the Holiday Inns story. There had never been anything like it before, and I don't believe there has been anything like it since.

You acknowledged the difficulties in trying to follow through on your Christian commitment in the midst of corporate pressures. What were the toughest issues you had to deal with?

As I mentioned, I had set a personal goal of becoming chairman of the board at Holiday Inns. I had risen to president and vice chairman; my goal seemed well within reach. Then came the Arab embargo and the oil crisis, causing many of our new stockholders to push for broadening our investment base. In 1975 and 1977, proposals for Holiday Inns to get into the gambling business were defeated, but in 1978, the makeup of our board of directors changed, and the vote was 14–1 in favor of gambling, with mine being the only dissenting vote. I knew at that moment that my hopes of ever becoming chairman were gone forever.

I had spent fifty years climbing my "mountain" and had nearly reached the top. The summit would have been mine if I had just voted "right." Although I knew I had done the right thing, I wasn't happy with the consequences. In business, success is generally measured by material accumulation, wealth, fame, and power, and I'm not sure my thinking was much different at that point. But I had to think of the many people I had counseled and of all the years I had willingly held myself up as a role model for Christian businessmen. I knew that if I had given in on the gambling issue, I would have betrayed all those people. Most of all, I would have betrayed my Lord.

Still, it was hard to accept. I had envisioned that God was building a great corporation to attest to how He answers prayer. I didn't realize that His story with Holiday Inns had ended — and with it, my career.

And you didn't have an opportunity to sit back and enjoy the financial fruits of your labors, did you?

At that point in my life, I had accumulated $1.3 million in personal debts, money that had been borrowed against Holiday Inns stock options based on a per share price of sixty dollars. After the Arab embargo, the stocks dropped to four dollars a share.

Suddenly, I was in the same position my family had faced in 1929 — the thing I said would never happen again. As it turned out, I didn't lose my house, but I was bitter for a long time — including toward the Lord. I once had 115,000 shares in the corporation; today I have six. "Why would He let that happen?" I kept asking myself. What I couldn't see was that although He was through with Holiday Inns, He was still developing me. God knew how much I liked the Lear jet, the red carpet treatment, the power, and being on a first-name basis at the White House.

How did you get over the bitterness?

I discovered that it was destroying my life, just as effectively as drugs or alcohol could. Finally, I remembered what Grandma had always told me: "The Lord is always with you." I saw that I had been trusting myself most of my life, even though I always asked God for wisdom in dealing with the needs of each day. He wanted me to stop relying on myself and place my complete trust in Him.

A major turning point came in 1976, when I was speaking to the Los Angeles Association of Corporate Executives annual meeting. I told that Holiday Inns story, as I had for years, but a sharp, young black executive asked a question. He suggested there might be more to the story than I had already related. That was the first time I ever told the complete account of God's involvement in the formation and development of Holiday Inns, and I discovered it was the story God wanted told.

Today, Holiday Inns is purported to be the largest purveyor of pornography films in the world. Christians have been urged to boycott the chain. That didn't happen until after you were no longer involved in day-to-day operations, right?

Yes. In the early days of in-room movies, we had three hundred thousand rooms, and we were obviously the first call the movie companies made. But we wanted to maintain the wholesome, family atmosphere of our motels, so the board voted not to accept the movies. I was accused of costing the company $9 million dollars in clear revenues, which would have been our share of the royalties. It seemed like a poor business decision financially, but it was consistent with the values we believed in.

But your success rate in upholding principles wasn't 100 percent, was it?

There is an inherent danger in compromise, no matter how slight. Our business started out to absolutely prohibit any type of gambling, pornography, and alcohol. Somewhere along the way, our marketing people convinced us that although we didn't need to get into the whisky business, we definitely needed to have a little room where a man could get a drink at the end of a long day. So we turned our heads and bent the stick a little bit, and today Holiday Inns' bars generate many millions of dollars in revenue each year. In that instance, I'm sorry I didn't put up a stronger fight.

In the Christian community, we often hear the phrase, "full-time Christian service." How does that relate to Christians pursuing careers in the business world?

What I think this refers to is a businessman — or businesswoman — who seeks to walk with God twenty-four hours a day. The proper priorities are God, family, and your fellow man, then your job. Being a Christian businessman means showing people that I care for them and doing those things that are most pleasing to the Lord. Wherever we work, we *all* are called to full-time Christian work. If we don't keep that perspective, seeking to follow Christ every hour of our lives, we may well find anguish, bitterness, and unhappiness.

What is the outlook for true Christian commitment in the marketplace?

Today, the importance of our personal relationship with God is being discussed more openly, and we have greater opportunities than ever to communicate God's message of salvation. But I'm not sure that the business community is as open spiritually as it once was. And many of the Christian businessmen I meet don't seem as eager to demonstrate their faith. That is perhaps the greatest need in the marketplace today.

*"For even the Son of Man did not come to be
served, but to serve."*

Mark 10:45

14

POWER, PEOPLE, AND POLICY
(A CEO builds a strong case
for participative management)

Robert J. Tamasy

I mmediately upon introduction, Nevius M. Curtis casually shatters the
stereotype of a chief executive officer. Affable and direct, he shrugs
off all formality he might command as chairman of Delmarva Power, a
gas and electric utility company with $1.7 billion in assets serving Dela-
ware, Maryland, and parts of Virginia. "Call me Nev," he smiles to his
visitor, thrusting out a hand of greeting.

Unlike some of his peers who might feel a need to assert their corporate rank, the fifty-seven-year-old Curtis leans back in his chair, tie
slightly loosened, shirt sleeves rolled up. His sportcoat is out of sight,
hidden away until absolutely necessary. This relaxed exterior, however,
belies the inner workings of an intense, deliberate top executive. During
his tenure, Delmarva—with two thousand and six hundred employees
covering a five thousand and seven hundred square mile service area—
has passed on to its four hundred thousand customers three rate reduc-
tions and two rate refunds over the past three years.

Another unusual aspect of Nev Curtis is his approach to corporate
management. His leadership philosophy at Delmarva Power, ironically,
does not include excessive use of "power." His style is not to mandate

or manipulate. Instead, he strongly advocates "participative management" throughout the company.

"To me, participative management is more than a buzz word," he asserts. "We have an abundance of talent at all levels here, and I believe each person should be involved in decisions that affect his or her job. Participative management means you work through teams, and that has proved very effective for us. Ultimately management is the process of helping subordinates get their work done. And who knows more about their jobs than the people performing them?"

Curtis held his attitude long before it became popularized through such books as *In Search of Excellence* and *The One-Minute Manager*. For that reason, in 1980, when he was named president of Delmarva Power, he did not rush to exert his authority.

"I spent the first two weeks trying to decide what kind of president I wanted to be," he says. "I viewed my position as that of a coach, so I started analyzing the qualities of a good coach. He is one who knows the playing field, the rules, and players. I realized I didn't know enough about any of those.

"So I decided to go around the company getting to know many of my people, what they did and how they did it. Soon afterward I was in a service center, talking to one of our line men—a big fellow, about six-foot-six. I had gone out wearing casual clothes, and after we had been talking for about fifteen or twenty minutes he asked, 'By the way, Nev, what do you do for the company?'

"I shuffled around for a few moments and then said, 'I'm the president of the company.' 'To h— you are!', he replied, pointing out he had never heard of a president who would be up at 6:30 in the morning, talking with men on the line dock about one hundred miles from his office. 'And no president asks a lineman what's wrong with the company and listens to the answer.' It was then that I understood what tremendous walls there are between top leadership and the hourly workers. In their eyes, they are the ones who do all the work—and we are the ones who mess it up."

Curtis has not always been a considerate, compassionate executive. There were many years when he would make decisions and then see that they were carried out. Another significant event occurred in his life during 1980, however, that has helped to reshape his perspectives on management. He committed his life to Jesus Christ, accepting Him as his personal Savior. "The way I look at the world has never been the same since."

In particular, Curtis learned that on earth, Jesus acted as a servant, even though He could have demanded to be served. "As I studied the life of Christ, I became fascinated with servant leadership. That's where participative management fits in. You are helping people, not only to do their jobs, but also to find satisfaction in what they do, to make them feel a valued part of the team. Sincere Christian concern does not mean mushy softness, but rather loving people enough to expect them—and help them—to do their best.

"Of course, in addition to the servant, there is another Biblical model for the leader—the shepherd. A shepherd doesn't consult his sheep about which pasture they would like to graze in. He is a better judge than they are. If the shepherd leaves the decision up to the sheep, soon they will be wandering in every direction.

"In a similar sense, if there is a fire at an electrical substation, that is not the time to call a team meeting and brainstorm. That is a time for definitive action. Even with a smooth-working, cooperative team there has to be someone who is responsible to the corporation and able to speak with authority when a decision must be made. Otherwise, a sense of uneasiness will develop among the team members.

"The test of leadership, then, is to know when to be a shepherd and when to be a servant—in whatever form that might be."

Ultimately, Curtis sees himself not as the top official for a midsized utility company, but as a man whom God has placed in a very prestigious position. "After I became a Christian, I recognized so clearly that I had this job solely because God put me here. Looking back over my career, I can see that each piece of my life and career is like a jigsaw puzzle. Everything that I have is the Lord's, and I am responsible for handling it properly, even the people who report to me.

"I remember a situation some time ago. We were re-evaluating the format of our monthly bills. Basically, our bill is a communication of how much gas and electricity a person has used and his obligation to pay for that amount. Therefore, it is important that the information is communicated clearly. Since our old bill was very confusing, we decided to develop a new format.

"I assigned a committee to research the matter. Frankly, I wanted to use bar charts, but I didn't want to bias our team members' judgment. When it was time for a report and recommendation, I sensed my manager was about to tell me something I didn't want to hear. I was right. Our research clearly showed our customers preferred numbers, simply presented, and that is what we did.

"In the old days, we would not have known what the customer thought, for we would not have asked him. Now we have learned to ask. In the world of problem-solving, everyone has different abilities and insights. It's important that everyone involved be given the opportunity to contribute, regardless of where they are on the organizational chart.

"I've told our people at Delmarva that God created us all and has given everyone some gift or talent. Since He did not give anyone all of the gifts or talents, we need each other. Most people will buy into that. A second corollary, that all people are equal in God's sight, isn't accepted as readily. The blue-collar worker sees the executive wearing a tie and having his own office, and has trouble with that idea.

"To be honest, I was troubled with that concept, too, after I became a Christian. I felt guilty because I had so much, while I saw others who had so little. I began asking myself, What is a good Christian? What does a real Christian do? Become a missionary in India? Surely not be an executive of a power company, I thought. It took me a long time to work through that issue, but I've come to realize that we are where the Lord puts us, and He wants us to be faithful to the responsibilities we are given.

"As a CEO, there are people God can use me to reach that others cannot. I also play a major part in shaping our company's policy, and through participative management we strive to make jobs more meaningful to our employees. It's amazing the difference it makes when people feel they have a say in decisions made concerning their jobs."

"For even the Son of Man did not come to be served, but to serve. . . ."

Mark 10:45

_____ *15*

THE HEART AND SOUL
OF EFFECTIVE MANAGEMENT
(Merging the corporate mind
with the servant heart)

James F. Hind

What does Jesus Christ, dying on a cross early in the first century, have to do with my trying to achieve economic growth for a company late in the twentieth century? That question haunted me for more than thirty years of my business career.

I saw a huge gap between the church and the boardroom, the sacred and the secular. I wanted to determine how what I learned in church during a couple of hours each Sunday morning could be applied in a practical, acceptable way during a forty to sixty hour work week. It seemed many other people also desired to find a way to bridge that gap.

About three years ago, I began to formulate an answer to my question, after I left full-time corporate life to become a consultant. Recording my thoughts on paper, they eventually became the nucleus of my book that was published earlier this year, *The Heart and Soul of Effective Management.*

Studying the life of Jesus through the Scriptures, interpretative works, and commentaries by both clergymen and knowledgeable lay people, I focused on how He trained and developed his twelve disciples, molding and shaping ordinary men with different personalities, appetites, and ambitions.

As Christ interacted with these men, He met their individual needs and also nurtured them in a caring manner. Christ, although a tough-minded realist, motivated His followers through softness, sensitivity, and generosity — He combined a corporate mind with a servant heart. He fully understood and faithfully practiced the most important principle of human motivation: *People want to know how much you care before they care how much you know.*

The management trait Christ demonstrated that impressed me the most was *servant leadership* — His willingness to give of Himself for the benefit of others. The more I studied His life, the more I became convinced that He embodied management at its best, a style that can easily be translated into today's business environment.

Managers should view themselves as *developers of people*, rather than "take charge" heroes. They should help others to thrive and flourish; in the process, they themselves will succeed to their utmost.

Meeting Needs of Others

Servant leadership does not mean subservience; it is not weak and submissive as the name might imply. Rather, it is filling a supportive role that puts self-serving interests and ego gratification aside, choosing instead the goal of meeting the development needs of others.

Neither does servant leadership abolish the demands a good manager must place on others — such as competency, obedience, discipline, excellence, and hard work. It adds an important dimension to effective management, linking corporate pragmatism and compassion.

The keystone of servant leadership is concern for others and an eagerness to communicate this attitude through actions that say, "I'm for you." Management's dedication to this higher spiritual purpose brings special significance to the workplace, inspiring a sense of devotion among the workers, breeding both quality productivity and effective management.

Feelings—not compensation, a corner office, a title on the door or carpet on the floor—are the greatest human motivators in the workplace. In His daily interactions with the disciples and other people, Christ showed that He understood this principle; contemporary research has confirmed its validity.

With pressures of merger-mania, takeovers, competition, and self-interest, American management is largely losing the art of caring for and motivating people. It is shifting away from a caring attitude for its people, concentrating solely on economic growth and survival.

Recognizing People's Worth

While business books, videos, and seminars teach the how-to's of achieving excellence, encouraging innovation, managing change, learning to lead, gaining power, negotiating, and handling finances, few—if any—tell how to help the other person develop and succeed. Business America has neglected our Lord's second greatest commandment, "Love your neighbor as yourself." There is a great need for the recognition of people's self-worth and value to each other. Unless business can learn to use work to help people grow, it will be reduced to a lost soul, insensitive to people's needs, known only for its power structures and bank accounts, and driven solely by self-interest and economic considerations.

The marketplace desperately needs a new approach for people to manage themselves and others, one that returns spiritual values to the workplace and gives people a sense of "calling." Christ's teaching and actions can show us the way.

As Christians, our ultimate goal should be the advancement of the Kingdom of God, and a servant leadership approach to managing people helps us to do this. It provides a positive witness for Jesus Christ because if we live and manage like Christ in character and feeling, people around us will get to know Christ better—and be more receptive to His ways.

*"For even the Son of Man did not come to be
served, but to serve. . . ."*

Mark 10:45

16

TRADING PLACES

Jim Hartsook

L eadership is an area in which I've had my share of on-the-job
training. In high school I was president of the student council, captain of the basketball team, a main character in school plays. I continued
to be called on to lead a number of activities in college and on into my
adult life.

Perhaps one reason I consistently found myself in leadership roles
was because I was an achiever. I liked being in front, gaining the recognition that comes with leadership. Whenever I took on an assignment, I
made sure it was done — and done right. I took pride in my ability to
make things happen, and I suppose if you had asked me, I would have
told you I knew enough about leadership to write a book on it. That
conviction continued into my business career, doing personnel work for
the accounting firms of Deloitte Haskins & Sells, and now with Price
Waterhouse.

In mid-1977, a series of events caused me to re-evaluate my life,
eventually resulting in the decision to commit my life to Jesus Christ.
That was an important step for me in many ways, and it significantly
altered my views on leadership. Until then, I must admit, I employed all
my skills in interviewing and training to use people, getting them to do
what I wanted them to do.

I sincerely thought that was my primary responsibility.

After becoming a Christian, I discovered what God expected of me as a leader was much different. Activity, I realized, had been a salve for what was missing in my life. I had been *doing* rather than *being*. My concern shifted from things that people did to the people who did them. As I read the Bible, it became clear that God wanted me to encourage the people around me to become the persons He intended for them to be.

That new understanding led to significant changes in my approach to leadership. For instance, I found that my priorities were out of whack. Since I felt it was up to me to get everything done, I was over-involved in the office, church activities, anything that interested me. I was a leader at work and in the community, but I had failed at being a leader at home. That began changing when I discovered God's design for the family.

The Lord taught me to be more selective about what I got involved in. We tend to view ourselves as so important, but the truth is, God can find others to do whatever He wants done. In the past, whenever I was asked to take on a project, I hesitated to say no, since I felt people were depending on me. Now I have the freedom to decline so I can spend sufficient time with my family, which I know is a high priority with the Lord.

One of the keys to leadership, I believe, is recognizing God's priorities and not letting our desire to be at the front get in the way. If we're trusting solely in our own abilities, we're certainly not relying on the power of Jesus Christ.

This has helped me in another important area of leadership — delegation. All we have to do is look around us, at this amazing world God has created, to realize He has more leadership ability than all of us have together. He knows everything that needs to be done and has all the necessary resources, people, and elements at His disposal. One of the principles of effective Christian leadership, then, is getting yourself out of the way and letting God do His work.

I think of the Houston Mayor's Prayer Breakfast in 1985, which I was asked to chair. At first I didn't feel comfortable with the responsibility, even though I had helped with similar events in the past, because it came at one of the busiest times of the year for me. Finally I concluded that if God wanted me to do the job, I would have to trust Him. As it turned out, it was the easiest job I have ever done. All our planning and preparations for the event, which attracted well over one thousand people, were accomplished in five meetings.

Realizing God is in control has helped in another aspect of planning. I used to get very uptight when someone I was depending on did not show up, or when details did not go as smoothly as I had anticipated. The Lord has shown me, over and over, that He will always provide the people He needs to accomplish His purposes — to His glory.

That is a hard lesson, however. I still find myself lapsing into old habits from time to time, trying to control and manipulate people and circumstances. That is not God's way.

Another important element of leadership is setting a good example. When I was young, my father was ill much of the time, so I spent a great deal of time with my grandmother. She was always positive and happy, never cross, an excellent example for me. She didn't know it, but she was serving as a model for me that would continue to impact me as an adult.

People constantly watch their leaders, and they are quick to pick up any inconsistencies. Leadership is not just a matter of what you say, it's also what people see in you and the things you reflect as important by your actions. I have had an opportunity to disciple a new Christian who also works in our office. Regularly, we meet to discuss what the Bible teaches about how we should conduct our lives, but throughout the week he can observe me to see if I'm living out what I teach him. It's quite a challenge.

Maybe the most important thing I have learned is that walking closely with Jesus Christ day to day takes the tension out of leadership. There are not so many unmet expectations, nor so many disappointments. Knowing God is in charge, I no longer feel as if the weight of the world is on my shoulders. And that enables me to be a better leader, serving as an encourager and helper, rather than a dictator. One of the best ways I can honor God is by assisting others in knowing Him and reaching the potential He has for them.

*"For even the Son of Man did not come to be
served, but to serve. . . . "*

Mark 10:45

17

A REVOLUTIONARY APPROACH
(An automotive executive talks about change)

Don Mitchell

S ince February of 1986, I have been involved in a fascinating project. The General Motors (GM) plant which I manage in Wilmington, Delaware, has undergone a $311 million renovation, changing it
from a traditional auto assembly plant to the most technologically advanced automotive facility in the United States. The plant, which had
produced large Chevrolets, has been redesigned for our newest market
entries, the Corsica and Beretta.

If I were not so closely involved in the work, I would find the statistics hard to conceive: twenty million pounds of steel and old equipment
had to be removed, replaced by nine hundred truckloads of new equipment, and we used twenty-four thousand gallons of paint to cover
twenty-three acres of ceiling during the renovation process. We have
invested more than twenty million dollars in personnel training, in teaching our workers how to operate the new equipment, as well as extensive
instruction in interpersonal skills. We also provided career placement
training for those employees whose jobs were made obsolete by our new
technology.

These figures are impressive, but I believe the most exciting part of
the entire project has been our radically different approach to decision-

making and problem-solving. Traditionally, decisions in our industry have been made by management and carried out by the hourly rate workers. In this case, however, we knew it was important to have personnel at all levels integrally involved for a number of reasons.

First of all, we knew that in making such revolutionary changes in our plant, we needed the support of everyone. Secondly, we needed to overcome problems resulting from the old system of decision making. We saw the necessity of driving the decision-making process down through the organization. The best quality decisions will be made by those closest to the problem, which frequently is the operator on the assembly line.

These steps actually began in mid-1985, when thirty-eight production workers were hand picked by management and the union. They did advanced planning with our engineers in Detroit and prepared training programs for the balance of the work force. These people had been putting parts on cars for twenty-five years, and knew many of the production and design problems that engineers don't always understand. This provided a critical base for our problem-solving and training process. Since then, this group of employees has literally solved hundreds of problems even before actual production began. Their effective involvement has been contagious throughout our plant.

When I was moved from our Linden, New Jersey, assembly plant, where I was production manager, to Wilmington, many of the mechanics for the transition already were in place. Over the succeeding months, we held weekly meetings with all personnel levels, knowing how critically important it was to maintain proper communications throughout the changeover. This intensive emphasis on communications has been the key to facilitating employee involvement.

It has been truly amazing to see this whole process in action, as management people and assembly people have crossed long-standing boundaries in a united effort to create an enjoyable, efficient working environment which produces a top quality product.

Perhaps even more astonishing, to me, is that I could even be a part of all this. It wasn't too many years ago that a participative management approach was contrary to my style of management. In one of my earlier plant assignments, soon after graduating from the General Motors Institute, I was a compulsive workaholic and an overbearing supervisor. I frequently found it easier to replace people than to develop them or re-solve problems.

I did not see it then, but my lifestyle and approach to work was anything but conducive to team building—either on the job or at home. It was not uncommon for me to work sixteen hour days, and I always worked at least six days a week. Although I had gained a reputation throughout GM as a person who carried a pretty heavy load, I was caus-ing tremendous problems around me. I had virtually no compassion for those working under me, and with the number of hours I spent in the plant, I obviously had little time to spend at home with my family. As a result, my wife and children suffered tremendously from neglect.

After twelve years at one of my earlier plant locations, with my home life decaying and sensing that I wasn't getting the level of produc-tivity at work that I once did, I decided it was time for a change. I quit my job with GM and took a job as manager of a large industrial plant in central Mississippi. I was excited, feeling the change would put some pizzaz in my life and would help me feel better about what I was doing with my life.

I spent exactly 357 days working for that company, but nothing in my life changed. My lifestyle was the same as it had been, I was work-ing just as many hours, and what I had thought was an opportunity for things to get better turned out to be a chance to make them a little worse.

Knowing that this job was not my answer, I was fortunate enough to be one of the few guys to make it back to GM after leaving the corpora-tion. I was sent to Detroit, where I worked as an engineer on the 1980 X-car, and on a team to design a new plant to be built in Oklahoma. I saw the job as a good opportunity to get my feet back on the ground and put some sanity back into my life.

Unfortunately, nothing changed. The situation in my household was becoming serious; my wife and I were beginning to talk divorce. So when I was offered an assignment with a new plant in Oklahoma City, I eagerly accepted, hoping once again that a fresh start would straighten things out for me. Once again, my expectations proved unfounded.

By the time I got to Oklahoma City, my divorce was in the final stages, and I spent most of my time traveling. I was on the road for forty-two weeks in a row, going back and forth to Detroit sometimes twice a week, and putting in extraordinarily long hours, even for me.

One night after flying back home, I stopped to get a soft drink. Suddenly, my heart started beating very rapidly, something I had never experienced before. I ended up in a hospital intensive care unit. After four days, the doctor came in and told me that, although the medical staff had been unable to find anything wrong with my heart, I could not keep up my work pace indefinitely.

That should have been enough to prompt me to slow down and clean up my act, but I didn't make any positive changes. In fact, in addition to resuming the same non-stop work schedule, I added another habit—drinking. As could be expected, I began to have significant health problems.

It was about that time we started production in the plant, and a new boss was transferred in to whom I reported directly. He was different from any boss I had ever worked for, particularly in a crisis. When problems arose, he would very methodically go in, work through the difficulty and resolve it, without any fanfare. He never seemed to get ruffled.

His lifestyle also was unlike other management people I had been associated with. Over time we got to know each other well, and he proved to be a true friend. When my divorce became final, I felt like I was suffering from a kind of social leprosy, but Dick stuck by me when nobody else would. I can't fully express the great impact he had on my life. As we became better friends, he would invite me over to his house all the time. I started taking my children over there on Sunday afternoons.

One particular Sunday, we were sitting outdoors, enjoying the sunshine when Dick asked, "Don, would you like a mixed drink?"

I was a bit surprised by his question, but I said, "Sure." My policy by that time was never to refuse a free drink. Dick went inside and came out a couple of minutes later with the drink. I took a sip and almost choked. "Dick, what in the world is in this glass?", I gasped.

"Didn't you ask for a mixed drink?", he replied.

"Yeah."

"Well, it's iced tea and lemonade." That gives you an idea of the kind of guy Dick was.

After I had recovered from my shock, he said, "Come on over here, Don, I want to talk to you." We walked under a large tree he had in his back yard and sat down. After a few moments, Dick commented, "Don, God has a perfect plan for your life." That's all he said. I did not respond, but my immediate reaction was consternation. I thought, *The audacity of this man to tell me something like that. I have lost my family, I don't have the kind of visitation rights with my children I would like, I'm living in a lousy apartment and basically all I have are the clothes on my back. And he has the nerve to tell me God has a perfect plan for my life!*

The interesting thing about Dick was that he had a sense of when to stop whenever we got into a discussion about God and spiritual things. He never pushed too hard or too long. About a week later he invited me to attend church with him and his wife, Sharon. I agreed, and went with them again from time to time. The things I heard there moved me deeply, but I wasn't sure what was happening. I didn't understand exactly what it was, but there was something that I needed.

Dick had told me that he read from the Bible every day, but that was about as religious as he ever got with me. I observed his "religion" by the way he acted, not by what he said. It occurred to me that, if Dick benefited from reading the Bible, it might have something for me as well. I bought a Bible and started reading it. From time to time I would ask Dick a question about it, and he would answer it, but he never pressed me. As I read through the verses and chapters, I started to realize some truths about life that I had never known or understood.

For instance, although I had attended church regularly for most of my life, I discovered that going to church does not make a person a Christian any more than watching a football game on TV makes someone a professional football player. Christianity, the Bible told me, is not a spectator sport.

As I read about Jesus Christ, I learned that a Christian really is someone who has a personal relationship with Him. The Bible also made it clear what the admission requirements are for going to heaven and achieving eternal life — it lays it all out perfectly clear.

It says, first of all, we have to be sorry for our sins. Looking back at my life, I had no problem understanding that I was a sinner, and I had a lot to be sorry for. Secondly, the Bible says we must ask forgiveness, believing that Christ died on the cross for our sins. It astounded me to think that Jesus had done that for me. Third, we need to turn our lives over to Christ, asking Him to take control. Three simple — but crucial — steps.

There is a verse in the Bible that says, "Behold, I stand at the door and knock; if anyone hears My voice and opens the door, I will come in to him, and will dine with him, and he with Me." Suddenly, it became evident that God *did* have a perfect plan for my life, a plan He had completed nearly two thousand years ago! Yet, it also was clear that the decision was mine, that God would not force Himself on me or anyone. I knew I had to accept it willingly, without coercion.

I made that decision in October of 1978. I may not have used all the right words, but I remember very vividly telling God that I was sorry for the wrong things I had done, sorrier than I ever had been before. I told Him that I knew He couldn't make a bigger mess out of my life than I had, so I asked Him to come into my life and take charge.

From that time, my life began changing in an incredible way, not dramatically, but steadily. I met Nina, who would become my wife. At the time, I didn't realize that it was important for me to marry a Christian woman, but after we married, I prayed for Nina day and night until she also committed her life to Christ nearly a year later. In the Bible, a verse states, "the husband and wife shall cleave together as one flesh." That suddenly made sense when Nina became a Christian. I found out what true beauty can be in a marriage, when a man and woman are united spiritually as well as legally.

Other changes in my life after becoming a Christian included being able to cease drinking and smoking, even though I had tried to stop dozens of times before. I also cut back substantially on my work load. One of the driving forces in me had been a feeling that if anything went wrong, I was personally accountable for it. Once I realized that Jesus Christ was in control of my life, I recognized that when things go well, God deserves the credit, not me. And when things are not as successful as I would like, I can still have the peace of knowing I have done my best in serving God through my job.

My faith carries me through the usual anxieties of changing jobs and moving the family. When my boss in Oklahoma City called me in and informed me I was being transferred to the plant in Linden, New Jersey, I have to admit that my idea of heaven was not seven miles south of the

Newark Airport. I was thankful again for my friend Dick's assurance that God had a perfect plan for my life. Over the past eight-plus years, I have seen that God doesn't let me get into anything that He hasn't first looked over and approved. That is a truly comforting thought, and it provides me with an indescribable peace, no matter what the situations may be at home or at work.

Ultimately, participative management in our plant is really God's way of operating our business, which He has established through the centuries. We have found that, instead of putting management on a pedestal, it is more effective — and makes good business sense — to work on a peer level with our employees. This is a principle which is stated well in the Bible: "Thus the last shall be first, and the first last."

Do not be yoked together with unbelievers.
2 Corinthians 6:14

18

REDUCING THE RISK OF BUSINESS

William D. Bontrager

E very year hundreds of Christian businessmen enter into partnerships or other business ventures with fellow Christians. Many times they meet the other person at church, through an organization like CBMC, or some other form of business or professional association.

Many of these same Christians, within the next year, find themselves locked in conflict. The promising business that started with prayer, fasting, and unity ends in anger, bitterness, fractured relationships, and sometimes even churches becoming divided. At such times the usual question is, "Where did we go wrong?"

Based on my experiences—twelve years practicing law, five years as a judge, and three as director of the Christian Conciliation Service of Minnesota—that question could have any number of answers. But rather than seeking to rectify past failures, I think it would be most helpful to consider some practical suggestions to begin implementing now, in an existing business relationship or in one about to be formed, to prevent failures from occurring.

- First, enter into a written contract, but *call it a covenant*, the Biblical name for an agreement.
- Second, remember that *your agreement is ultimately with God*, so that your yes may be a yes, your no a no, and so that you will do all

97

that you promise to do. State in the formal agreement that you are making a covenant with God, as well as with the other party.

- Third, each of the parties should formally profess Jesus Christ as Savior and Lord in the written document. Then each party acknowledges and accepts the other individual's faith profession as genuine. The reason for this is simple: Once a dispute arises, we often declare the other party is an unbeliever and use that as justification for not dealing with him in a Biblical fashion. The document will serve as a reminder of where you began.

- Fourth, acknowledge to one another that, should a dispute arise, you might not "listen" to the other when they come to confront you in a specific fault (Matthew 18:15). Therefore, you each should list the names of potential witnesses (in accordance with Matthew 18:16), persons to whom you do listen, such as your pastor, a prayer partner, or another Christian businessman.

- Fifth, each partner must covenant to practice the principles of Matthew 5:23–24 or Matthew 18:15–16 as soon as they become aware that a dispute exists. If after speaking personally the issue is still unresolved, the one who initially identified the problem should call on the other person's "witnesses" to assist. *Note:* In calling on the witnesses, do not tell them the nature of the offense, since that amounts to gossip. Wait until you are all in the presence of the other party.

- Sixth, provide for final and binding resolution of the dispute, should the other steps fail in eliminating the problem. One good way would be for the four "witnesses" to select a Christian attorney to join them as arbitrators. If there is a Christian Conciliation Service near you, that service could serve as arbitrator.

- Seventh, covenant with one another in the words of the Apostle Paul in Romans 8:38–39, "For I am convinced that neither death nor life, neither angels nor demons, neither the present nor the future, nor any powers, neither height nor depth, nor anything else in all creation, will be able to separate us from the love of God that is in Christ Jesus our Lord," and add the phrase, "or my love for my brother, _____." (NIV)

- Finally, follow the Biblical practice of taking communion (breaking bread) together as you both sign the covenant.

These steps are not a guarantee that conflict will be avoided. But they will lessen the impact of the conflict and will provide a means for resolving it before a crisis exists. Rational, acceptable solutions are much harder to find after a conflict has developed. Most importantly, if these steps are carried out and observed, our Lord will be glorified through our obedience to the guidelines He has offered in His Word.

Do not be yoked together with unbelievers.

2 Corinthians 6:14

19

AN UNEVEN MATCH
(Knowing when to throw in the towel)

Scott McReynolds

Soon after I became a Christian, I made the unsettling discovery that lofty ideals are more easily professed than practiced—particularly when they are not shared by business partners.

I was in charge of a small mortgage company, a subsidiary of a holding company. Although my partner did not share my beliefs, we had always gotten along, and I felt he was a fair, high integrity type of guy. The trouble began when he brought in another partner as vice president of the holding company, effectively making him my superior.

This new partner was openly opposed to even the mention of spiritual matters. His values and mine were very different, and as time went on, it became increasingly difficult for me to function effectively under his direction. As I prayed, asking the Lord for help, I guess I lacked the nerve to get out. But neither could I stay.

God worked a miracle, not only enabling me to get out of that situation with my self-esteem intact, but actually enabling me to purchase the company outright, gaining a new financial partner in the process. He since has become a Christian, and I now have two other Christian partners.

I can't explain how much it means to be involved in a partnership that is centered upon Jesus Christ. Through His wisdom and guidance, we have been able to resolve numerous disagreements amicably.

Perhaps the most serious occurred recently, when two of the partners were engaged in a strong dispute regarding business philosophies and practices. Each had strong opinions on how the other's department should be run. Individually, each man met with me and suggested that I should seriously consider firing the other. Now if I had acted on their counsel, I would have had to dismiss both of them.

Rather than taking immediate action, I committed the entire circumstance to prayer. The Lord prompted me to bring Oswald Chambers' great book, *My Utmost For His Highest*, into work for our weekly devotional. That day's message happened to be called, "Pull Yourself Together." After discussing that, I was impressed that the best way of resolving the problem was for the two men to work it out themselves.

Telling them I had no intention of firing either one or modifying their responsibilities, I directed them to meet for half an hour each day for a week, committing at least half of that time to prayer. At the end of that time, they were to come back to me and tell me the solution they had reached. I even told them that if they decided they wanted *me* to leave, I would. Ultimately, they did reach a compromise and their interactions are substantially improved.

The relationship with my original partner has not been nearly as good. After I had purchased the company, he had not talked to me in ten months, even though we still were in the same building. Finally, two months ago he called, and we had lunch together. During our conversation, he pointed to a big change in me after I became a Christian. He told me he did not agree with it, but he respected it. I just told him that I hope one day to have the opportunity to explain in detail what my faith has meant to me.

As I left, I thought about the lesson I had learned. This partner had been reliable and respectable, even though he had not been a Christian. Unfortunately, because we could not make decisions according to the same spiritual framework, he had brought in another factor which had destroyed our association.

As the Bible says, "Do not be bound together with unbelievers; for what partnership have righteousness and lawlessness, or what fellowship has light and darkness" (2 Corinthians 6:14, NAS).

Do not be yoked together with unbelievers.

2 Corinthians 6:14

20

DISJOINTED VENTURES

Larry Burkett

We hear a great deal in Christian circles about not being "un-equally yoked." But what does that mean when applied to fi-nances? First, we must define a "yoke" to understand why this analogy was chosen.

There are two distinct types of yokes presented in the Bible. One is a collar used on slaves to show their total subjugation. The second, which is of concern here, is a harness used to link two working animals together. In 2 Corinthians 6:14, the Apostle Paul writes, "Do not be bound together with unbelievers," (NAS). The word he chose was *zugos,* a yoke serving to couple two things together. Paul also used the word, *heteros* thereby creating the word, *heterozugeo,* meaning to be unequally yoked. Thus, we are admonished to not be unequally yoked with unbe-lievers.

A yoke in Jesus Christ's day was a common device used to couple oxen together for plowing or hauling. The oxen were matched as closely as possible so the burden would be distributed equally. The two animals had to be trained to work together, even walking stride for stride so the heavy wooden bar would not rub holes in their backs as they worked.

Once connected by the yoke, the oxen were no longer two—they were one working unit. Hence the analogy of a yoke to a marriage is an accurate one. A marriage should be two people pulling in common bond toward compatible goals and sharing the load equally.

What is a financial yoke?

Let's first define what a financial yoke is not:

When two or more people are related in work by an employee/employer relationship, they are not yoked. They are not carrying an equal load, and either is free to leave at any time. There is an authority relationship, perhaps even bondage, but not a *heterozugeo*.

What about ownership of stock in a corporation?

This may be a yoke if, for instance, there were an equal ownership of the stock, because then the stockholders are, in essence, partners.

In a minority/majority stockholder relationship, there is no yoke created (although there may still be an authority relationship, and even bondage).

What about partnerships?

There definitely is a yoke created in a partnership arrangement. What one partner does, the others are responsible for. The law deals with them jointly and/or individually for acts of the partnership.

What about limited partnerships, syndications, etc.?

These probably create yokes for the managing or general partners because they literally are partners in every respect.

For the limited partners, there is an investment relationship, limited in liability and authority. Again there may be an authority relationship, but not a yoke-type bond.

Summary

There is no absolute method of predetermining what creates a yoke and what does not. Marriages and partnerships fit the description of yokes nearly perfectly, so we are admonished not to be bound to unbelievers. However, a yoke can be created even in a non-partnership business arrangement if the intent is for two or more people to share equal or unlimited authority, as well as rewards or liabilities.

The fact that we are not to be yoked to unbelievers should not imply that non-believers are less honest than believers. Many are very honest, ethical people. The principle is given because the believer must be willing to pay any price to serve God, while the unbeliever will not be willing to do so. Thus, their attitudes are incompatible, and ultimately they will clash (1 Corinthians 2:14). When a believer and non-believer can maintain a partnership without conflict over the spiritual goals of the company, it is normally because the believer has compromised God's principles.

Just because we can have partnerships with other believers does not mean that we should. Paul wrote, "All things are lawful for me, but all things are not profitable" (2 Corinthians 6:12a, NAS). Stretching that principle some, then I can say, "Any two Christians can be partners, but not all should be" (2 Opinions 2:1).

There are different levels of maturity, commitment, and human compatibility. You should choose a business partner with the same caution that you would choose a spouse.

If you already are in an unequally yoked situation, observe the principles taught by the Apostle in 1 Corinthians, chapter 7, and pray that God will use you to bring your partner to salvation.

*Though he stumble, he will not fall, for the Lord up-
holds him with his hand.*

Psalm 37:24

21

THE ARTFUL MANAGEMENT
OF FAILURE

Fred DeFalco

We all are familiar with failure and setbacks, but how many of us
see them as the only real opportunity to practice and experience
real success? Instead, most of us expend great amounts of energy trying
to avoid or eliminate failure from our lives.

Experience has taught me that since some degree of failure is inevitable, our efforts would be better used trying to manage it in an artful
manner. When the Apostle James wrote his letter to Christian Jews scattered abroad, he didn't tell them to moan about their problems. Instead,
he urged them to "Consider it pure joy, my brothers . . . " (James 1:2).

Learning how to manage failure and setbacks artfully takes time —
I've been working on it for seventeen years and still have a long way to
go. But during that time, I have found that while I still may not have all
the answers, I've done a good job of researching the important questions.

Learning From Experiences

As I stand in front of a group, leading a business seminar, no one would
guess my troubled background. I was born the last of six children thirty-
five years ago, raised in a lower middle class neighborhood in Baltimore. I had many bad examples to follow and encountered failure early.

An eighth grade dropout, I spent time in reform schools, became involved in drugs, and was jailed four times by the age of sixteen. Then before I had reached my nineteenth birthday, I was married, had enlisted in the Merchant Marines and still had no direction in life.

Somewhere there had to be a better way of life, I reasoned, but where? My answer came when someone explained to me God's simple plan of salvation. From the moment I put my faith in Jesus Christ, I started building on that Rock.

My adventures with success started slowly. One of my first jobs was that of a "teller" behind a garbage truck. (I was the guy who would tell the driver, "Move it up, Joe.") After ten months behind that truck, I concluded there had to be a more appealing way of making a living, and I got a job in a steel mill, where I worked for three years. I moved on to telecommunications and then, in 1978, I went into real estate. Over the next eleven years I advanced from leading salesperson to sales manager to regional manager/senior vice president.

Failures of the Famous

One of the most important things I did as I got started in real estate was to study biographies of great people of the past—business people, missionaries, political leaders. To my surprise, I discovered that each of these revered individuals had encountered more failure than any of us could ever imagine. But they had the tenacity, faith, courage, and character to manage it and use it to their advantage.

After seeing that pattern repeated over and over, I adopted the philosophy that success is the artful management of failure. I used this philosophy in building people, which resulted in rapid growth within my areas of responsibility. It worked so well, I applied this philosophy to my personal life. My relationship with my wife, Dot, was as weak as it could be. She had been raised in foster homes and had suffered from repeated abuse. Coupled with my background, we didn't have much to work with. Yet, over the years we learned to artfully manage our failure and today we are truly in love—it only took about fourteen years of practice! And so we don't forget, our children frequently remind us to continue developing our failure management skills.

I've had many opportunities to implement my philosophy in business. I virtually lost all that I had in several land development projects, and I'm still paying my way out six years later. Even with the career successes and promotions, I had more than enough failures and setbacks to keep me in practice.

Ten Key Principles

So what have I learned about artfully managing failure and setbacks? I have discovered ten key principles:

1. You need courage.

It is the one thing that can turn any situation around—whether it be in business, marriage, or other relationships.

Courage is defined as mental or moral strength; willingness to venture, persevere, and withstand danger, fear, or difficulty; resisting opposition or hardship; and firmness of mind and will in the face of danger or extreme difficulty. God told Joshua to be courageous, even when the odds seemed insurmountable. The Bible promises that if God is for us, who can be against us?

2. Start saying you have a *situation* instead of a *problem*.

Situations are normal, a part of living. They are designed for self-propulsion, not self-pity. *Respond* to situations, don't *react*. Learn to work a situation until it works out.

A caterpillar goes into a cocoon and starts to turn into a butterfly. Then to become free, it must beat its wings against the cocoon wall. In the pounding, the butterfly is gaining strength so it can fly away after the cocoon opens.

Situations are our chance to show the world that we believe God when He says all things work together for good. I'd rather have business problems in the United States than be in the Soviet Union without a business.

3. Gain a true understanding of success.

Success *is not* the four P's: possessions, position, power, and pleasure. Making a living is just the means; life itself is the goal. As Oswald Chambers wrote, "Success in life does not come from holding a good hand, but playing a poor hand well."

In baseball, you only need a .300 average to do well. That means for one hundred times up to bat, you only hit the ball safely thirty times. You don't concentrate on the outs you have made, only the hits. If no one else is counting, why should you?

4. Renew your mind.

The present input into your head and your past conditioning determine your output. Concentrate on quality input—one hour of sermon will not override ten hours of negative TV programming.

5. Learn to live your life from the inside out.

Don't live like a thermometer that only reflects what is going on; be a thermostat that controls the environment around you.

6. Don't live for yourself.

Live your life for the glory of God and the benefit of others around you.

7. Be a student of all areas of life.

Look deeply into the eyes of your loved ones; listen for the unspoken word. Life is a long-term project, for which God has a long-term plan. Stay still on God's easel when He's trying to paint. If we move all around or jump off, He has to start over and repeat the same strokes.

8. Try to compartmentalize your life.

If you are having extreme challenges at work, don't carry them home. If you have difficult situations in your personal life, try to keep them out of your work. Give each area unyielding commitment, but only when you are in the midst of it.

9. Be a go-giver before a go-getter.

Go out and give more than you are paid to give. Don't hold anything back when it comes to service. Balance time commitments in all areas, but give as hard as you can when you're involved.

10. Dare yourself to be much better in everything you are doing.

As a boy growing up, I did every negative thing that someone would dare me to do. Now I apply that to life in a positive way.

- Dare yourself to be a better spouse!
- Dare yourself to be a better parent!
- Dare yourself to be a better business person!
- Dare yourself to be a better son or daughter, or a better friend!
- Do the basics well!

Though he stumble, he will not fall, for the Lord upholds him with his hand.

Psalm 37:24

22

A MATTER OF OPINION
(What is success? What is failure?
It depends on who you ask)

James R. McClure

O ne of the deceptive aspects about failure is that often it looks so much like success. And success can seem suspiciously like failure.

I had determined from childhood to be a "success." So once I decided that I wanted to pursue a career in computers, I went after it with great intensity.

After college I was commissioned as an officer in the Army, and while many of my friends were in Vietnam, experiencing the horrors of war, I was working eighteen to nineteen hours a day at Fort Bliss, Texas, overseeing the work of 250 civilians and military personnel at the post's twenty-four hour per day data processing center. This proved to be a great initial step for my computer career.

When I got out of the service, I hooked up with H. Ross Perot's fledgling company, Electronic Data Systems Corporation (EDS), where I saw the company grow from three hundred to three thousand employees in less than three years. Eighty to one hundred hour work weeks were the norm for me. I hardly ever saw my wife, Alice, since I often would work straight through the weekend.

Different Views of Success

I rapidly gained recognition within the organization. Large raises enabled me to buy bigger things and nicer housing. I was a success, right? Alice would have answered an emphatic *No!* While I was accumulating recognition and emotional strokes for my work, life for her was miserable. She was married to a man who came home only long enough to get a few hours sleep and a change of clothes before heading back to the office.

I left EDS to join a small consulting firm, envisioning a repeat of the EDS success story. That did not happen, although the company did mark substantial growth. From that firm, I moved on to work as a young, fast-track executive for two large, regional commercial banks.

During all of these experiences, I found that if you are willing to put in the extra hours to get results, most bosses heartily approve. So I continued working eighty to ninety hours per week, even though I was now the father of two daughters. My job was that of a "fire fighter," solving critical problems or undertaking major projects. I did my work well and was rewarded accordingly.

At home, however, things were not so great. One particular incident caused me to start reviewing my priorities. It was rare that I would be home on a Saturday morning, but on one such occasion my two-year-old daughter, Shannon, was toddling across the living room, and I reached down to pick her up. Instead of coming to me, she turned around and ran, crying to Alice. At first, I thought Shannon was sick, but Alice tersely pointed out, "No, Jim. She just doesn't know who you are."

Her words hurt, but I knew what my wife said was true. I was gone from home, 6 A.M. to 10 P.M. on weekdays, working every Saturday and even going to the office Sunday afternoons after church. But the shock of this incident soon wore off as I continued to focus on building a successful career.

After ten years in banking, I decided it was time to try my hand at an entrepreneurial venture by joining a small, fast-growing computer consulting firm. Over the next two years, the business grew from $3.5 million to $12 million, but one event forced me to re-evaluate my attitude toward success and failure.

Goal Was Missed

When the second year after I had joined the firm ended, I reviewed my growth goals for the year. We had achieved 99 percent of the objectives. But it was devastating to me that in spite of all my hard work, I had failed to fully reach the goal. Instead of being euphoric that we had come so close to a very ambitious target, I felt deeply depressed. That was when a partner in the firm pointed out that whatever you commit your life to is your god; I realized that for me, *work* had become god.

My reaction to the narrowly missed goal, the partner's comments and the memory of Shannon's rejection several years before, dramatically showed me how completely out of whack my priorities were.

I can see now that God was trying to get my attention, showing me how shallow my life had become. I had a prestigious job, big salary, company car, a nice house, lots of "things," a wife and two children, and yet I was desperately lonely. I was considered a good manager and had helped others advance in their careers, but I had no real friends. I was too busy getting results to invest time in building friendships. My work shaped my self-worth.

I started rethinking what was really important. As a ten-year-old boy, I had asked Jesus Christ into my life, but as an adult—except for weekly church attendance—I had excluded God from my day-to-day activities. As I thought about it, I concluded that God needed to be central to everything I did.

Sick with fear and anxiety, and even considering suicide, I got on my knees for the first time in many years and prayed, "God, I've really messed up my life. Life's success isn't what everyone says it's supposed to be. I don't want to live this way anymore. Lord, take my life and do with it what you want."

My first step was to submit my resignation from the company, effective June 30, turning my back on the potential of a lucrative partnership. I didn't know where I would go, but I sensed that God wanted me to make a clean break from my job-is-everything lifestyle.

Income Dropped Dramatically

I also expected God would soon provide another "cushy" job for me, but June ended without another job materializing. Early in July, I was asked to do some private consulting work, so I pursued that—but my income was reduced to a fraction of what it had been, necessitating some dramatic lifestyle changes.

God still had much to teach me. A year later, I was invited to join a partnership with three other men. I prayed about this decision, but even when God seemed to say "No!" and put roadblocks in every direction, I was determined to go ahead—and I did. I became a partner in a custom manufacturing company. The business had nothing to do with computers or anything else I knew about, but it sounded like a potentially good business.

I couldn't have been more wrong. Within three months, the company was struggling; at the six-month point, it had lost a considerable amount of money; and after one year, we were several hundred thousand dollars in debt. Once again I felt devastated, and this was far worse than falling one percentage point short of a company growth goal. I owed more money than my house and everything else I owned were worth. Losing the business seemed almost like a death in the family.

God had let me have my wish to be a partner in that business, even though He had tried repeatedly to warn me against it.

Crisis Drew Them Closer

The positive aspect of this crisis was that Alice and I were able to weather it together, and it actually drew us closer. Several years before, it would have destroyed our already shaky marriage. But having endured some very tough times, especially Alice's faithfulness through the years of neglect, we were strong enough to survive.

I then returned full time to working as a computer management consultant and God saw that we had just enough income to meet our obligations each month—not 23 cents more or 15 cents less.

From the world's standpoint, I was experiencing the consequences of failure, but spiritually, it was perhaps the greatest success that I had known to that point. Actually, it was God's success, because He finally had my complete attention and dependence.

My vocational struggles did not suddenly come to an end—1988 was one of the most difficult years of all. Yet, it was also one of the most exciting. I was convinced more than ever that I needed to put my family first, so I declined to take consulting assignments that required extensive travel and long periods away from home. As a result, my consulting business was extremely inconsistent. Alice, the kids, and I learned to live on a tighter budget than ever.

New Job Opportunities

At the same time, God gave both Alice and me some incredible ministry opportunities. She got a part-time job with Search Ministries, whose national headquarters is just a couple of miles from our house. And while I was developing spiritual traits such as trust and faithfulness, I was able to assist with a ministry to needy inner-city people.

Joe Ehrmann, a former tackle with the Baltimore Colts, had established the ministry in Baltimore. He and I have been friends for years, and when I learned that he was renovating an old warehouse, I decided to help out while my business allowed me a more flexible schedule.

I had never had much exposure to or empathy for inner-city people, but after working alongside of Joe and others, I began to sense the needs and the importance of God to those living in the inner city. The warehouse project, which was started in September of 1988, was completed the following April. Also in April, God opened a new vocational opportunity for me—a corporate computer management position.

God's Timing

Over the past several years, I have gained a new appreciation of God's faithfulness. As He says in Jeremiah 29:11–13, "For I know the plans I have for you . . . plans to prosper you and not to harm you, plans to give you hope and a future. Then you will call upon me and come and pray to me, and I will listen to you. You will seek me and find me when you seek me with all your heart."

Working eighty to one hundred hour weeks and gaining corporate recognition, I thought I was a success, but as a husband and a father I was an absolute failure. When I tried to remedy that by making some career changes, many observers would have called me a failure in business, but I was finally beginning to succeed in those things that are really important — relationships — first with God, and then with Alice and the kids.

Though he stumble, he will not fall, for the Lord up-
holds him with his hand.

Psalm 37:24

23

LOSING IT ALL
(What do you do when you are about to lose everything you have worked for during your entire life?)

André W. Iseli

From the time that I was a boy, I had worked twelve hours a day. For most of my life, money had been my only scoreboard. Suddenly I was confronted with the very real prospect of losing the fruits of all my labors.

I had become partner in a corporate venture in 1974, and from the beginning it had been a classic example of being in the right place at the right time. Being an entrepreneur, I was involved in several other businesses, but I was pleased to see this company doing so well.

Then, in 1984, the bottom fell out. A series of lawsuits were filed against the corporation, and I was named in those suits, even though I had nothing to do with the disputes that had triggered the court action. A corporate obligation was being interpreted as a personal obligation.

The magnitude of the suit was inconceivable. During the two years the dispute dragged on, I experienced every anxiety imaginable. The sum total of every bad thing that had happened in my life prior to that time seemed miniscule.

I had always prided myself as being a hard-working, honest businessman and resented being accused of something I was not responsible for. Faced with the possibility of losing my livelihood and the ability to provide for my family was nearly more than I could bear.

However, in keeping with the adage, things did work out for the best—and not just in a material sense. The case eventually was settled out of court, with the monetary cost to me far less than it could have been. Even more importantly, I discovered that my relationship with God was not what I had thought it was.

I had given my heart to Jesus Christ at the age of sixteen, but there is a great difference between just knowing the Lord and truly serving Him. By nature, I was a street fighter and a loner. I prided myself on being able to "do it myself," and although I knew that God was always there, He certainly wasn't near the top of my priority list.

Philippians 4:6–7 talks about not being anxious for anything. We are to submit our concerns to God, so we can experience His peace during times of adversity. But as I went through that difficult time, I knew nothing about that. All I knew was how helpless I felt.

Looking back, I can appreciate how the Lord was at work throughout that time and how He was using it to draw me and my family closer to Him. By the time the crisis had been resolved, I had learned for the first time about real trust in God, realizing that He wants the best for me.

I've also learned what a blessing it is to get on your knees to pray with your wife. Gail and I literally were driven to our knees as we sought strength to endure that horrible time. I kept asking, "Why me, Lord?" Since I was a boy, I had accepted accountability for my actions. When I did wrong, I expected correction. But why was this happening, when I had done nothing wrong?

Eventually, I could see that God was allowing this trial to mold us, to soften us so we would be more useful in serving Him.

Two years later, I was again the target of multiple lawsuits—and again I was being accused of something I had nothing to do with. I was associated with a brokerage firm, and another broker with the firm had become overly enthusiastic about what he regarded as an outstanding investment situation—to the extent that the bulk of his clients' money was invested in the one stock. When that stock failed, his clients all lost a lot of money and many of them sued for damages.

Each of the twenty-eight suits included me, since I was construed to be the branch manager at the time the problems occurred, although I was not. From the beginning I felt that I was not personally responsible, but my family and I had the great embarrassment of having a number of subpoenas served at our home and seeing newspaper accounts written that contained totally false information. On the advice of my attorneys, I did not reply, so I had to quietly endure being assassinated by the press.

Tallulah Bankhead once said, "I don't care what they say about me, as long as they spell my name right." I can attest, from personal experience, that she was wrong.

In time, several of the suits were dismissed, and the balance is being settled through arbitration. In each case, it did not appear that I would have any personal liability. But once again there was a high emotional toll on our family. The positive result was being drawn much closer to God, and to each other.

I've been involved in more than forty businesses, and not all of them have succeeded. But my biggest failure was not fully committing my life to Christ more than thirty years ago. Early in my business career, I set a goal to become "filthy rich." Now, that seems like a foolish decision, knowing that Jesus admonished us not to lay up treasures on earth, but in heaven. I could have avoided the pressures and anxieties of striving for the wrong priorities.

I'm thankful, however, that God used these circumstances to show me that He alone deserved to be top priority in my life. There has been one additional benefit: I have gained a great sensitivity to people who are hurting, being able to counsel with and encourage many of them during the past four years.

I have fought the good fight, I have finished the race,
I have kept the faith.

2 Timothy 4:7

24

WORK'S END OR SECOND WIND?
(Weighing the options for retirement)

Ronald W. Blue

The word "retirement" conjures up all sorts of pictures. One dictionary defines retirement as "withdrawal from one's position or occupation, or from active working life." From that we can draw two conclusions: retirement could mean ceasing to work altogether, or it could simply mean a change in vocation or occupation.

Only in the United States is it possible for large numbers of persons to quit working at some age so they can retire. Retirement plans funded by companies, unions, and other groups, as well as Social Security and the general affluence of Americans, have made retirement or quitting work a live option to a majority of people. That situation is unique to our society.

In the rest of the world, quitting work is generally not an option. Looking at the Bible, it's hard to think of anyone who retired. The real question probably is not "can you retire?" because most will have that option. The question, instead, becomes, "should you retire?" By retirement, I mean quitting work.

To help in answering this question, let's look at the Bible—specifically, Luke 12:16–21:

And he told them this parable: "The ground of a certain rich man produced a good crop. He thought to himself, 'What shall I do? I have no place to store my crops.'

"Then he said, 'This is what I'll do. I will tear down my barns and build bigger ones, and there I will store all my grain and my goods. And I will say to myself, "You have plenty of good things laid up for many years. Take life easy; eat, drink and be merry." '

"But God said to him, 'You fool! This very night your life will be demanded from you. Then who will get what you have prepared for yourself?'

"This is how it will be with anyone who stores up things for himself but is not rich toward God."

We could learn many lessons and principles from this parable, but let me draw one conclusion: the man in the parable had a life purpose, which was to take life easy — eat, drink, and be merry. But God said to him, "You fool." I don't believe Christians are called to a life purpose of eating, drinking, and merry-making. Instead, God has given us a life filled with purpose, meaning, and accomplishment for the cause of Jesus Christ.

My perspective must be that I am here on earth as a pilgrim and sojourner for a limited time, and during that span all my energies and activities should be directed toward accomplishing God's plans and purposes for me. Therefore, I may retire from a particular occupation or vocation, but it would not be to live a life of ease for the rest of my days. Rather, it would be because God had called me to another activity, ministry, or vocation for His purposes.

Many people confuse financial independence and retirement. They are not the same. I know a number of people who are financially independent but far from retired. I think of one good friend who sold his business a couple of years ago to devote himself to developing a ministry to businessmen. He is now so busy ministering to businessmen, he has little time even to manage the wealth God entrusted to him. This is hardly retirement!

We must answer a fundamental question of life: Why am I here? One day we each will stand before God to give an account for the time He entrusted to us (2 Corinthians 5:10). I would hate to have nothing more to report than, "Well, my golf handicap dropped ten strokes after I retired," or "My major accomplishment was to try thirty-seven different restaurants offering a senior citizen's discount." Or even, "Lord, I visited every continent in the world and took in all the beauty of Your creation." None of these activities is necessarily bad in itself, but they can become wrong if they are one's motivation for life.

I believe one of the greatest wastes of natural resources available to the Christian community is older people who have so much to offer in the way of wisdom, knowledge, and perspective, but do not make that available to those of us who are much younger. Our perspective should be that, in light of eternity, we have so little time and so much to do!

Consider Moses, who didn't even begin his work for the cause of God until age eighty. And in Psalm 90:12 he prays, "Lord, teach us to number our days aright, that we may gain a heart of wisdom." Let's make that our prayer as well.

I have fought the good fight, I have finished the race,
I have kept the faith.

2 Timothy 4:7

25

COMING OF AGE
(A sixty-eight-year-old insurance executive talks about "taking it easy")

Robert J. Tamasy

During the late 1970s, the energy crisis dramatically affected American lifestyles. There were so many places to go and so much to do, but with gasoline being rationed, there was widespread fear of not being able to get there to do it.

In a similar way, advancing age creates an energy crisis of its own. One of the great inequities of life is that children, who seem to have so little of importance to do, abound with energy, while adults, with so many commitments and responsibilities, see their energy levels decline with the passage of years.

One response to that reality is a relatively new innovation in western society, the concept of "retirement." Although not in widespread use until the early 1900s, retirement has become an accepted stage of life in America. Pensions, Social Security, Medicare, and various forms of investment are geared toward the day when an individual "stops working" and begins to reap the fruits of his labors.

Retirement, however, is not a part of Lorin Griset's vocabulary. While many of his peers are actively pursuing post-vocational interests such as traveling, fishing, reading, or just "relaxing," the vibrant, sixty-eight-year-old insurance executive from Santa Ana, California maintains many of his same activities of twenty years ago.

"I'm fortunate in that my business is one I don't have to retire in," Griset points out. "It's not like working for a major corporation, where you might face mandatory retirement at age sixty-five.

"In the insurance business, we're able to dictate our own time, so I haven't had to face the adjustments many corporate executives must deal with. Today, although in terms of age perhaps I should be retired, there is nothing particularly new or different in my regular activities."

Griset's activities, in addition to selling insurance as he has for most of the past forty-six years, include serving on the boards of trustees for Westmont College and Biola University, two boards affiliated with Wycliffe Bible Translators, his church board, and playing golf three times a week (walking the full eighteen holes).

He is also a regular participant with the Christian Business Men's Committee of Santa Ana, the city where he once served as mayor and city council member.

While he may move at a pace somewhat slower than that of thirty years ago, Griset is not aware of a personal energy shortage. "I hope I never get into the 'I worked hard, so now I'm going to take it easy for the rest of my life' frame of mind. Since I became a Christian as a student at UCLA in 1936, I've strived to make the Bible my guide for living. Do you know what the Bible says about retirement? Absolutely nothing. Therefore, I've concluded that retirement is not intended as a part of the Christian mindset.

"To the contrary, I believe God expects us to continue actively serving Him as long as we live. For instance, 1 Corinthians 15:58 tells us, 'Therefore, my dear brothers, stand firm. Let nothing move you. *Always* give yourselves fully to the work of the Lord, because you know that your labor in the Lord is not in vain.' As we read God's Word, I believe its principles apply to all Christians, whether they are young or old. And we should never stop following them."

Griset sees each day of his life as an investment. Just as a good financial counselor will advise a client to put his money to work in some profitable manner, he believes in using each hour of his life to its greatest advantage.

"The Bible teaches about laying up treasure in heaven. I don't believe this refers just to dollars. It also pertains to our time and the focus of our lives," he says.

Much of his time expenditure is directed toward CBMC activities. "In the Christian life, it is not easy to do many things well, no matter how old you are. My philosophy is to find that one thing I do best, and then focus on it. Having been a businessman all my life, I feel my greatest effectiveness is working with other business and professional men, helping them to discover what it means to have a personal relationship with Jesus Christ, and then assisting them as they try to apply Biblical teachings to their everyday lives.

"As someone once said so appropriately, our primary objective as Christians — and certainly my objective — is to take as many people to heaven with us as we can.

"I have found CBMC to be an ideal instrument for providing that kind of opportunity, bringing together businessmen who are young, old and in between."

Griset concedes that advancing years may prompt the need to shift gears, but not to quit. "My physical abilities are on the decline, but I'm thankful to God that my spiritual life is not. One of the keys for ongoing spiritual growth, I've found, is to remain in areas that challenge me, such as teaching a Bible class or discipling a man. Without these to spur me on, I know I would begin to lag spiritually.

"And at the end of my life, I want to be able to say, like the Apostle Paul, 'I have fought the good fight, I have finished the race, I have kept the faith.' "

I have fought the good fight, I have finished the race,
I have kept the faith.

2 Timothy 4:7

26

FUTURE SHOCK

Ted Benna

For twenty years, I had helped build a successful employee benefit consulting business, but one fact bothered me. While the plans I designed were producing large tax advantages for business owners, non-owner employees were frequently receiving only minimal benefits.

Since becoming a Christian, I have learned to trust in God's personal involvement in every area of my life, including my vocation. So I prayed, asking for His guidance in finding a program that would be more useful to both employers and workers. God's answer came one Saturday afternoon in January of 1980, while I was trying to revise a benefits program for a client company. I discovered how Section 401(k), which had been added to the Internal Revenue Code in 1978, could offer substantial employer/employee advantages.

That section provided for employees to save a portion of their salaries on a pre-tax basis, but I knew that tax savings alone would not be a sufficient incentive for most employees to tie up money in a long-term investment plan. So I structured the plan to include "matching" contributions from the employer as an additional incentive to increase participation.

We tried out the plan first with our own company, and were surprised to see more than 90 percent of the eligible employees join the plan. Even after it received IRS approval in 1981, many were skeptical about the 401(k) plan, but slowly it gained interest. Over the next several years, it became the hottest development in the employee benefits field. Today, roughly half of all full-time U.S. workers are covered by some form of the plan. I'm thankful that God directed me to an idea that will help in meeting people's financial needs for years to come.

Of course, besides 401(k) plans, there are many other investment options. They all fall somewhere within what the financial industry terms the "three-legged stool": government-sponsored plans, employer-sponsored plans, and personal savings plans. But there is one consideration that most people seem to overlook. While preparing financially for retirement, they neglect to make the necessary psychological preparations.

It's not unusual for a retiree to die shortly after retiring; others spend their retirement years in misery. It isn't easy to spend forty-plus years going to work every day and then suddenly turn it off. All of us, regardless of age, want to be needed.

For that reason, individuals who have little productive involvement outside of work should move into retirement gradually. One good way to do this is by adjusting from a full-time to part-time work schedule. That may mean working three days a week instead of five, even if it means changing jobs.

As we move from an industrialized society, age becomes less of a factor since more and more jobs are not dependent on physical stamina. With a shortage of qualified workers in many parts of the country, employers are eager to hire experienced, retirement-age workers on a part-time basis.

Other factors in society also are beginning to reshape retirement as we know it today. A large portion of retiree income is currently being funded by the succeeding generation of workers. The so-called "baby boom generation" is moving rapidly toward retirement age, and that will place an unprecedented strain on this transfer system. The next generation will be unable, and probably unwilling, to bear the cost of the baby boom retirees, especially since the present, younger generation of workers is not expected to achieve the same level of financial success as their parents. Faced with increasing difficulties in buying single homes, new cars and other costly items, post-baby boom workers are not likely to transfer much of their income to help the elderly maintain a standard of living higher than their own.

As a result, many of today's workers who are anxiously looking forward to retiring in their late fifties and early sixties will not realize their expectations. Considering the fact that the average sixty-year-old will live for another twenty years — and many will live thirty or forty more years — it is unlikely that many sixty-year-olds will be able to accumulate a sufficient amount to maintain their standards of living for the rest of their lives.

It would be wise to begin considering how to invest the post-retirement years. For that reason, here are several recommendations:

- Continue working as long as possible. God did not intend for us to spend one-third of our adult years (or more) in idle leisure, and society urgently needs our experience and expertise.
- Make the transition from high-pressure, full-time employment to less demanding part-time employment during your sixties and seventies.
- Avoid going from full-time employment to total retirement, unless your time will be productively occupied in other ways.
- Do not retire until your level of retirement income is at least 150 percent of the amount you currently need to maintain a comfortable standard of living.

PART TWO

HIS PRIVATE WORLD

Let us run with perseverance the race marked out
for us.

Hebrews 12:1

27

FINDING THE RIGHT PURPOSE

Gayle Jackson

A ll around us, people seem to be engaged in a lifetime search for meaning and fulfillment. Some are looking for it in other people, while others grasp for it through personal achievements. Still others think meaning can be found in material things. I have concluded that the answer can best be found through the use of three words: *purpose, vision,* and *objective.*

Purpose is *what we want our life to add up to — and why.* Vision follows in that it is *seeing ourselves move toward the accomplishment of that purpose.* Finally, objectives are *measurable milestones as we are moving toward that purpose.*

It is common as people come toward the close of their lives to look back and add up what they feel they have accomplished. I would submit that their tallies would be much greater if they had conducted their lives in reference to a clear understanding of their personal purpose.

There are four classic approaches we use to discover our purpose:

The first approach, *deduction,* actually is a "non-purpose." This one, unfortunately, is the category most people fit into. They conduct their lives without any clear purpose or direction, with little or no thought as to what they are doing or why. Only later in life do they deduce what their purpose was, making it what we might call a "postmortem purpose."

Second is *association,* in which people gain a sense of purpose through their associations in life—family, neighbors, business, church, or organizations they belong to such as CBMC or the Rotary Club. In complying with the corporate purpose of one or more of these groups, they gain an "adopted purpose."

Third is *emulation,* in which people follow the model or example of others. Many of us have "heroic models" we seek to be like, whether it be emulating their hairstyles, manner of dress, or the ways they talk and act. The result of emulation becomes a "vicarious purpose."

Fourth is *personalization,* which I believe is the only way of determining one's purpose, the approach used by only a small minority of people. This involves developing deep, personal, purposeful concepts of what God wants me to do with my life.

In each of these approaches, however, a wrong purpose can be reached. It is important, therefore, that one arrive at his purpose not by technique, but by consulting the proper source. The only time that lasting and meaningful purpose will be found is if God is its Author and Source.

The Bible reveals that God's purpose for His people has three dimensions: that which is *ultimate,* that which is *universal,* and that which is *unique.* God's ultimate purpose includes the whole created order, of which we can catch only glimpses. By and large it is God's "secret." His universal purpose, however, is shared by all His people—to glorify God as we participate with Him in the process of being prepared for an eternity in heaven. God's unique purpose takes into account the individual roles we fill in our lives, such as being a husband, father, son, brother, employee, and neighbor; our spiritual gifts; our temperament; skills; and the environment in which we find ourselves each day.

Once we realize that we each have a specific purpose, however, it is important that we keep a few things in mind:

- Purpose is not something we can measure, since it involves intangibles such as glorifying God and serving others.
- It is also a process which takes an entire lifetime, not an isolated event.
- There will never be enough time to do everything we would like to do, so we must realize it is God's plan—and not ours.

- We each have a purpose, and as we strive to carry it out, it always will develop our dependence upon God.
- The longer we live, the clearer our purpose will become, even though we may never see exactly how it all will work out.

If we seek to determine God's purpose for our lives, what can we expect? Several things, I believe — namely contentment, a clear focus for our lives, a recognition of our dependence upon God from day to day, and the ability to say at the end of our lives, "It is finished."

Questions To Consider

The following are some questions you might consider in evaluating the direction you want your life to take from this point on:

1. What is the purpose for your life? What do you see as the purpose for your family, or for your relationship with your spouse?
2. What is the purpose for your job position?
3. If someone were to examine your calendar, entertainment activities, or checkbook, what would they communicate about how you perceive your purpose in life?
4. Are you more concerned with the product of your life, or the intangible process God is taking you through?
5. Are you content?

The world tells us that we should be motivated by discontentment, but the Apostle Paul wrote that "godliness with contentment is great gain" (1 Timothy 6:6).

Perhaps the bottom line question should be, do you want to be in the game of life, developing a deeper relationship with God in the process, or do you want to be a spectator sitting on the bench? From my observations, it's apparent that 75 percent of the people we meet each day will never get into the game!

*Let us run with perseverance the race marked out
for us.*

Hebrews 12:1

28

REACHING YOUR GOAL
(Five steps for developing
an effective game plan)

Jim Dudleston

R esearch has shown that only 5 percent of adults actively set goals
for any area of their lives. Since I teach goal-setting, I typically
ask the participants at my seminars why they think so few people take
the time to set personal goals.

Basic responses include: "Some people aren't convinced of the need
to set goals or are content with things as they are." "Many are specta-
tors, not 'players' in the game of life. It's easier to watch others and
wish than to get on the field and run." "Counterproductive habits like
procrastination and lack of self-discipline undermine the achievement of
goals." "Some people never try anything new because they are afraid of
failure. Maybe they have a poor self-image."

One final comment is the one most frequently expressed by people
who don't set goals yet sense a desire for personal and professional
development: "I never learned how to set goals." Many people have
never been shown how to make a written plan to accomplish what they
want. For those people who desire a Biblically sound method for setting
goals, I offer what I call the "Five-Step S-M-I-L-E Formula."

Step 1

Survey the current condition of your life (Proverbs 27:23). A good survey will take stock of each of the following seven categories. (In Step 2 they will become target areas for goals). For each category, ask yourself, "How satisfied am I with this area?"

- *Mental goals.* Self-improvement goals related to educational areas, such as reading books and attending courses.
- *Physical goals.* An exercise program or goals designed to enhance one's appearance or health.
- *Spiritual goals.* Bible reading, personal evangelism, church attendance.
- *Social goals.* Development of relationships outside of one's family, such as friends and club memberships.
- *Family goals.* Activities done to build stronger family relationships.
- *Financial goals.* Management of financial resources and selecting items to purchase.
- *Career goals.* Objectives related to professional or business growth.

Step 2

Make a specific goal in an area that has a high priority for you (Colossians 3:17). Now that a survey has been taken, select specific areas where you would like to see improvement or results. Develop these target areas by considering the following checklist:

- Is the goal written in specific terms?
- Has a date for completion been chosen?
- Is the goal sufficiently challenging, but not overwhelming?
- Has the goal been worded as a positive result for which you are willing to assume responsibility?
- Is the goal reasonably achievable with resources that are available to you?
- Can the goal and plan for its accomplishment be monitored in the daily calendar you carry?

A comparison of some vague goals, followed by a more specific statement of the same objective, may be helpful here:

Vague: "I wish I could be better at my job."

Specific: (Management of meetings is the area selected.) "I will prepare and distribute an agenda for every staff meeting, and we will start punctually and end on time. I will implement this strategy starting next Thursday."

Vague: "I'll try to lose some weight in the next few months."

Specific: "I will weigh 175 pounds on December 31."

Step 3

Identify the activities and resources needed (Luke 14:29–32). This is the creative step of the planning process. Simply "brainstorm," jotting down all the tangible resources (such as money and equipment), intangible resources (such as time), and activities to do on a piece of paper in random order as they occur to you.

Step 4

List all the activities and other considerations in a logical order (Proverbs 24:27). Planning is the way God expects us to accomplish our goals, even though it is He who ultimately decides the outcome (Proverbs 16:9).

Step 5

Establish a time frame for the accomplishment of the goal (Psalms 90:12). If the goal is simply a one-step activity, such as taking your wife out to dinner, then a single completion date is all that is necessary. However, if the goal requires a multiple step process, such as making a family budget or landscaping the back yard, then not only does the whole project need a due date, but each step needs intermediate checkpoints to assure steady progress from one step to the next. My research indicates that the calendar or organizer one uses should be in a loose-leaf notebook so that goals and plans can be filed for references and due dates monitored along with your daily appointments and "to do" lists.

ใง ใง ใง

You have probably noticed that the Five-Step S-M-I-L-E Formula is an acronym. It's no coincidence that those who make decisions to achieve a balanced life based on godly priorities have more to "smile" about. But keeping an eye on God's larger purposes of evangelism, godly conduct, and discipleship is what gives life meaning — and without which all goal-setting deteriorates into selfish striving. Certainly all Christian businessmen desire to be models of excellence in their homes, organizations, and communities. Setting godly goals is one step in the right direction.

Let us run with perseverance the race marked out for us.

Hebrews 12:1

_____ *29*

STOP SIGN, MILEPOST, OR FORK IN THE ROAD?

Ted DeMoss

Have you ever stood alongside a casket, gazing at the body of a deceased businessman and thinking, "Did it really matter whether he lived or not?"

Apparently, Jehoram was such an individual. He died at the young age of forty, and following his death these words were written in 2 Chronicles 21:20: *"He reigned in Jerusalem eight years and, to no one's sorrow, departed,"* (NKJV).

Contrast Jehoram to Jim Elliot, one of five missionaries who died at the hands of the Auca Indians. Before leaving for South America, he was asked why he would waste his life among ignorant savages. He responded, "Why do you think it's so strange I would give up that which I cannot keep in exchange for that which I cannot lose?"

At another point in his life, Elliott wrote, "Lord, make me a crisis man — not a milepost in the way, but a fork in the road, so when people meet me they will have to decide about Christ in me."

Every business or professional man, I believe, could be looked upon in one of three ways: first, he might be viewed as a *stop sign* or even a *dead end*. This man has no answers and was described by the psalmist who wrote, "The fool has said in his heart there is no God." A man who has not earnestly sought the Creator of the universe is just existing—much like Jehoram, whose death made no difference to anyone!

Years ago in New York City I asked a businessman, "What, in your opinion, is the bottom line of life?" Without hesitating, he answered, "To make enough money this month to pay the bills I incurred last month." What an empty life! This man may have been committed to his family, but when I talked briefly with him about Jesus Christ, he responded he had no time to look for God.

A second kind of individual is like the milepost signs we see along interstate highways. These signs often tell us useful information, such as how far it is to our next destination, but once we pass them, we forget about them completely.

Until I got involved with CBMC in 1951, I was just having birthdays and passing time. I could have told you about my becoming a Christian and the circumstances of my conversion to Jesus Christ. But I was like the milepost sign that is encountered and quickly forgotten. No one who ever met me, believer or non-believer, was touched by the fact that I belonged to Christ. Although involved in church work, I knew nothing about the work of the church.

I think of a man who once told me that he had averaged being in his church for six nights per week for more than twenty years. His only night "off" was Saturday night when he prepared to teach the Sunday school lesson. He even was a CBMC member. Sadly, he could not identify one life that had been influenced through his church work. He, too, was like a milepost to Christians and non-Christians.

The third type of individual is like Jim Elliot, the man who seeks to be a fork in the road, one who prompts people to make decisions for Jesus Christ when they meet him. How does the "Fork" differ from the "Milepost" or "Stop Sign"? I believe the forks in the road are strong, spiritual individuals. Oswald Sanders in *True Spirituality* defined spirituality as "the power to change the atmosphere by one's presence; the unconscious influence that makes Christ and spiritual things real to others." "Unconscious" is the key word in that definition. It means influencing others without trying. He doesn't need three points and a poem to share Christ; his walk is so ordained by God that he becomes unusual—and unforgettable.

The Bible teaches that a man becomes a truly spiritual man by spending time alone with the Lord. A man or woman who is in the Word each day comes to doubt his doubts and believe his beliefs. A person who does not spend time each day in God's Word, however, will soon start to believe his doubts and doubt his beliefs.

A man or woman of the Book gains the correct priorities, putting God first not by lip service, church attendance, or activities, but by getting to know Him better each day. As a result he or she will be a more faithful husband or wife, parent, church member, employer, or employee, and this will produce a ministry in the lives of others.

I have often prayed that I never lose sight of God's goal for my life: to know Him better and to help make Him known to others. I have learned the Lord often answers this kind of prayer through situations we cannot understand, but we have this assurance: "Since God is directing our steps, why try to understand everything that happens along the way?" (Proverbs 20:24, TLB).

Are you content to go through life as a Stop Sign, a Dead End, or a Milepost? Or do you want to be, with God's help, a Fork in the road?

*Consider it pure joy, my brothers, whenever you face
trials of many kinds.*

James 1:2

30

STRESS

Eric Allen

You wake up and look at the clock. It reads 8:35 A.M., and you have to be at work at 9 A.M. Instantly you're a blur of flailing limbs and flinging bedsheets. You race to the shower, then to the sink to shave, and come away with more nicks than one hundred episodes of The Big Valley. How could you have slept so late? After all, the kids are up and have already turned your home into a miniature Vietnam, or so it sounds.

Since you don't have time to eat, you pour a glass of juice, then clumsily dip your tie in it. Then it's out to the car and into traffic that reminds you uneasily of a Driver's Education film you saw back in school.

Finally, you make it to the office at 9:25 A.M., hoping against hope everyone will think that's a "designer" tie you're wearing. Your trip past the receptionist's desk leaves you a-bloom with little pink "While you were out" slips.

And then, the final blow — your boss is waiting for you in your office, and he's arranged for a team of medics to be put on stand-by outside your office. Because today you were supposed to have that report ready for him, but you had just a few finishing touches to put on it this morning. The problem is, he needed it for a managers' meeting at 9:00 A.M.

Ever had a day like that? Perhaps not that extreme, of course, but it may sound too familiar. Before you even get to your desk, you feel like

149

you've been before the Grand Inquisition — your heart is pounding, your hands are clammy, and your mind is in chaos.

What you're feeling is a well-known phenomenon — *stress.* Everyone has it, even when their days don't go quite that badly. Stress is normal — it is a healthy physical release of hormones (such as adrenaline) which enable your body to cope with tense moments that require the "fight or flight" response.

Unfortunately, "fight or flight" may have been viable alternatives for earlier civilizations, but not anymore. Now it's something more like "move or get trampled." And in today's American workplace, tense moments have turned to tense hours, or days, or even weeks. That is not healthy.

After prolonged periods of stress, the hormones, which were once so helpful, turn against the body, suppressing the immune system and permanently speeding the body's metabolism. As a result, you become more susceptible to illness, and because your concentration is lowered, more prone to injury.

Excessive stress has been linked to many kinds of health problems — cancer, diabetes, arthritis, heart disease, infertility — even the common cold. In addition, prolonged stress can reduce productivity at work, foster a bad attitude, and stifle creativity. One study concluded that the effects of stress are costing about $150 billion a year in the United States.

But notice: it is only *excessive* stress that poses all these hazards, not *normal* stress. We require a certain amount of stress just to wake up in the morning, and most people work best under mild pressure. Even being born is a stressful event. In fact, the only true stress-free state is death . . . and that won't get you to the top of the corporate ladder very fast.

What causes stress? Almost everything. Most people know that major crises, such as moving, being fired, and losing a close friend or family member can put a strain on the body's system. But many researchers now believe that much of the excessive stress in our lives comes from the "little things." And in America, we are surrounded with little things.

For example, the average person entering today's workplace must know twenty-four times as much information as he did only forty years ago, according to one study. That in itself is enough to "stress out" a lot of people. But compound that with traffic jams, computers, airline delays, waiting in lines, irate customers, radios and TVs chattering constantly, telephones ringing, huge crowds—even the most stalwart businessman may have trouble coping and be unable to understand why. "My life is normal," he says. "Why do I feel so rotten?"

So what's a businessman to do—take a vacation? Not so fast. Another thing many people don't know is that "bad" stress is not the only type that can harm them. "Good stress," such as a vacation or wedding, can strain the body's system too.

The real question is, "How much stress is too much?" And the answer to that depends on the person. Some people are born to take the heat; they seem to thrive on the pressure as it closes in around them. Others disdain pressure; they would rather spend a year in a broom closet than thirty minutes in a corporate boardroom.

Both types, however, must learn to *deal* with stress in some way, because it exacts a high toll on the body, even from those who thrive on it. Most researchers agree that the "solution" to stress is not getting rid of it—the solution is dealing with it in a productive, healthy way.

Consider it pure joy, my brothers, whenever you face
trials of many kinds.

James 1:2

31

ARE YOU ADDICTED TO ADRENALIN?
(How to handle pressure when "the squeeze" is on)

An Interview with Dr. Archibald D. Hart

L ike the weather, stress is something we often talk about but feel we can do little to remedy. Yet, something can be done — and must be done — about stress, if we are to avoid the severe physical consequences that millions are suffering each day, according to Dr. Archibald D. Hart, author of *Adrenalin & Stress* (Word Books, 1986).

Dr. Hart, dean of the Graduate School of Psychology and professor of psychology at Fuller Theological Seminary in Pasadena, California, is a clinical psychologist who has done extensive research into how the mind affects the body and, conversely, how the body affects the mind. After years of studying people under stress in a variety of environments, he has concluded that the chief cause of most stress-related diseases is overproduction of adrenalin and other stress hormones.

Long-term overarousal and excessive flow of those hormones, he states, lead to psychological and physiological distress, eventually resulting in maladies ranging from heart and arterial diseases to headaches, gastric problems, ulcers and high blood pressure. High cholesterol levels, often blamed for many of those ailments, actually are a results of

excessive stress hormone production. The solution then, according to
Hart, is "adrenalin management."

**I understand that your book, *Adrenalin & Stress*, has been an
eye-opener for many of your readers?**

Yes, it has been rather remarkable. I receive a steady stream of letters
from ministers, businessmen, and others who have been to doctors for
stress problems. The people writing tell me, "I have never had anyone
explain my problem as clearly as you have."

How would you summarize what you are saying in your book?

The essence of stress is overarousal. We live in an overaroused culture — we invented electric lights so we can prolong the day, noise levels
are high, we are bombarded with media, people are losing the ability to
be alone and be quiet. The Christian evangelical church has, to some
extent, bought into this without realizing what it's doing. Most churches
incorporate tremendous stimulating and arousing properties. I think we
are confusing worship with entertainment.

So the essence of my message is that overarousal is what kills us.
We can look for stress in tensions, anxieties, and life's catastrophies, but
that's not where the more subtle hidden danger is. The body knows no
difference between what is positive or negative stress, pleasant or unpleasant. If we get angry, we arouse the same mechanism as when we
are at a dinner party with some nice people.

**Is all stress bad and detrimental? After all, just getting up in the
morning produces a certain amount of stress.**

The only good stress, in my opinion, is arousal that is short-lived. The
model I try to present is one of hills and valleys: climb as high a mountain as you want to, get as much adrenalin going as you need, as long as
it's followed by a valley of rest and low arousal, a "sabbath valley," if
you will, allowing the body to restore itself. Then it doesn't matter how
much arousal you get, because the recovery time is built in.

It's when there is not an adequate valley following the mountain that
a system of adaptation takes place, where the system starts to wear and

tear at a faster rate. It doesn't have the resilience and doesn't bounce back as quickly. We then adapt to a higher level of energy, which is our adrenalin — a whole group of stress hormones — circulating in our bodies, resulting in a depletion of our immune system, making us more vulnerable to cancers; it increases circulating cholesterol, making us more prone to cardiovascular disease; it depletes our natural brain tranquilizer, so we become more anxious.

Christians are just as guilty and vulnerable. There's no Sabbath anymore for many Christians. Theologically, we know that Jesus Christ is the fulfillment of our Sabbath, but the penalty in the Old Testament for not keeping the Sabbath was death. That's how seriously God took it. Christians today need the equivalent of that Sabbath rest, Biblically and biologically.

What, in your opinion, is the extent of illnesses that are stress-related?

Up to 50 percent of the people who go to general physicians, as high as 70 percent in some cases, are there primarily because of some stress-related problem.

It was recently reported that of the five most popular prescribed drugs for the last year, three of them were for blocking adrenalin to lower blood pressure. The other two were used to lower stomach acid, and the sixth most common drug was a tranquilizer. A vast amount of dollars, hundreds and hundreds of millions, are being spent to lower our arousal. Unfortunately, they are merely treating the symptoms, rather than the disease.

Today there is much written about controlling cholesterol levels through diet and exercise. In your book, however, you state those are only of limited value since high cholesterol is primarily produced by stress.

That's right. Studies have shown, for example, that at most, through diet you can only reduce your cholesterol level by 11 percent, meaning that if your cholesterol level is 280, the best you can hope for is 250, which is still very critical. There are new drugs that fantastically reduce cholesterol, but we don't know what the long-term consequences of that will be. Where else will the destruction of prolonged stress show itself? We're still treating just the symptom and not the cause.

You use the term "hurry sickness," referring to our response to a fast-paced society. Is it true that someone can become addicted to his own adrenalin, much as an individual becomes addicted to alcohol or drugs?

There is a whole area of addiction beyond drugs — gambling, jogging, and other compulsive-obsessive behavior. When we operate at higher and higher levels of adrenalin, our system adapts to it and needs the stimulus of adrenalin all the time. So much so that when such a person relaxes, his heart beats erratically and he suffers symptoms of withdrawal.

I am convinced that many of our compulsive behaviors are a result of the addictive effects of adrenalin. A gambler, for instance, experiences an adrenalin surge, which is one reason why he continues to gamble even when he is losing.

What would be some tell-tale signs of adrenalin addiction?

Fidgeting, shaking, inability to concentrate. Symptoms of adrenalin withdrawal are much like that of coming off of cigarettes or drugs. When you are addicted to adrenalin, you cannot tolerate low levels of stimulation. Silence is intolerable. That is something we commonly discover in business executives. An attorney I work with regularly falls asleep in front of the TV; but he can't sleep without it.

Is there any hope for the adrenalin "addict"?

Certainly, but since the process of withdrawal is very slow, I would recommend a good, long vacation, two or three weeks long. That's long enough to go "cold turkey" successfully.

We need to teach ourselves how to relax. First of all, I believe God created a valley for us each day — called sleep — so we can recover from our mountaintops. I am a "Type A" personality, but I have found that I need nine to nine-and-a-half hours of sleep a night. When I do that, I can tolerate anything. When I get less sleep, my tolerance level drops sharply.

In addition, we need valleys of recovery each hour, taking a few minutes to just relax the tension. And every week we need an extended period of relaxation. I do that regularly with great benefit. My wife tells me I am much easier to live with now.

Do you have any final words of advice about dealing with stress?

We need to learn to rest more. That must not be confused with idleness. Take long walks, listen to the birds and smell the flowers. We need to follow the model of Jesus' life, which was one of calmness, peace, un-hurriedness and balanced priorities. What makes us think we will finish all we want to do before we die? We must remember that a successful life will always be unfinished, and the more successful it is the more will be left undone.

Help For Healing "Hurry Sickness"

Here are Dr. Archibald D. Hart's suggestions for healing "hurry sickness" disease which results from excessive, continual stress arousal:

- Find the source of your stress, the most common causes being people, sin, and pain. When possible, deal with the source to reduce your stress level.
- Monitor your adrenalin arousal by regularly measuring heart rate, blood pres-ure, skin temperature, and muscle tension.
- Determine to reduce unnecessary stress arousal by relaxing your body, quiet-ing your mind, and asking God for His peace.
- Learn to deliberately slow down. Behavioral change begins in the mind.
- Review your life goals and determine if they are creating excessive stress.
- Relax your expectations and enjoy the world around you.
- Prepare for times of stress, and plan for recovery time after periods of high stress.
- Get sufficient sleep. "We need all the sleep we can get if we are to avoid stress disease. The average adult needs between eight and ten hours of sleep each night."

Taken from *Adrenalin & Stress,* by Dr. Archibald D. Hart, Word Incorporated, Dallas, Texas, 1986 and used by permission.

Consider it pure joy, my brothers, whenever you face
trials of many kinds.

James 1:2

32

THE CRASH OF '87

Robert J. Tamasy and Eric Allen

O ctober 19, 1987. That date will long be remembered by all men and women involved in the stock market. For many of them, the end of the world could not have been more dramatic. With the Dow Jones Industrial Average plummeting an unprecedented 508 points during that single, incredible day, stress became personified.

How bad was it? Steven Schultz, who has been with Shearson-Lehman Brothers in Phoenix, Arizona, for seven years, used this analogy to explain the crisis to a friend who teaches school. "It was like if you reported to school one day and every child in your class got sick—all day long."

Schultz said the avalanche in stock prices came so quickly that there was little to do but watch and wait. "What a feeling of helplessness. We were all so tied to it, it seemed like the end of the world. When I stepped out of the office, I fully expected to see cars stopped and abandoned in the streets. I was amazed to see life proceeding normally."

Whitney Lyon, assistant vice president with Merrill Lynch in Los Angeles and a broker for twenty years, termed the day "quite unbelievable. It was a kind of pressure you just can't imagine."

Although he lost a substantial amount with his own investments, Lyon said the greatest stress was in having to deal with frantic, confused clients. "The phones began ringing at 5:45 A.M. and didn't stop until well after 6 P.M. All five lines on my telephone were continuously lit up.

"I was concerned about my own losses, but the worst part was the responsibility I felt for my clients. How do you explain something like that to people who just don't understand? The experts had predicted a major correction, but no one expected it to come so soon or be so extreme."

Edward Britton, first vice president with Drexel Burnham Lambert in Washington, D.C. and a veteran of the stock market for more than nineteen years, said the cataclysmic events of the day intensified already high daily pressures. "I go home every single day fighting the tendency to be drained absolutely dry. This thing exacerbated it to the nth degree."

Weeks after "Black Monday," the three men — all committed Christians — reflected on their responses on that day.

"I went home that night with the same grim face of everybody in our office," Schultz said. "I was affected like anyone else, but the difference was that I could look past the devastation of the day, going beyond the sorrow to the hope we have as Christians. The Bible says the things that are seen are temporal, but the things that are not seen are eternal. That day gave me and my wife, Anita, a greater appreciation of the eternal."

He said Anita was a strong source of support in dealing with the day's stresses, as was another Christian broker in Grand Rapids, Michigan, whom he had met indirectly through the Christian Business Men's Committee. They reviewed the events of the day over the telephone, offering one another support and encouragement.

Lyon, like many other brokers, found it "hard to sleep that night, or the next few nights, but I did a lot of heavy praying. There was nothing any of us could do, and ultimately it was a reminder that it is God's money anyway. All we do is serve as caretakers. He provides it, and He can certainly take it away. Each night, as I prayed and read my Bible, I rediscovered the 'peace that passes all understanding,' in spite of the market's chaos."

Britton describes himself as "an aggressive, feisty guy, and knowing the Lord made a tremendous difference. If I hadn't been a Christian, I would have come right through the phone at some of the people. I had to ask God for His patience, calmness, and discretion. Unfortunately, I didn't do that with every call, and the ones I didn't ended up being strained and tense. The ones when I did pray before went much more smoothly because the Lord was in it.

"A number of my clients called me a week later. They said, 'Ed, I know you're probably going through tremendous problems. I pray for you every day. I needed to talk with you, but I waited for things to calm down.' That, more than anything, strengthened me tremendously.

"Psalm 139:23–24 says 'Search me, O God, and know my heart, test me and know my anxious thoughts. See if there is any offensive way in me, and lead me in the way everlasting.' And Galatians 6:9 says, 'Let us not become weary in doing good, for at the proper time we will reap a harvest if we do not give up.' Well, I felt like giving up a lot. It's tough. But the Lord helped me go through the whole thing."

Consider it pure joy, my brothers, whenever you face
trials of many kinds.

James 1:2

33

STRESSED FOR SUCCESS

Bruce Neuharth

D id you know that pizzas cause stress? They can if you are involved in making and selling them.

I discovered that fact in 1973 after I became the manager of a pizza restaurant in my hometown of Pierre, South Dakota. I had left college, concluding that my time would be better spent working in business than in studying books about it. My career's frantic pace began just two weeks after my wife, Mary Lou, gave birth to our first child. I worked seventy to eighty hours a week, determined to be a success, and my efforts paid off.

From the start, my goal was corporate advancement, and the Pizza Hut Corporation was pleased to oblige me. I was promoted to a management position covering eastern South Dakota and Texas, and eventually accepted an upper management position with the company, supervising fifteen restaurants in suburban Chicago. I jumped at every opportunity to advance within the corporation to earn a bigger paycheck.

My commitment to building a career caused a lot of stress for me, but I actually enjoyed it. I gained a reputation with our company as the man to call on to send into an area where restaurants were struggling. I would go in, find out what the problems were, correct them, and turn the business around. Life was a continual pressure cooker for me, but I relished that.

Unfortunately, the stress began taking a physical toll. I started drinking heavily to relieve the pressures of each day, and medical problems began to develop. For a while I thought all that I needed was a change of scenery, but that was not the answer. We moved eleven times in eleven years, but my health continued to decline. The hectic, demanding corporate life that I loved so much seemed determined to kill me.

Between 1976 and 1979, I made more trips to the hospital than I can remember. At one point a doctor brought in a psychologist, hoping he could help me in dealing with the stress I was facing each day. Instead of being grateful, I became furious. I insisted that he leave my room.

As the pressures of striving for success in business continued to build, my condition worsened. The doctors began treating me with cortizone to offset my intestinal problems, but the medication began eating away at my bone structure. After a while I could hardly walk because of a deteriorating hip. Eventually I had to undergo a bone graft to the hip to replenish my blood supply.

I spent six weeks of a six-month medical leave from Pizza Hut in the hospital. When I went home, things did not get better. One day I slipped in the bathtub and fractured a vertebra in my neck. I did not remember what happened until several days later, but I narrowly avoided becoming paralyzed from the neck down.

It was during one of my hospital stays that I began to take a fresh look at my life. A seventy-eight-year-old man was sharing my room, having undergone prostate surgery. He had a sparkle, a joy in his life that I envied but could not understand. The man was a Russian immigrant and spoke in broken English, but I sensed there was something in his life that mine lacked.

On the day he was to leave the hospital, he was standing by my bed, saying good-bye, when suddenly he grabbed his chest and collapsed. I watched, horrified, as the hospital staff tried futilely to revive him. As they worked desperately on him in the bed next to mine, I could see all the activity going on. I saw them leaning over him, placing a large needle in his chest.

About that time someone realized I was still in the room. I was wheeled into the hallway while the life-saving efforts continued. The old man could not be revived, however, and his body was removed. Upon returning to the room, I saw it had been cleaned up and a newly made bed with clean sheets stood where the old man had been just hours before. It almost seemed as if nothing had happened.

Reflecting on my own life, I realized what a mess I had made of it. I had been trying to do everything on my own, being stubborn and thick-headed, but where had it gotten me? Just into a hospital bed, reaping the physical consequences of a life driven toward success.

I began thinking about what some friends, Dave and Colleen Jensen, had told Mary Lou and me not long before. When we lived in Pierre, Dave and I had been drinking buddies and had traveled quite a few miles together in the "fast lane." However, after our family moved away to Illinois in 1978, Mary Lou and I heard that the Jensens had had some kind of religious experience. When we went back to visit, we could see that they had indeed changed, but I couldn't understand what that change was. All I knew was that Dave had given up his old lifestyle for something I could not identify with.

After we were in Chicago, Dave and Colleen came to see us. Over dinner they told of how they had come to know God in a personal way, through Jesus Christ, and how that had literally changed their lives. Nearly two thousand years ago, Jesus had died on a cross, not for any crime he had done, but to pay the penalty for the sins of all mankind, they said. By accepting that payment, they had received forgiveness for failing to follow God's laws. The Jensens explained that they loved me and Mary Lou so much, they wanted us to know how we could have a personal relationship with Christ, too, and spend eternity with them and Christ.

At the time, I had felt I was being polite, pretending to be listening but presuming that what they were saying was going in one ear and out the other. But lying in my hospital bed, still distressed by seeing a kind old man pass so quickly from life to death, I discovered that I had not forgotten all of what the Jensens had told us.

I remembered them saying something about the wages of sin—disobedience to God—being death, but also that God offered eternal life through Jesus Christ. Recalling the special peace and joy the old man had exhibited just moments before he died, I wondered if he might have had the same relationship with God that the Jensens had. I knew that I didn't.

Not long after that, on March 8, 1979, in the privacy of my bedroom at home, I offered a simple prayer to God, inviting Jesus to come into my life. I confessed that I was a sinner and asked for God's forgiveness. Recognizing that I had failed miserably in trying to control my own life, I asked Jesus to take over.

Two weeks afterward, Mary Lou also prayed to commit her life to Jesus Christ. We later found out that Dave and Colleen had been praying faithfully for us for more than two years!

My decision to become a Christian did not immediately solve my problems. Because my bone structure had continued to deteriorate, I had to undergo yet another operation, a total hip replacement. But immediately following the surgery, the pain I had suffered for two-and-a-half years was gone completely. And that evening I was out of bed, walking with my new hip, to the amazement of my doctor. I haven't had any problems since.

My marriage and family life improved dramatically. Although I still greatly enjoyed my work, I began to see how much I had neglected my wife and children. They became much more important to me, and I worked hard to set aside more time to be with them.

I viewed our 1981 relocation to Wichita, Kansas, as arranged by God. The move brought me into the corporate environment as national training coordinator with Pizza Hut. At the same time, I sensed the challenge to begin sharing my faith in Jesus Christ with my fellow workers.

In 1983, I changed companies, moving after eleven years with the same company to Godfather's Pizza, Inc. I guess you could say they made me an "offer I couldn't refuse." In Wichita I became director of training for Godfather's, and two years ago moved to the corporate office in Omaha, Nebraska, to become national director of training and development, responsible for the staff and materials needed to train managers and employees of five hundred franchise restaurants and two hundred company-owned establishments.

Our time in Wichita also was very significant to us spiritually, since we became part of a strong, Bible-centered church and became close

friends with other committed Christians. We soon could see God's involvement in the relocation, both to enhance my career skills and enable
me to grow closer to Him.

It was in Omaha where I first encountered the Christian Business
Men's Committee. Through CBMC I have not only learned how to become more effective in telling others about what Christ has done in my
life, but have also established new friendships with businessmen who
share my convictions and care enough about me to hold me accountable.

Stress? It's still with me and all around me. The difference is in how
I deal with it. In the past, I would keep it bottled up until I reached a
breaking point, try to drown the stress with several drinks, or just not
handle it at all, allowing a situation to boil over into uncontrolled anger.
Now I turn to God, praying for His wisdom and insight. The Bible tells
us to "cast all our anxieties upon him, because he cares for us" (1 Peter
5:7), and that has proved to be a better remedy for stress than any of the
medications I took for several years.

For instance, I recently concluded the two most difficult weeks of
my four years at Godfather's or at any time during my management
career, having to dismiss several members of my staff due to a substantial budget cutback in my department. God taught me a lot of important
lessons as I wrestled with the responsibility of laying off several key
people, including two managers. In the past, the stress would have been
almost unbearable, but in this situation, I realized I could call on God
for help. One of the first questions I asked myself was, "How would
Christ handle this situation?" That did not remove the unpleasantness,
but it enabled me to deal with the people affected in a more caring,
sensitive manner, offering whatever help I could.

The Bible, which I believe to be God's revealed word to mankind,
has been a great resource for me. Whenever I find myself struggling in
my job, I am always reminded to check my focus, determining whether
I am trying to deal with my circumstances from God's perspective—or
going back to my old ways of trying to handle them myself.

I can see now that although many people work hard to succeed,
most of them do so without any purpose other than to achieve success
for its own sake. I see my job at Godfather's from a different perspective. It is my responsibility to do the best job I can for the company. In

fact, the Bible says that "Whatever you do, work at it with all your heart, as working for the Lord, not for men . . . " (Colossians 3:23). So I am actually called to work according to a higher standard than my human bosses might set.

Ultimately, I see my real purpose at Godfather's as sharing my life with Jesus Christ with other people, as the opportunities present themselves. I find much wisdom in the verse the psalmist wrote, "Commit your way to the Lord, trust also in Him, and He shall bring it to pass" (Psalm 37:5, NKJV).

*But pity the man who falls and has no one to help
him up!*

Ecclessiastes 4:10

34

KEEP OUT!

Walt Henrichsen

W e hear the word "accountability" a lot more today than when I
first came in to the Christian life more than twenty years ago.
Today, it's hard to have a serious discussion about the things of God
without someone raising the question of accountability.

Why is this? I believe it's because we are living in a fragmented and
lawless society, an age that can best be characterized by the last verse in
the Book of Judges, which says, "everybody did what was right in the
sight of their own eyes." Most people today are not tied to a geographic
locale and longtime friends who hold them accountable, even without
that word being used. So the tendency is to start doing things you normally would never do. Unfortunately, this has been true even among
leaders in the Christian community.

Trying to shore up this sagging wall of responsible behavior, the
body of Christ has begun talking a lot about the importance of personal
accountability. Everyone is clamoring to let other people know that they
are accountable. Since accountability has become the "in" thing, I think
it is helpful to look at it from a Biblical perspective.

To begin, we need to understand the kinds of accountability. First of
all, there is the area of *overt sin*. This involves obvious breaking of

God's commandments, and the offender is approached whether he wants to be or not. A good example is in 2 Samuel 12, after King David has committed adultery and murder. Nathan the prophet goes to rebuke him, and David does not offer any excuses. He simply says, "I'm guilty. I have sinned against the Lord."

Then there is the situation when someone comes to you and offers help or counsel regarding *impressions that have been created.* These are not necessarily sins, but actions or attitudes that are counterproductive either to the cause of Christ or to the individual's personal life. Again, David is a good example of this. In 2 Samuel 19:1–8, he bemoans the death of his son, Absalom. Joab comes to the king and tells David that he seems to be more concerned about his dead son, who was his enemy, than about the loyal, valiant men who saved his life. There was no sin involved, but David's behavior was clearly counterproductive.

One key point about this second form of accountability: you must have a man's *permission* to work in his life. You come because you are asked. A man may say, "I want you to be brutally honest with me. If you see anything in my life that is counterproductive, promise that you will call it to my attention." But unless you are asked, it is usually pointless to do so. Men don't want others breaking into their lives without being asked. I have gone unasked to men involved in overt sin on numerous occasions, and I have yet to hear even one man repent.

The third kind of accountability is in the area of *decision-making.* Note the distinction between decision-making and counsel. In seeking counsel, you already know what you want to do. You go to someone and say, "This is my plan. I want you to evaluate in case there are some gaping holes in it. But unless you can show me something that I've missed, I'm going ahead." In decision-making, however, you don't know what to do, so you go to your accountability partner (or group) and ask, "Should I do this or that? Help me make the decision."

We find a Biblical example in 1 Kings 22:6–8, where Ahaz and Jehoshaphat are seeking advice on whether to proceed with a battle plan. All the prophets of Baal say to proceed, but the prophet of God says no. Because Ahaz didn't like God's prophet, they disregarded his counsel and went into battle. As a result, they both lost their lives.

In seeking help in decision-making, there are two important considerations:

- We need an attitude of surrender. We need to say, as Jesus did in John 5:30, that I have no will of my own; my will is to do the will of Him who sent me. If that's not how you feel in your heart, you're not ready to make a decision.
- Decide what you are going to do with the information before you get it. If four people say do it and one says don't, how are you going to act? Make that decision before you ask and, having made that decision, don't go back on it.

Now that we know about the kinds of accountability, let's consider how people view accountability. First, there are those who say they want it—but they really don't. That's where most Christians are. They have no intention of being accountable because they don't want people meddling in their lives, but we have created an evangelical environment in which saying "I don't want accountability" is like saying "I hate motherhood and apple pie." So instead, we make excuses: "I don't have anybody who will enter into an accountability group with me." One man even told me, "I don't know of anyone who's as far along in the Christian life as I am to whom I can be really accountable."

Then there are those who argue that accountability is found in the organization. Someone might say, "I'm accountable because I'm part of CBMC (or whatever ministry). They are my accountability group." The truth is, that's just a guise, a smokescreen.

A third view is that accountability can only be found through the elders of the church. I don't believe this is true Biblically or theologically, but let me make one practical observation: in all my years of walking with Christ—and I attend church regularly and know the pastor and elders of the church—*not once* has any of them ever inquired into my soul. There may be some out there who are concerned with a man's walk with God, but I have not met any.

Fourth are those who freely admit they don't want accountability, don't think they need it, and have no intention of getting involved in it. I know a few businessmen like this, who are very secure and don't care who knows it.

Finally there are those who understand the need for accountability, seek it out, and develop it. Unfortunately, the guys I know who fit into this category I can number on two hands — and maybe have a couple of fingers left over.

With all of our desire to see more accountability, there are some basic indisputable facts we must accept. First, it is conferred or delegated, but never usurped. You can't go to an individual and say, "Okay, Bob, I want *you* to be accountable to *me*." You can't do that with your wife, your children — or your brothers in Christ. People are accountable only to the degree that they want to be held accountable — they decide that, we don't.

For instance, people can easily resist accountability by withholding information. When I talk with my son, I might ask, "How are you doing?" "Fine," he replies. "What's going on?" "Nothing much." "Care to talk about it?" "Nope." What are you going to do then? Absolutely nothing. I can cry a little bit, yell, or throw something, but if I think I can *make* a teenager — or an adult — be accountable, I'm fooling myself.

Accountability does not have to be reciprocal. I can be accountable to someone without him being accountable to me. People say, "I'm not in an accountability group simply because I'm not able to find someone willing to enter into that agreement with me." You don't need it. Reciprocity is not essential or necessary. All you need is to find someone willing to hold *you* accountable.

One final point: ideally, those to whom you are accountable should have no vested interest in your performance. Once there is a vested interest — if what you do affects their reputation, income, their ministry, or whatever — people lose objectivity. The guys who hold me accountable can afford to be objective with me, since their lives are not affected in any way by what I do.

If we could always know the will of God, we wouldn't need to ask an accountability group. But so rarely do any of us clearly know His will, we need to ask many questions. I can think of many times when I made decisions on my own and regretted it; I can't think of *one* time where I have submitted to my group, followed their leadership, and regretted it.

Reasons for Accountability

There are basically two reasons for accountability, according to Walt Henrichsen:

- "God gives us accountability to protect us from ourselves. There are only two people who can destroy your life — yourself and God. And I've got good news: God has your best interests at heart. So that narrows the field. As Pogo, the cartoon character, said, 'We have found the enemy, and it is *us.*' "
- "To be a model for the rest of your family. The man who comes to his wife and children and says, 'You are accountable to me, but I want to go on record. I am accountable to no one,' has either an incredibly submissive wife or has a grenade in his hand with the pin pulled out. It's just a matter of time before the thing blows up on him."

But pity the man who falls and has no one to help him up!

Ecclessiastes 4:10

35

TWO HEADS ARE BETTER THAN ONE
(Men serious about following God are willing to be held accountable)

Tim Philpot

As I understand my role as a Christian businessman, one of my primary responsibilities is to be a personal witness for Jesus Christ. There is a problem, however, with the general perception of what a *personal witness* is. Generally we associate the term with a lonely event, sort of a "Christian against the world" mindset.

Business and professional men, including most of the men I have met over the years through my involvement in the Christian Business Men's Committee, love to think of themselves as independent, fully able to accomplish their objectives without the help of anyone. We regard ourselves as "lone rangers," riding the trail for God with no need of assistance from other men.

I was like this myself for a number of years. I tried to survive as a Christian man in a demanding, secular environment without the support of other Christians. It was me and Jesus against the world and the devil. It sounded noble, but all I accomplished was to become tired and lonely. Even though I had a desire to serve God and attract others to Him, I

175

couldn't think of one person who had come to know Christ as a result of my first three years of involvement in CBMC.

In the fall of 1982, I became involved with three other men in a small accountability group. We met weekly to pray, study the Bible, and hold one another accountable in certain spiritual disciplines. As time passed, we began to trust each other and were able to confide our frustrations in life openly and honestly. We discovered how much easier life can be when there is someone else to share the load. God had brought us together as a tremendous gift, as men who could encourage and support one another. As Ecclesiastes 4:9–10 tells us: "Two are better than one, because they have a good return for their work. If one falls down, his friend can help him up. But pity the man who falls and has no one to help him up."

For me, the accountability group filled a great need. Despite my Christian activity, I had not seen anything really good happen through my efforts. Through these men, I was motivated to become more consistent in my time each day with God, praying and studying the Bible. Our mutual accountability gave us the encouragement to exercise regularly, memorize one scripture verse each day, attend church regularly, fast by skipping one meal per week, and to pray for one another.

In addition to the personal benefits I received through this relationship, I saw my personal ministry through CBMC start to bear fruit. I began to see other men committing their lives to Christ and have had the opportunity of discipling some of them.

Since 1982, the other three men in my group have all moved to other cities, but after learning the principles of accountability, I have been able to carry them on to other groups. Today one of my primary interests is in helping other men discover the benefits of personal accountability. It has proved very significant in my life and in the lives of other men I have met with.

Ultimately, as Christians we are accountable to God, but I'm convinced that some form of accountability is a *necessary* part of the Christian experience. *It's not just an option.* On the outside, men like to act independent and self-sufficient, but on the inside, if we're honest with ourselves, we know what failures we are and how much we need to be accountable to someone who is sincerely concerned about our well-being.

I'll admit that in my worst moments, at times when I'm struggling the most, I don't want accountability. Ironically, that's when I need it the most. But it's been my observation that *men who are serious about following God are willing to be held accountable.* If not, it's usually a sign that there are some areas of a man's life that haven't been turned over to God.

Within the CBMC context, it's overwhelming to think what would happen if the local committee leaders could be spiritually accountable to one another. Not only could they pray and study God's Word together, but they also could discuss how the CBMC ministry is functioning. "Joe, who are you bringing to the next luncheon?" "Bill, how can we be praying for you?" "Jack, how is your 'Timothy' doing?"

The way I see it, true evangelism is a result of true togetherness. When we hold each other accountable to spiritual disciplines and to living a life that is worthy of God, evangelism will be a natural result. As Proverbs 27:17 says, "Iron sharpens iron; so one man sharpens another."

But pity the man who falls and has no one to help him up!

Ecclessiastes 4:10

36

HELPING THE OTHER GUY WIN

Joe Crawley

Accountability? What's that?

Most men, including myself, respond that way when first presented with the concept. In a society where people love to boast, "I did it my way," without anyone's help, the idea of being accountable to someone else is as alien as a green-skinned, three-eyed visitor from outer space.

Even after I became a Christian, I prided myself on my independence and self-reliance. Through business and church activities, I was trying to have a ministry in others' lives, but I was working alone. When John Shoop invited me to meet with him once a week to discuss the Bible, I initially turned him down. It seemed more of a commitment than I wanted to make, but eventually he persuaded me to try it.

Those meetings did several things for me. While in high school, I had earned a national Bible quiz award, but John helped me to realize that much of what we truly learn—and apply—can come only through experience. Through our time together, the Scriptures became more real and practical to me than ever. I learned the value of being accountable to another man on a consistent basis. He also showed me a structured way to pass on spiritual truths to others and encouraged me to find another man to help grow spiritually.

Before long, the name of a specific man came to my mind. When I asked him about meeting regularly to discuss spiritual things, his response was similar to mine. The thought of establishing a relationship with another man for reasons other than business or hobbies was totally foreign to him. But eventually he agreed to meet with me once a week to talk about the Bible. It was exciting to discover that my friend had many questions about God but had never known who to ask.

Of course, accountability—even for a Christian—is much more than a Bible study. I used to regard it as "bean counting"—having someone check up on you to make sure that you've gotten all your jobs done. But true accountability is encouragement: encouraging another person to do what he really wants to do, not legalistically pushing him into doing something he is not committed to.

The Book of Ecclesiastes includes a wonderful passage on accountability: "Two are better than one, because they have a good return for their work: If one falls down, his friend can help him up. But pity the man who falls and has no one to help him up! Also, if two lie down together, they will keep warm. But how can one keep warm alone? Though one may be overpowered, two can defend themselves. A cord of three strands is not quickly broken," (Ecclesiastes 4: 9–12).

What this describes is individuals who are in agreement, putting plans of mutual interest into action. They don't have an attitude of, "You do your thing and I'll do mine." They want to help one another win.

An accountability relationship is special because it requires openness and trust. For it to work, it can't be based on legalism, fear, or guilt. The motivation must be love—a genuine concern for the other person's best interests.

In our society, true friendships are rare. Intimacy generally is not encouraged. I have found that people will come around when you're hurting, but not many are eager to share your joy. In fact, "friends" often seem to resent good things happening to you. And in business, competition is so fierce that the general attitude is, "I'd rather that we both lose than see the other guy win."

That is where accountability relationships are different. Men come to see themselves as a team, as partners. I expect men I meet with to "remind me" rather than "make sure" that I do what I intended. And in holding another man accountable, I try to remember that *my* role is to help him achieve *his* goals. Success is not a threat, but a mutually satisfying accomplishment, just as all the members of a football team share in a victory. Ideally, then, being accountable is an all-win situation.

But pity the man who falls and has no one to help him up!

Ecclessiastes 4:10

37

ACCOUNTABILITY: HOW AND WHY
(Most men are too macho, independent, and prideful to risk letting down their "masks")

Gayle Jackson

I have had the opportunity to speak at conferences and seminars on the need for personal accountability, and inevitably one basic question surfaces: "How do I go about establishing an accountability relationship — and with whom?"

Obviously, that is an important question, but I believe before we set out to become part of an accountability group, we need to be clear on why we are doing it. As I have studied the Bible, I've discovered four primary reasons for accountability.

God's Law of Injury

We can be injured by four entities — others, Satan, God, and ourselves. But Jesus tells us not to fear physical harm, but only the one who can kill us spiritually. In an eternal sense, others cannot hurt me. And in reading the Book of Job, I find that although Satan is powerful, he is under God's control, so even he cannot hurt me. He may "sift me like wheat" (Luke 22:31), but he can't kill me spiritually. That leaves only

God and me, and since God is clearly committed to my good, I can be assured that He will not hurt me. The one person I need to be concerned with, then, is me. *The reason I need accountability is to protect myself from me.*

God's Law of the Body

When Jesus sent out the disciples, He directed them to go in two's. The Apostle Paul even found it necessary to travel as part of a team. Throughout the Scriptures we see that God created in us a need for others. In His priestly prayer (John 17), Jesus emphasized the importance of unity. Therefore, *to keep our focus on the eternal, we need accountable people around us.*

God's Law of Negotiability

There is nothing negotiable in the Law of God. Truth is truth. But man seems determined to negotiate God's Word. *Without accountability, the history of man is a story of negotiating away God's truth.*

God's Law of Submission

Although the Bible underscores our need for a submissive attitude (Ephesians 5:21), men in our society do all they can to avoid authority in their lives. But God's plan is for all to be under authority. We require accountability, then, *not only to fulfill the need to submit but also to model authority in our lives to others.*

With such convincing reasons for being accountable, we see the need to comply. So what are some of the rules of accountability?

To be truly accountable to others, we must be willing to accept their authority. That requires the sometimes painful experience of letting people see below the surface of our lives. Like most men, I have no problem with surface relationships, because I can make sure people see me only when I look good. Even in Bible studies, there is a tendency to protect the image that we want others to see. But in an accountability relationship, people must be allowed to see us as we truly are—warts and all! This necessitates an open, honest exchange with the group, especially in the three areas men are almost never open and honest about: money, private fears, and sex.

God has commanded us to be submissive to others, but most men today are too macho, independent, and prideful for submission. But since God has commanded us to submit especially to Him, it is our job to execute His command. And we need to take the initiative; we should not expect to be recruited into a submissive, accountability relationship. He expects *us* to do the recruiting.

Basically, a successful venture into personal accountability requires the willingness to be transparent, a commitment to obedience to God, and the desire to find godly men to look over our lives. Presuming these three prerequisites are present in your life, here are some simple guidelines on what to look for in accountability partners:

- You need to share the same basic vision.
- You should not be financially vested with each other, since accountability should not be tied to financial gain.
- You and your partner(s) should have no hidden agendas for the relationship.
- You must pray faithfully for one another.
- You need to make time for each other. The fact is, consistent follow-up is tiring.
- You must be willing to ask the hard questions of each other.

I would advise you *not* to seek accountability with celebrities or pastors. Although we may regard them as authority figures, we need to seek men we can relate to—and who can relate to us. Pursue men of God who clearly demonstrate God's control in their lives, men whose spiritual maturity is communicated through their actions, not their positions.

All information in an accountability exchange must be held confidential unless *explicitly* stated otherwise. *Don't confuse sharing with gossip.* With this clearly understood, accountability partners can feel free to submit all critical decisions for review and be willing to share weak and vulnerable areas of their lives. Our openness also demands that we be teachable, willing to consider and accept what God is trying to show us through the wisdom and insights of others.

You may be thinking, "All right, I'm willing to become accountable to someone. But what things should I become accountable for?" This is by no means a complex or minutely detailed list, but some suggestions would include: your commitment to God; a commitment to faithful, daily time in prayer and reading the Bible; and a commitment to establishing a personal ministry. We each should be willing to be held accountable for our relationships with our wives and children, as well as our jobs. Sexual vulnerabilities and the use of our money also should be vital accountability concerns.

I believe that one of the best passages on personal accountability is Hebrews 10:24–25, which has much more to say to us than an exhortation to attend worship services regularly. We are to "consider how to stir up one another to love and good works," (RSV). This passage also tells us that we are to meet often with an attitude of encouragement, ultimately focusing our thoughts, words—and actions—on the things that are eternal.

Accountability is not something God intends as an additional burden for us. It is for our own good. As we recruit godly people into our lives for accountability, they will actively affect our growth and thinking. Accountability, without a doubt, is God's plan for people to assist other people—it is one of His best ways for helping us stay on course for Jesus Christ.

No soldier in active service entangles himself in the
affairs of everyday life, so that he may please the
one who enlisted him as a soldier.

2 Timothy 2:4, NAS

38

LIKE A PUPPET ON A STRING

Clyde Hawkins

Have you ever felt like you are being yanked around like a helpless puppet? Family obligations, personal and vocational commitments, friendly demands. They can do that to you. All of them are good, except when they are in direct competition. When that happens, you find yourself in a state called "entanglement."

I have observed that in the Christian life there are actually three states: *insularity*, in which you effectively isolate yourself from the world; *perfect balance*, which happens so rarely that Dr. Howard Hendricks claims the only balanced Christians he has ever seen were those en route from one extreme to another; and *entanglement*.

Because of their goal orientation, businessmen tend to lean more toward entanglement than insularity. It seems we are on a pendulum in constant motion, never staying in balance for long. As a new Christian, my life must have been the epitome of entanglement. I had been heavily committed as a nonbeliever; once I committed my life to Jesus Christ, I simply added more activities.

There were times when I felt like I was drowning in a sea of good things. One night—actually about three in the morning—unable to sleep and unable to determine how I could get my life under control, I decided it was time to act. The next day I resigned from every board and committee I was serving on. The only solution, I had concluded, was to start from scratch. Then I prayed, asking God to show me which things He wanted me to do and which things were good things that someone else was far better equipped to carry out.

Over the years, God has honored that decision. I was so busy, I had become unable to function properly as a father. As I sought to re-establish the Biblical priorities in my life of God first, then family, business, and ministry, I was able to rebuild relationships with my children. I even saw two of them come to know Christ during the next two years.

Perhaps you suspect that you, too, might be entangled, but aren't sure. Some of the symptoms are thoughts preoccupied with money, debt or achievement; reacting rather than acting; thoughts that are out of control; making emotional decisions; body present, mind absent; physical exhaustion and lack of exercise; no scheduled times for family, recreation or leisure; no time for reading the Bible and praying; little or no giving to God's work.

To me, entanglement means becoming totally caught up with things of the world—things that are not lasting—rather than with things of eternal importance. That certainly is not God's desire for us. As 2 Timothy 2:4 states, "No one serving as a soldier gets involved (entangled) in civilian affairs—he wants to please his commanding officer."

Once we recognize the dangers that entanglement can present, the question is simple: How can we avoid it? I believe there are three steps that we need to follow if we are ever to achieve the type of balance in our lives that Jesus Christ exhibited in His own.

Determining Our Purpose

In John 17:4, we see Jesus praying to the Father, "I have brought you glory on earth by completing the work you gave me to do." His purpose was clearly defined; He knew what God had called Him to do.

Amazingly enough, the Lord accomplished this without a house, car, or checkbook. He didn't have a DayTimer, Rolex sundial, or Montblanc quill. Without a Fax or cellular phone, He moved steadily toward the goal that had been set for Him from the start.

Doesn't this make you wonder about why we burn out our lives in the quest of things which have such little significance in terms of accomplishing God's purpose for our lives?

If you want to get a handle on what your life's purpose is now—and what it should be—here are some questions you might want to ask:

- What is my life adding up to? (Especially in terms of family, job, others, and yourself.)
- Is this what I want it to be?
- What are the reasons for the commitments I make?
- What are the activities that rule my life?
- Why do I spend time doing what I do?
- If someone examined your checkbook and calendar, and interviewed your spouse, children, and associates, what would he conclude your life's purpose to be?

Finding Accountability

We need at least a few people with whom we can sit down and talk honestly, although it may not come easily. In recent years, a lot of godly men have fallen. A significant number of them said that if they had had other men with whom to be accountable, their personal tragedies probably would not have occurred.

In Hebrews 10:24, we are told to consider how we can "encourage (or stir up) one another toward love and good deeds." Ultimately, we are accountable to God, but this verse tells us that He wants us to support one another.

The world seems to constantly try to pull us off track, and we desperately need someone who cares enough about us to ask tough questions and to pray for our spiritual well-being.

We all have blind spots, whether it be obvious areas of sin or just the tendency to become overcommitted in the everyday affairs of life. That's why the words of Proverbs 27:6 are so true: "Faithful are the wounds of a friend," (RSV).

Spending Time With God

Finally, and most importantly, entanglement can be avoided through times of solitude — regular time alone with God. But to do this requires planning. We need:

- A specific place.
- Equipment, including a Bible and notebook, maybe even a hymn book.
- Scheduled time, not only daily but also extended times, perhaps monthly or quarterly.
- A sincere desire to spend time with the Lord.
- The discipline or commitment to follow through in doing it.

As J. Oswald Sanders wrote, "We know God as well as we choose to. Arrange your life to accommodate Him."

In Jeremiah 9:23–24, God says, "Let not the wise man boast of his wisdom or the strong man boast of his strength or the rich man boast of his riches, but let him who boasts boast about this: that he understands and knows me, that I am the Lord, who exercises kindness, justice and righteousness on earth, for in these I delight."

One of the hardest parts of the Christian life, particularly in the area of entanglement, is learning how and when to say "No!" I'm a people-pleaser and would love to be on every committee I'm asked to serve on, but I have found that in understanding my purpose, being willing to be accountable to a few other men, and having regular time with God alone, I'm not as entangled — or frustrated — as I used to be.

No soldier in active service entangles himself in the
affairs of everyday life, so that he may please the
one who enlisted him as a soldier.

2 Timothy 2:4, NAS

39

LIVING WITH ENTANGLEMENT

Robert J. Tamasy

M ost of us would like to find a book called, "How To Keep Your Life in Perfect Balance Without Really Trying." Unfortunately, such a book does not exist—and probably never will. It seems we are destined to live somewhere between over- and under-commitment.

William Bonner, a forty-five-year-old attorney in Media, Pennsylvania, a suburb of Philadelphia, has resigned himself to this reality. In addition to the law practice he has maintained with his father, Hugh, since 1971, he is married and has four daughters and one son, ranging in age from three to nineteen years old.

Parachurch Involvement

In addition to his local church, he has been active in a number of parachurch ministries, including the Christian Business Men's Committee, Gideons, Fellowship of Christian Athletes, and the Billy Graham Evangelistic Association. For several years he also served as chairman of the Delaware County Prayer Breakfast.

Over the past several years, however, the greatest tug on Bill's time has been his growing involvement with The Rutherford Institute, a nonprofit legal and educational organization based in Charlottesville, Virginia. Attorneys associated with the Institute take on *pro bono* (no fee) cases in Federal court involving religious speech, sanctity of life, and family autonomy.

Recently he was named regional coordinator for the first, second, third, and forth Federal circuits, which means he is responsible for supervising cases being defended through the Rutherford Institute along the Eastern seaboard from Maine to South Carolina, as well as the District of Columbia, Puerto Rico, and the Virgin Islands.

Obviously, Bill is well-acquainted with entanglement. You might say they know each other on a first-name basis.

"The temptation to become overcommitted is constant, and I admit there are times when I don't handle it as well as others," he says. "The demands of work are always pressing, and clients are anxious for solutions to their problems. There are so many ministry needs I don't see around me. And that doesn't even include the responsibilities of being married and the father of five children."

No Fixed Formula

Bill agrees that a simple, effective formula for avoiding entanglement would be nice, but feels it is an impossibility. "Entanglement is a common problem, particularly for self-employed businessmen who sense a deep burden to be involved in serving God and others in ministry.

"One area of my law practice is domestic relations, and I have concluded that the temptations of adultery, drinking, and other negative, wasteful activities do not compare with the serious temptation of becoming overcommitted. The worst thing about it is that our society even condones it. You can look very good and feel very responsible, and yet have your life totally out of control and have a family that is suffering.

"We can take a certain pride and satisfaction in what we are doing—whether it be work or ministry—but the cumulative effect of not relating to wives and children, not being closely involved in their lives, finally comes home."

The Reputation Trap

There is a saying that if you want something done, find a busy man to do it. Bill believes there is truth in that adage, and his own life reflects it. "If you have developed a reputation for getting things done, you'll be called on to do more and more in the future."

So how does *he* handle the multiple demands on his time, especially when such a high premium today is placed on individuals willing to engage in Christian activism? Bill concedes he has no easy answers and is not a candidate to write a how-to book on the subject.

"When I got into legal activism, it wasn't because I had nothing else to do with my time. Actually, it was my wife, Jane, who encouraged me. She had done a lot of reading about social issues that are undermining America's Judeo-Christian heritage and kept after me to get involved. My own convictions are pretty well shaped, but my children are still developing theirs. Our society has become so entrenched in relativism. I didn't know what else to do but get involved in the fight. I felt I needed to be on the front line to help preserve what's left of our traditional values."

Yet Bill hasn't lost sight of the ideal for a balanced life, one which is not controlled by the tyranny of the urgent. There are times when he must work late into the night preparing for a court case, but he tries to avoid making that a lifestyle. "Cases are so open-ended; there's so much investment you can put into them. You want to be well-prepared, to make sure that you have a winner. But you also need the discipline and wisdom to know when to stop. I don't always have that wisdom, and my family suffers from my mistakes."

At such times, strong, honest accountability relationships help in making course corrections, he says. "We don't dare operate like loose cannons, without a network that keeps us accountable for what we are doing—and why. My wife and family are part of this network for me, but they can be too tolerant, seeing that the things I do are worthwhile. For that reason, I know that I also need friends as part of my accountability system.

"There are times when I've gone too far and Jane will draw the line, but she is generally very supportive of what I do, especially since she believes in it so strongly too. So I need a few friends who care enough about me and my family to ask hard questions about how much time I should be giving to the various areas of my life. One question that always stops me short is, 'How's you family doing *right now* while you're working so hard?' "

Another key, Bill pointed out, is maintaining a prospering relationship with God regardless of external stresses. "When the pressures of work come, the spiritual life is usually the first thing to go. But if we're not spending time in the Bible and in prayer, before long it starts to come apart. That's one reason I try to make a point of meeting in Bible study each week with other men. Our discussions remind me of how God's truth relates to everyday life, and that helps in calling me back to accountability."

That still does not guarantee a forty-hour work week and free, uninterrupted weekends with family, he notes.

"I find it extremely difficult to keep everything in my life in order. I find myself so concerned. I feel responsible to be sharing the gospel verbally with others, but I also sense a very real responsibility to the social gospel—our response to pornography, abortion, freedom of religious expression, home schooling rights, and other concerns. It takes a disciplined spiritual life to keep some semblance of balance.

"The key is to always be searching out whether God wants us involved in a particular area. There are so many worthwhile causes within the body of Christ, but we are not called to get involved in them all."

Perfect balance will only be achieved briefly, if at all, Bill contends. "If we truly care about the things that concern God, we will become burdened. And we will overinvest ourselves at times, without question. But being willing to be held accountable will protect us from making fatal mistakes. Most of all, we must make sure that we don't spend our lives in ways that we have not been called upon by God."

No soldier in active service entangles himself in the affairs of everyday life, so that he may please the one who enlisted him as a soldier.

2 Timothy 2:4, NAS

40

HOW TO SAY "NO"
(When you want to say "Yes")

Ken Smith

We often talk about overcommitment (or entanglement), but what is it exactly? A simple definition might be the inability or unwillingness to say no when we should. So why would anyone get overcommitted when all he needs to do is say "No!" at the right times? I think there are four reasons:

- Most of us aren't organized well enough to know when to say no.
- Often we don't want to say no.
- Many of us don't know how to say no.
- Most of us don't understand what we should say no to.

Suppose someone approaches you at church and asks you to assume a responsibility. How do you react? If you're already so overcommitted that you're experiencing anxiety, you might say no in a very inappropriate way. You might be defensive or become angry. You may cry. You might respond with a lecture, or wither the person with your meanest look. What you probably would not do is thank him for being offered an opportunity to fill that need.

If you're not already anxious despite being overcommitted, you might go to the other extreme. You know you shouldn't say yes, but you might anyway. You may conceal your discomfort, even though you resent being asked.

There is a third category: If you're the rare individual who is not already overcommitted, you may feel like someone who is not in debt. Have you ever just paid off a credit card bill and felt the irresistible urge to go out and charge something? That is exactly what overcommitment is—attempting to spend time that you don't have, going into debt with your time.

Thankfully, God did not make provision for either saving up time or for spending it in advance. Instead, we suffer at the point where we would borrow if we could. Overcommitment, then, is our futile attempt to "borrow" time. Each of us, at one time or another, fails to say no when we should. But that is no excuse for being overcommitted as a way of life.

The average person finds himself overcommitted far too often. Many people don't know what it would be like not to be overcommitted! Ironically, among Christians the person most likely to overcommit himself is one who reflects much of the fruit of the Spirit as expressed in Galatians 5:22–23—love, joy, peace, patience, kindness, goodness, faithfulness, and gentleness. Eagerness to serve and exercise spiritual gifts can prompt a detour to the path of unrighteousness because of overcommitment.

You may have noted that the one fruit of the Spirit that I didn't mention was self-control. The Christian without self-control or self-discipline (actually Holy Spirit-directed discipline) can display all the outward signs of a Spirit-led life and yet be ineffective due to poor discipline. Our strengths almost always relate to our weaknesses. Lack of self-control can neutralize even those whom God could use the most, despite how many good traits they have.

A different kind of person often guilty of overcommitment is the self-centered individual who wants it all—and right now! He constantly drives for success in the secular sense. He never has enough time to accumulate all the wealth, acquire all the knowledge or achieve all the power that he feels he needs. This person suffers from greed; he will never have enough. He refuses to say no for the opposite reason as the servant. He fears missing something for himself, rather than an opportunity to serve someone else.

Then there are the rest of us. We are at neither extreme; we just haven't learned when and to what we should say no. Our yes or no is haphazard, a response to circumstances of the moment rather than planning. Generally, we attribute overcommitment to lack of personal organization, but even the most organized person finds himself overcommitted once in a while. Here are some ways you can avoid the trap of entanglement:

Establish Goals and Priorities

If you know enough about yourself and how you use time, you should avoid chronic overcommitment. You know where you've been, where you are and where you're going. Based on your goals and priorities, you can be prepared to say no to things that are not consistent with those objectives.

For instance, an opportunity for career advancement almost always comes with a cost attached. You may be asked to devote 75 percent of your time over the next year to travel. If you haven't set goals and priorities for yourself and your family, you have no rational basis for turning down such an opportunity. You suspect this will create problems at home, but you have no objective way to analyze the consequences. (And let's face it — that's not something we like to do in advance.) But if you have specific goals and priorities, it is much easier to recognize potential conflicts and arrive at the right decision. In this way, we can be more confident about knowing when God wants us to say yes and when He wants us to say no.

Seek Accountability

We frequently become overcommitted because we aren't accountable to anyone. If you are married, make a habit of consulting your spouse before making commitments. A friend of mine has spent half of his life making unrealistic commitments—and the other half undoing them after his wife finds out.

Consider Other Factors

Sometimes the reasons for overcommitment are beyond our immediate control. If your boss is unrealistic about your workload or abilities, you may stay overcommitted without fully understanding why. Or you may have physical or emotional problems which inhibit your performance. These must be identified and addressed before you can do anything at a reasonable rate.

Put God's Desires First

Disobedience is the underlying problem with overcommitment. We don't do what God wants and we do what He doesn't want. So the first step in dealing with overload is to understand what He is saying now. You may have to follow through on commitments that you now know were not in God's plan for you, but you need to go back and say no to other commitments. The cost may be high, and it's difficult to break commitments, but if that's what God wants you to do, you must be willing—if not exactly tickled pink about doing so.

Wait Before Saying Yes

Form a habit of never saying yes until you have had time to pray about a request. When asked to do something, give a specific time when you will be able to give an answer. Make a note of the request and pray about it during your next quiet time.

God is seldom, if ever, in a hurry. Even when you know your answer will be yes, don't respond immediately. If it's important to God, it will wait at least one day. It's surprising how much difference a one-day delay can make. You may still say yes, but you will have much more insight into your decision. For example, you may determine that a different completion date for a project is needed, or someone else should also be involved.

One final word: Follow the axiom, "If in doubt, don't." You may occasionally miss a blessing, but you also will avoid tons of grief. I find it's much better to run the risk of missing God than to bear the pain of getting ahead of Him.

No soldier in active service entangles himself in the affairs of everyday life, so that he may please the one who enlisted him as a soldier.

2 Timothy 2:4, NAS

41

LIFE ON A ROLLER COASTER
(Managing the ups and downs of priorities)

Randy Schroeder

It's been said that if you want to get something done, find a busy person to do it. There seems to be an unwritten law that whether it is in business, community activities or the church, a "doer" must always have more to do than he has time in which to do it.

In one respect it is flattering to be asked to take on a new job, since it implies that people see you as capable and dependable. However, being jack of too many trades can result in being master of absolutely none of them as you strive to run several directions at the same time.

This is a particular problem for me, since my tendency is toward overinvolvement. In college, I was committed to activities every night of the week. My mother realized this was a problem long before I did, and she once warned me that when I married, I would drive my wife crazy if I didn't change.

After graduating from college, I maintained my high activity level. But when my wife, Staci, and I married in 1984, it soon became evident that some changes would be necessary. Staci also likes to be active, but I discovered that we had a need for quiet times at home together.

For the first time in my life, it became apparent that I would not be able to do everything I wanted to do. The question was, "How do I distinguish between the things I should and shouldn't do?

The problem can become like a roller coaster. You get over involved with too many things. You push yourself to peak capacity and then find yourself plunging downhill under the load of over commitment. Exhausted and ineffective, you reach bottom and start cutting back on activities. Eventually, your schedule seems too light, so you take on more obligations and start inching up the hill again.

I concluded that although I may not be able to eliminate the "roller coaster" entirely, at least I needed to learn how to flatten out the hills and valleys. Aided by the counsel of some good friends, Staci and I found several considerations which have helped a great deal.

First of all, Staci and I established a joint life goal, "To know God and to make Him known." Whenever we are asked to become involved in something new, we sift those decisions through that goal.

Secondly, I've realized that there are only two things in life that are eternal: the Word of God and the souls of people. We are convinced that the things we need to be involved in as a husband and wife should center around those things. That's one reason I'm involved in the Christian Business Men's Committee — to reach and disciple business and professional men for Christ.

My third help in keeping my priorities balanced is my wife's discernment. For instance, soon after we married, someone asked if Staci and I would teach a Bible study for single adults. I said yes, without consulting her first. When I finally took the time to get her opinion, I realized that we shouldn't do it.

That lesson taught me that even though God wants me to be the spiritual leader in our family, I can't provide leadership in a vacuum. I need my wife's input — and I need to be a *good* listener. Her reasons may not always be expressed in what I think is concise, logical terminology, but God's Spirit can speak through her as my sounding board.

My fourth key in preventing my priorities from being upstaged by potential commitments is a simple one: Learn to say, "No." Staci and I have found that the majority of the things we are asked to do could be considered within the realm of our life goals, so we have to distinguish the *good* things from the *best* things. That may mean having to say no to some very good things.

Saying no can be very difficult, because we are afraid the people asking will feel rejected and we don't want to let people down. Sometimes, it takes what I call a "gut check," testing how secure we are in Jesus Christ, to risk not always pleasing others. For the person who cannot say no, life will be a roller coaster. He either feels guilty for saying no, or he says yes too much and winds up overworked.

I suppose the best guideline was provided by Christ in Luke 9:23, when He said, "If anyone would come after me, he must deny himself and take up his cross daily and follow me." In other words, if I follow Jesus — and not men or organizations — He will direct my involvement.

*But grow in the grace and knowledge of our Lord
and Savior Jesus Christ.*

2 Peter 3:18

42

MARK OF A TRUE DISCIPLE

LeRoy Eims

The search goes on. Relentlessly, doggedly, hopefully, eagerly. And yet all too often the search is in vain. Time and again the searcher is left emptyhanded. Who is this searcher? GOD. And for what is He searching? He is searching for a rare commodity. God puts it this way: "I sought for a man among them." The operative word here is "among." Not a missionary who will cross the seas and bring God's message to a people, but for a man who is already out there *among* the men and women to whom God is trying to communicate.

I can hear you asking, "What's so tough about that? There are Christian businessmen out there in the giant corporations, the great department stores, on the staffs of the hospitals, in the law offices, the real estate offices, educators in the universities — all over the place. These men are *all* out there among them — hundreds of thousands of them."

Yes, I agree. But here's the catch. God is looking for a *certain kind* of man. Men are a dime a dozen. We are knee deep in Christian businessmen who are happy to occupy a church pew once a week — or attend a Christian concert or even go hear a missionary during a church mission week. But God is looking for a man who will live as a true disciple of Jesus Christ day by day in the marketplace, a man who will stand in the gap for God.

The eyes of God scan the horizon for such a man. The Bible says, "The eyes of the LORD move to and fro throughout the earth that He may strongly support those whose heart is completely His" (2 Chronicles 16:9, NAS). And how does a true disciple of Christ demonstrate that his heart belongs completely to God, and that he lives for the Lord alone? Six things come to mind:

1. He daily puts Christ first in his life by obeying the Word of Christ. "If any man would come after me, let him deny himself and take up his cross daily and follow me." (Luke 9:23, RSV)

2. He continues in the Word through Bible study and scripture memory, in response to the challenge of Jesus: "If ye continue in my word, then are ye my disciples indeed." (John 8:31, KJV)

3. He is faithful to maintain the practice of morning prayer and Bible reading. He has learned the value of starting the day with God, even as Jesus did. "And in the morning, rising up a great while before day he departed into a solitary place and there prayed." (Mark 1:35)

4. He is openly identified with Jesus Christ through two primary means. First of all, by his life. Jesus taught, "Let your light so shine before men that they may see your good work and glorify your Father which is in heaven" (Matthew 5:16). Secondly, by his lips. He is an ambassador of Christ who faithfully, "declares the excellencies of Him who called him out of darkness into his marvelous light." (See 1 Peter 2:9)

5. He attends worship services regularly, and joyfully carries his fair share of responsibilities in the life of his local church. His attitude is that of the psalmist: "I was glad when they said unto me, let us go into the house of the LORD." (Psalm 122:1, KJV)

6. Through *Operation Timothy* or some other discipling tool, he is committing that which he has learned to another faithful man who will in turn repeat the process in the life of another. Paul told Timothy, "And the things that thou hast heard of me among many witnesses, the same commit thou to faithful men, who shall be able to teach others also." (2 Timothy 2:2, KJV)

Here then is a sketchy picture of God's man among them. By God's grace, you can be that man.

*But grow in the grace and knowledge of our Lord
and Savior Jesus Christ.*

2 Peter 3:18

—————————————————————— *43*

UP CLOSE AND PERSONAL

Dr. Win Ritchie

O ne summer, some friends joined me for our own version of Southern reconstruction. A hurricane had swept through our area the previous summer, pummeling everything in its path—including the pier and the pavilion that stood on it behind my home along the banks of Mobile Bay.

None of us were expert carpenters, but we figured we knew enough to replace the pier and restore the pavilion and boathouse. The frame went up surprisingly fast, and we started securing it in place.

It occurred to me that it might be a good idea to step back and examine the work before we proceeded too far. I remembered a booklet I had read, called *The Art of Backing Off* by Robert Foster, and the wisdom it contained had stuck with me.

As I "backed off" and took another look, I noticed the pavilion had a decided 10 degree tilt to it. From inside the little building, everything had looked plumb, but from just a few yards away, that was obviously not the case. Since our goal had not been to construct an Alabama replica of the Leaning Tower of Pisa, we had to correct this problem.

As an optometrist, I have made similar discoveries in working with children who are visually impaired. Initially, they seem to be poor students with limited academic abilities, but careful eye exams show that many of them have high IQs—their inability to see properly causes serious learning problems. One of my goals in correcting their vision, then, is to narrow the gap between their learning potential and actual performance levels.

The pier rebuilding project was completed without much difficulty, but over the next weeks, my insights about "backing off" began to percolate in my mind. I began to see that there was a spiritual application to this principle. Looking at myself as objectively as possible, I realized that there was a tremendous gap between the man I was and the man I knew that God intended me to be.

In a real sense, I am actually four men:

- The man the public knows.
- The man my family knows me to be (and they know me very well).
- My inner man — the guy only I know and don't reveal to anyone else.
- The man God knows (as we understand from Psalm 139).

How could I begin closing this gap between spiritual potential and spiritual reality? My answer was to take a "spiritual inventory." I've found it helpful, even fifteen years after I first had the idea, to periodically conduct an inventory, much like is done in the retail business. My inventory has consisted of the following eight questions:

1. Have I had a personal relationship with Jesus Christ?

Even though I became a Christian as a boy of twelve, there have been times when I have doubted where I stood spiritually. If that isn't settled, you really cannot move ahead until it is. For me, 1 John 5:11–13 has given me the assurance of an eternal relationship with God through Christ.

2. What have I done about a system of values in my life?

That is, what are my priorities? What comes first in my life? There have been many times, after comparing my time in the office, my time with my family and time spent in other areas of interest, that I've recognized how out of kilter my life had become. In fact, I believe strongly in the CBMC ministry, but once, when I saw it was taking priority over my family, I knew it was time to make some changes.

3. Have I developed a root system for my life?

Until 1958, I had never once confronted anyone with the truths of Jesus Christ, and I had no consistent daily quiet time with God. Three things happened that year, however, that turned me around spiritually.

I attended a laymen's leadership seminar where the topic was "A Man and His Bible." I learned how essential it is that a man establish a regular quiet time to pray and study the Bible. Then, two members of CBMC—Art DeMoss and Harry Smith—came into Mobile to start a ministry to businessmen. They helped me learn how to share my faith with other men. The third thing involved a patient who had been coming to me for a number of years. After his eye exam, he began asking me about my church activities. Then he said something that hit me hard: "Doc, you've been taking care of my eyes for several years, but if Jesus Christ is so important to you, why haven't you ever said anything to me about Him?"

Those three events set my spiritual pilgrimage on an entirely new course.

4. What have I done about the problem of balance in my life?

In my early adult life, I boxed and then coached boxing. One of the most important things about boxing, and the most difficult to teach, is balance. The various areas of my life—physical, spiritual, wife, children, church, work, recreation—all compete for my attention, and I've always had a difficult time finding that right balance, too.

I often find myself getting busy doing good things and neglecting important things, like time with my wife and my children, even time alone with God. Balance and priorities are closely related, and I've found that they need to be closely monitored because they have a way of changing without our being aware of it.

5. Have I learned to sit in God's waiting room?

In my line of work, the waiting room is an important area. Most people don't like to wait. We expect everything in our society to be instant, and waiting is not a favored pastime.

By nature, I'm a mover and a shaker. I talk fast, and even sleep fast. But I've been in God's "waiting room" quite a bit as various problems and needs have come up. One hard lesson for me has been that waiting is a crucial element in spiritual growth. Isaiah 40:31 tells us that "those who wait on the Lord shall renew their strength," (njkv). We like things done according to our timetable, but sometimes God simply says, "Wait!" And unlike the waiting room at my office, which is comfortable, with nice furniture and an aquarium, God's waiting room may not be plush. But it has a way of molding the state of the inner man.

6. Can I afford the luxury of integrity?

This may seem like an unusual question for a Christian to ask himself, but in the health care world today — as in most types of business — there is a lot of dishonesty; half-truths are common. So I wrestle to maintain my integrity, since it's so easy to go the other way.

This can range from expense accounts and income tax reporting to being honest and transparent with wife and children. Especially when dealing with dollars and cents, it's so easy to throw principles out the window — even in the Christian community.

7. Is Jesus Christ the dominant force in my life?

Put another way, does He stand out in all the relationships that I have? As the Apostle Paul wrote in 1 Corinthians 2:2, "For I resolved to know nothing while I was with you except Jesus Christ and him crucified."

To evaluate this area of my life, I like to ask myself questions such as "What have I done today that only a Christian would do?" or "I may be doing good things, but what am I doing solely for the glory of Jesus Christ?" I used to lift weights, and although I was strong, it still was necessary for me to focus all my energy into getting the weight up or it wouldn't go. In the same way, if we're distracted and not concentrating fully on Christ, our Christian life won't go very far either.

I remember the first time I was called on at a service club meeting to give the invocation. Immediately I wondered, "Should I pray like a person who really knows the Heavenly Father, or should I pray so that I don't offend anybody?" How you answer a question like that is determined by whether Christ is truly the dominant force. (I did choose the first option.)

8. Am I a faithful steward of the gospel?

I take this final question from 1 Corinthians 4:2, which says, "it is required of stewards that one be found trustworthy," (NAS). Sometimes I utter this prayer: "Lord, I may be unfaithful in many areas of my life, but at least allow me to be faithful in sharing the Lord Jesus Christ with others."

As I indicated, I first began asking myself these questions about fifteen years ago, and I continue to ask them today—some of them every day. And my constant prayer, as I take my personal inventory, is that God will enable me to narrow the gap between the man I am and the man He wants me to be.

*But grow in the grace and knowledge of our Lord
and Savior Jesus Christ.*

2 Peter 3:18

44

QUESTIONS WE'D LIKE TO ASK GOD

An Interview with Joni Eareckson Tada

S trong leadership can be found in any number of settings, but seldom do we think of a seat in a wheelchair as a position of influence. More than twenty years ago, Joni Eareckson would have agreed. An energetic, athletic teenager, Joni gave no thought to disabilities, other than to avoid those who had them. Then came a moment which forever altered the course of her life—she dove into the Chesapeake Bay, misjudging its depth. Her head slammed against the bottom, breaking her neck and severing her spinal cord, leaving her a quadriplegic with no movement or sensation below the tops of her shoulders.

Joni's story since then has been chronicled in two films and three books, the latest of which, *Choices: Changes,* is currently nestled atop the Christian bestsellers list. One of the best-known disabled individuals in the world, she has had a phenomenal impact upon countless lives—inspiring, encouraging, and challenging both the healthy and the handicapped alike. Through example, and spoken and written word, Joni offers a truly unusual form of leadership—from a wheelchair.

Her life, in spite of paralysis, is one of victory and fullness. Today, she is a gifted artist and singer; an accomplished author; the founder of a ministry to the disabled—Joni and Friends; and for the past five years, the wife of Ken Tada. She even drives a specially equipped van.

Joni talks about some of the lessons she has learned about disabilities, suffering, and questions we would like to ask God.

In your talks, and in your books, you express your fears and struggles as you have adjusted to life as a quadriplegic. Isn't such openness unusual in our Christian society, where it is generally considered unspiritual to express personal doubts and uncertainties?

I agree that we often feel compelled to wear masks, to disguise our needs and concerns, but in the fifth chapter of the book of James, we are told to "confess your sins to each other and pray for each other so that you may be healed," (5:16). I believe this is not just for physical healing, but also for the sharing of hurts, doubts, and fears. Sin demands to have man alone. When we hide our weaknesses, they have a hold on us. When we share our shortcomings, we become accountable to one another.

There can be real strength in opening up to one another. At the same time, we don't want to be spiritual exhibitionists. Some things have to be private between you and God.

Some people would tell us we should never ask God,"Why?", regarding our circumstances. Yet in your book, *Choices: Changes*, you write of having "faith to doubt, and yet believe." Explain what you mean.

Sometimes we wrongly think God is intimidated, and a little fearful of our doubts. We feel guilty about our questions. The truth is, God is more than big enough for our questions.

Not long ago I met a little girl, Kitty, at an autograph party for my book. She was clutching an old, tattered copy of my first book, *Joni*, to her chest. Her mother had told me Kitty had a congenital heart disease.

When Kitty came up to me, I told her how glad I was to meet her, and then I asked, "Do you know God?" "Yes," she shyly replied, "but I've got a lot of questions for Him."

I didn't tell Kitty not to ask her questions, and I didn't try to dissuade her from going to God with her doubts. One of the great things about the Christian faith is we can have such doubt, and still believe. God needs no defense. He has done very nicely defending Himself for thousands of years, and He can certainly handle our questions.

Do you feel the Bible supports an honest, questioning attitude toward God?

All we have to do is read one of the Psalms that David wrote. There is such a range of emotions in a single Psalm! All he was doing was being real, unafraid to tell God how he felt. The Lord knows the thoughts and intentions of our hearts, anyhow, so why should we bother trying to fool Him?

When people first meet you, I imagine many of them feel sorry that you will be in a wheelchair for the rest of your life. Yet you write that you "shudder" to think what your life would have been like if you had not become paralyzed. Is that really how you feel?

Exactly. I shudder when I think of all the wrong decisions I could have so easily walked through, decisions that were open to me at the time of the accident. I might well have finished high school, started college, quit to become married, had children and gotten divorced, and never have grown close to God. Sometimes visible disabilities offer an advantage over invisible disabilities, such as broken homes, financial problems, etc.

Before my accident, I had prayed "Lord, bring me closer to you." A couple of months later, I broke my neck. I chose my words too carelessly perhaps, and I also didn't take God seriously. I would not have chosen that approach at the time, but looking back over the past twenty years, the Lord has certainly answered my prayer—far more than I could have ever imagined.

In Philippians 3:10, the Apostle Paul writes, "I want to know Christ and the power of his resurrection *and the fellowship of sharing in his sufferings* . . ." (emphasis added). It seems there are times when we would like to erase that last phrase from the

pages of our Bibles. I've noticed occasionally that people repeating that verse even leave that last part out.

I've noticed that, too. But as Christians, we don't have that option. If we truly want to be Christlike, we must participate in His sufferings in some way. I guess the closest insight I've ever had to that truth was a little girl who wrote me in a letter, "I told my mommy I want a wheelchair just like yours." She was just a typical kid, with no disabilities, but she wanted to share in the fellowship of my suffering, discounting the pain and hardship.

Generally, when we desire to present examples of Christians to an unbelieving world, we offer the "success stories." As a person who sees so much of the other perspective, the hurting side of the Christian life, what do you think of the tendency to give only the positives of Christianity?

I suppose it's natural to measure a banker by his assets, a professor by his brains, or a beauty by her looks. Jesus, however, is not the Prophet of the winners' camp; He is the Prophet of the losers. The Bible shows the paradoxes: the weak being stronger than the strongest; the lowly, greater than the greatest; the last being first; fools being wiser than the wise.

There is a subtle danger in parading the strong, the likely, and the lovely as role models of the faith. Take the successful businessman, for example. There is nothing wrong with seeking a good return on an investment or a reasonable profit margin, but even more important in God's eyes is the businessman's attitude toward the janitor who mops up the floor each night.

I remember when I was on my feet as a teenager. At that time, the mere thought of a handicap was an anathema; I didn't even want to be around disabled people. Now that I'm one of them, I hate to think that there are many others out there just like I was.

Why do you think it is so hard for many of us to be around the disabled, or to relate to them in a meaningful way?

I think it's because when we get around someone else with a disability, it underscores our own weaknesses and vulnerability. We prefer to associate with winners rather than losers. We don't want to let our insecurities show.

How can we change that attitude?

One problem is we feel uncomfortable around someone with disabilities. We don't know how to respond to them. Actually, there are many ways to demonstrate that we care. When someone touches my wheelchair, or my arm, that shows sincere caring. We need to learn to understand that people are not "cripples" or "handicaps," but individuals with handicaps or disabilities.

Jesus Christ didn't have pity. Pity is a strong emotion that stays at an arm's length distance. The Lord had compassion, a close cousin to pity, except that it reaches out, touches, and embraces.

Joni, in spite of your disabilities, you have achieved a status as a Christian "superstar" that few able-bodied persons will ever attain. What keeps all this recognition, across America and around the world, from going to your head?

Well, this wheelchair has a way of bolting me to the earth, whether I like it or not. There is something about this wheelchair, similar to the Apostle Paul's thorn in the flesh, that keeps me humbled. To be honest, I don't like life in a wheelchair—I was the least likely candidate to love life in a wheelchair.

But I also appreciate what it has meant in my life. Hey, I can deal with it by God's grace and smile because of it—not in spite of it. But I'm reminded, "Let's not get too used to this," because one day in heaven I'll have hands that work and feet that walk. The Lord has allowed this loss in my life to keep me from mistaking this world, as I know it, as home.

Something else that helps me keep a proper perspective on life is my family. I have the most down-to-earth, real family you can imagine. My mother won't let me miss a trick. I've got a new book out, right? She hasn't even read it! "I'll read it when I get around to it, don't worry," she'll tell me. She doesn't want me to get a swelled head or feel I'm indispensable to the Kingdom!

You've summed up the Christian life with the words of the old hymn, "Trust and obey." Could you elaborate on that?

It's been more than twenty years since my diving accident. I can remember holding an ice cold glass of orange juice, with the side of the glass sweating into my hand. I remember what it was like to peel an orange and hold a fuzzy peach. Perhaps most of all, I remember what it was like to ride on my horse, Augie.

The exciting thing about Augie was the absolute trust and instant obedience he had towards me, his rider. He was instant and complete in obeying my commands. The joy of his heart was to do my will. His response to me was not dependent on his approval of the course I set for him.

Unfortunately, as people we rarely demonstrate the same trust and obedience toward the Lord. We haven't changed much from the words of Isaiah 1:3, when the Lord said, "The ox knows his master, the donkey his owner's manger, but Israel does not know, my people do not understand." We doubt the wisdom of the one who is holding the reins of our lives. That means we really don't know who God is, that He is worthy of absolute trust and instant obedience.

As a Christian at age fourteen, my trusting in God and obedience to Him was subject to my approval. Since then, I've come to see that God owed me no explanations. He did enough explaining at Calvary. We Christians often talk about struggle, but sometimes "struggle" is nothing but a nice word for postponed obedience. We use our trials as excuses for not obeying, thinking that we are the exception, that we are unique. Our best bet is to seal the words of 2 Timothy 1:12 into our hearts: "That is why I am suffering as I am. Yet I am not ashamed, because I know whom I have believed, and am convinced that he is able to guard what I have entrusted to him for that day." I think that's what it means to trust and obey.

*But grow in the grace and knowledge of our Lord
and Savior Jesus Christ.*

2 Peter 3:18

45

COPING WITH CRISIS
(With our misfortunes mounting,
we couldn't help but ask, "Why?")

Bill Michael

When someone we know is facing personal problems or grief, we strain to find adequate words of comfort and assurance. We want to say, "I know how you feel," but unless we have gone through similar circumstances, we really can't know what it feels like. More often than not, however, my wife, Grace, and I can truthfully tell others who are hurting, "We *do* know how you feel."

During our thirty-six years of marriage, we have faced a succession of tough times, many of which we couldn't fully understand. We have learned — through hardship — the reality of Romans 8:28, "And we know that God causes all things to work together for good to those who love God, to those who are called according to His purpose," (NAS).

Almost from the moment we got married, Grace and I have had to go through deep waters together. On our honeymoon in Albany, New York, we were involved in a dreadful accident. We were driving and the tire of an oncoming car blew out, causing the driver to lose control. The automobile hit us nearly head-on. Fortunately, we suffered no permanent injuries.

During our seventh year of marriage we were away from home, speaking at a youth retreat, when our home near Westminster, Maryland, burned to the ground. Fortunately, our two children at the time both were with us, but the fire left us deeply in debt. That was the first of many financial struggles we have faced.

In 1963, after having three daughters, God gave us a son, Arthur William III. I had always wanted a son, but when Arthur William was seven months old he died during exploratory heart surgery at Johns Hopkins Medical Center. He had been born with congenital heart defects, but we had not realized how serious his problems were until he was six months old.

Both Grace and I had committed our lives to Jesus Christ as teenagers, but it still was a tough blow. We struggled to understand why God allowed our son to die.

Then in 1972, my wife and I were away from home, speaking at a lay witness weekend in Binghamton, New York. On October 29, our seventeen-year-old daughter, Sharon, was driving to Sunday school with her fifteen-year-old sister, Melanie. It was raining, and the narrow road they were traveling on was covered with leaves. Sharon lost control of the car and it skidded broadside into the path of another vehicle. Melanie received only a few scratches, but Sharon suffered severe head injuries.

I was to go to the pulpit and give my testimony before a large church in Binghamton when we received a telephone call from our family physician, informing us of the accident. The four-hour drive back to Hanover, Pennsylvania, was a time of real soul-searching, wondering why God was allowing us to go through something like that again.

Sharon was a senior in high school and an honor student. She had been accepted to nursing school, and had given her life to serving the Lord, probably as a nurse on the mission field. We could not understand how God could let this happen.

The night before I had been reading in Philippians 3, in the *Living Bible*, while preparing for my message. Somehow, some verses stood out for me, appearing as if in bolder print. That had never happened to me before, nor since. I underlined them, and had planned to share them the next morning with the congregation. The verses (1, 8, 11, 13, and 15) said this:

"Whatever happens, dear friends, be glad in the Lord . . . Yes, everything else is worthless when compared with the priceless gain of knowing Christ Jesus my Lord . . . So, whatever it takes, I will be one who lives in the fresh newness of life of those who are alive from the dead . . . Forgetting the past and looking forward to what lies ahead . . . I hope all of you who are mature Christians will see eye-to-eye with me on these things."

Sunday morning, after hearing about the accident and reading those verses again, I knew God had meant them for us.

We arrived at the hospital in York at 2 P.M., where we were met by a surgeon who told us Sharon was undergoing surgery. Her heart had stopped once during the operation, which took five hours, and doctors told us it would require a miracle for her to live. We went to my mother's home that evening, to tell her about the accident. While we were there, a pastor friend in Hanover called to tell us Sharon had gone to be with the Lord.

It was during the funeral, even as we grieved, that we began to see how God truly can and does cause *all* things to work together for good to those who love God. The church was jammed with people, including a good portion of Sharon's senior class. The pastor talked about the Savior that Sharon had loved and served, and asked those who would like to ask Jesus Christ into their own lives to raise their hands. Approximately one hundred people responded, including nearly all of the class members. One of them, Sharon's best friend, Chris, has since gone on to college and has been instrumental in winning many people to Christ. As we were preparing to go to the cemetery after the service, a woman in her forties walked up to our car. She, too, had three daughters and had driven down with a carload of people from the church in Binghamton. She told us she had attended church all her life, but that morning she had prayed to receive Jesus Christ for the first time.

Those events did not remove the sadness of losing Sharon, but we did see God was bringing good out of it and that He had a purpose in her death.

Our hurts did not heal quickly, although we sensed God's comforting presence during and after our ordeal. The first year after the accident was the worst, particularly for Grace. She had not been able to bring herself to view the body, and it was seven months before she was fully able to deal with the fact that Sharon was no longer with us. It was on Palm Sunday, while listening to our church choir sing glorious hymns of praise, that Grace faced the reality that Sharon was on the other side, singing with the Lord.

For four days the tears came, no matter what Grace did or where she went. But that was the beginning of her inner healing. It still was four years before her pain really went away.

Being a businessman, it had been a little easier for me since I could immerse myself in my work. Even in business, however, I haven't been immune to hardship. We've had so many setbacks — we have even faced bankruptcy, although the Lord enabled us to avoid it. And I have to admit, it's been hard at times to associate with other Christian business-men who have prospered beyond measure while I was fighting to meet my obligations. I can think of one particular close friend who has en-joyed nothing but success, while we had only struggle. I've had to turn again and again to Matthew 6:33, "But seek first his kingdom and his righteousness, and all these things shall be added to you," (NAS), to keep a right perspective.

Looking back, we can see God's involvement in each circumstance we have faced. Although times often have been hard, we never stopped believing that God is good — and we've never questioned His faithful-ness. The Lord has taught us many important lessons through our trials. In fact, the hard times have been our real times of growth as Christians, because we had no choice but to depend on God. To be honest, we haven't grown much during our good times, I guess because it's so easy to begin relying on ourselves rather than on Him.

In one sense, I believe we have actually been more fortunate than most because we have been forced to walk more closely with the Lord to endure our difficulties. Despite our financial problems, we have learned how unimportant money really is. We know a lot of very un-happy people who are wealthy, even Christians, and even some multi-millionaires. It never works when you trust in gold instead of God.

It has been a joy to encourage and help others who are going through many of the same adversities we have faced. For instance, we have had numerous opportunities to console, share with, and comfort parents who have lost children. Repeatedly, God brings them into our lives. He also has opened the door for me to counsel men dealing with serious business problems. After having nearly lost everything myself, I know what these men are going through.

When I first accepted Jesus Christ, I had the idea that life would get easier, that I would get all the breaks. After all, I had become a "King's kid," and look at all I was doing for God! But Philippians 3:10 says, "that I may know Him, and the power of His resurrection and the fellowship of His sufferings. . . ." God put that last phrase there, whether we like to or not, because as Christians we are "being conformed to His death," (NAS).

Right now, things in our life are going along smoothly. The Lord has resolved some very complicated business problems in an amazing way, and I am now general manager of a large construction company in Lancaster, Pennsylvania. No longer faced with the pressure of business ownership, my relationship with Grace is better than ever. And with more job flexibility, the Lord is opening up doors for us to travel and speak on His behalf.

With everything that has happened in our lives, I honestly have to say there are times when we wonder, "What's next?" But God has stood by us through everything. We have seen the reality of 1 Corinthians 10:13: "No temptation has overtaken you but such as is common to man; and God is faithful, who will not allow you to be tempted beyond what you are able, but with the temptation will provide the way of escape also, that you may be able to endure it," (NAS).

The Lord has shown us, over and over again, that we can trust in and depend on Him. Psalm 37 is filled with that assurance. It tells us, "The steps of a man are established by the LORD. . . . When he falls, he shall not be hurled headlong; because the LORD is the One who holds his hand. I have been young, and now I am old; yet I have not seen the righteous forsaken," (37:23–25, NAS).

We've also learned to take life one day at a time—sometimes less than that. Jesus said, "do not be anxious about tomorrow; for tomorrow will care for itself. Each day has enough trouble of its own," (Matthew 6:34, NAS). We have an appreciation for God's blessings that I believe many Christians who have not faced serious troubles cannot completely understand. As the saying goes, you can't really appreciate the mountaintop until you've been in the valley.

*But grow in the grace and knowledge of our Lord
and Savior Jesus Christ.*

2 Peter 3:18

46

IS AMERICAN SOCIETY FACING THE EVE OF DESTRUCTION?

An Interview with Charles Colson

When former presidential aide Charles W. Colson's 1973 commitment to Jesus Christ made national headlines, there were many who questioned the genuineness of his conversion. But more than sixteen years later, Colson has become one of the nation's leading and most respected spokesmen for criminal justice, evangelical Christianity, and Christian social action.

The founder and chairman of the Washington, D.C. based Prison Fellowship Ministries, he is a best-selling author, columnist, and conference speaker. In *Convicted*, written with Daniel Van Ness, he calls for a radical reform of the U.S. criminal justice system. His latest book, *Against the Night*, is a strong warning against a society rapidly losing its moral underpinnings and a call for the church to again bring light to oppose the gathering darkness.

In a few months, we will enter the 1990s. From a Christian perspective, what can we expect as we approach the twenty-first century?

The last decade of the twentieth century is going to be the pivotal time for the entire century. Looking over the twentieth century, it has been marked essentially by great ideological conflict, liberal Western democracy versus a romanticized version of Marxism that Lenin embraced. Through much of the century, liberal democracy was in retreat, while Communism captured idealistic notions in Third World countries, American campuses, even some segments of the church.

Amazingly, in the last decade Communism has been intellectually discredited. Liberal democracy and capitalism have proven themselves. Even Third World nations are being drawn to it. The issue is whether the West can survive long enough to reap the ideological victory.

One of the most prophetic speeches ever given was by Aleksandr Solzhenitsyn in 1978. In his commencement address at Harvard University, he predicted a spiritual revival in the East. We see this happening today in Russia, as well as in Poland, where the overthrow of the Communist government has been one of the most incredible developments in history. Without question, Solidarity was a spiritual, Christian, church-based movement which succeeded in displacing a government without a shot being fired. In much of the world, Communism is losing and Democratic capitalism is winning.

But it's the second part of Solzhenitsyn's speech that concerns us the most. He said the West was suffering from terminal spiritual exhaustion—the people had stopped looking upward. And that is exactly what is happening today, despite the increase in Christian activism. Our nation is exhausting itself spiritually and losing its moral authority at the same time. So I see the 1990s as the time when the great dialectic of the twentieth century will be settled. The question is, will we be strong enough in the West to provide the necessary spiritual and moral direction?

Do you think we will be?

You want to know if I'm optimistic. I can't answer that. There are so many other questions that first need to be answered. For instance, with all the influences to the contrary, is it possible to provide moral education in American society? Have Phil Donahue and Oprah Winfrey become the arbiters of our moral values? God help us if they are!

We are living in a society in which the church has largely conformed, the traditional family has dissolved, and schools are failing to teach anything. I wonder if we can relocate the props of virtue that support civilization in the West today, when secularism is so rampant. It's like trying to stop a train going eighty miles an hour. We will require a massive moral overhaul if we are to avoid, as Solzhenitsyn predicted, dying of spiritual exhaustion.

There seems to be a growing concern about our country's moral decay, even beyond the Christian community.

The best stuff being written and expressed on the subject is actually coming from people outside of evangelical Christianity, men such as Robert Bellah, John Silber, Allan Bloom, Alistair McIntyre, even TV commentator Ted Koppel.

It's ironic that although Christians have been much more active politically since 1980, the United States is in worse shape ethically and morally than it has ever been. What more can we do?

Our hope is not in the church being a political instrument. Our hope is in the church being the church, and thereby allowing God to use it to the maximum political effect. We need to be true to our calling, that of expressing the character and caring of Jesus Christ, and being a witness of God's invisible Kingdom. When the church tries to be what it is not — something other than the bride of Christ — it usually fails.

But what about trying to influence legislation, establishing laws that require a higher standard of moral behavior?

The sad fact is, despite the U.S. Supreme Court ruling in the *Webster v. Reproductive Health Services,* which was hailed as a major stride in the pro-life movement, there has been no reduction in abortions in Missouri. Women are merely crossing state lines to obtain them. Until we can change the moral vision of the people, even changing the laws will not help us.

Nor is our hope in electing the right political leaders. Leaders do not change people; in fact, it's just the opposite. The values in society generally bubble up from the bottom, not filter down from the top. Every fundamental spiritual movement has found its start at the bottom. We could elect hundreds of born-again Christians to the state and federal governments, and it would not change anything. There has to be a moral impulse that calls people to something greater than themselves.

Where, then, must change be achieved?

I believe the battleground of the future, if we are to somehow succeed in saving and resurrecting the family and invigorating the church, is in radically converting our educational system. That is an area that we can do something about. If we truly have 50 million born-again Christians, as surveys indicate, then we should have a lot more healthy families and more influence on local school boards than we do.

Do you sense a stronger polarization between the Christians and secular segments of society?

There is no question that there is much more hostility toward the Christian faith than there was twenty years ago. We have asserted ourselves. People now know where we are and what we think. As a result, there is open hostility from those who oppose our viewpoints. But maybe this open hostility is necessary — historically, the church has never done well with success and affluence.

In light of this widening gap between the religious and the secular, do you think it is possible for a strongly committed, openly Christian candidate to make a successful run for President?

Certainly. Senator Bill Armstrong of Colorado was given serious consideration early on in the last presidential race. He is making a strong Christian statement on Capitol Hill. He has achieved national prominence and is an out-and-out, unapologetic follower of Jesus Christ. Senator Dan Coats of Indiana, who was appointed to Vice President Dan Quayle's seat, is another one.

Regarding Mr. Quayle, the American public has been sucked in by all the bad press written about him. I have been in his home, and he is as evangelical about his faith as I am about mine. He still goes to the same Bible-believing church that he went to before he became Vice President. When people ask me, "Why can't we get evangelicals in high-ranking offices?" I simply tell them that we've got one in Dan Quayle.

What are the key groups in determining thought in America today?

The media comprises one of the strongest groups, along with those in education, government, business and, of course, religion. Today's barbarians wear pinstripes rather than animal skins, and wield briefcases rather than spears. CBMC is a vital, grass-roots organization targeting one of the elements of society that has the greatest ability to influence thought and behavior.

In your book, *Convicted,* you issue a strong call for radical change in our criminal justice system. Is that another area that the church needs to address?

Criminal justice is getting and deserves as much attention as the other issues in society, such as abortion, pornography, and poverty. Some 98 percent of all Americans will be victims of crime, and 80 percent will be victims of violent crime. The fact that the victims are being ignored by our system is scandalous. If we do not start to effectively apply the principles of criminal restitution and restoration, our justice system will collapse under its own weight.

Overall, what is your opinion of Christian activism?

We have a serious lack of education in the church today, resulting in too limited a Biblical perspective. We need to broaden that view. While we must be concerned about the welfare of the unborn, the drug epidemic and pornography, we should be equally concerned that our society apply the Biblical principle of gleanings, attending to the needs of the poor, the prisoners, the oppressed.

It's fine to be involved in single issues, because we all have different gifts and responsibilities, but we must do them in view of the full counsel of God's Word. If we don't do the basics, we will lose all the rest. But if we do as Christ said in Matthew 6:33, to "Seek first His kingdom and His righteousness," (NAS) then the rest will come.

We need to be beacons of character, living lives of righteousness, holiness, and integrity before society.

. . . and you will be my witnesses in Jerusalem, and in all Judea and Samaria, and to the ends of the earth.

Acts 1:8

47

GOOD NEWS FOR THE MODERN MIND

An Interview with Jim Petersen

Secularization, like a monstrous tidal wave, is sweeping across much of the Western world. Having already engulfed much of Europe and Latin America, the flow is rapidly spreading in the United States. This value system, which places man, and not God, at its center is having a dramatic impact in all areas of society. Its effect upon contemporary evangelism is increasingly profound, posing a formidable challenge to all who seek to communicate the Good News of Jesus Christ to individuals from non-religious backgrounds.

Jim Petersen, an authority on trends in world evangelism, in 1963 got his first opportunity to confront secularization firsthand. He was assigned by the Navigators to build a ministry to university students in Brazil, but found most of them during that revolutionary period were antichurch, antigovernment Marxists. Traditional approaches to evangelism were ineffective, causing Petersen to begin rethinking the whole process of winning people to Jesus Christ. As a result of his studies, he has concluded that some changes are urgently needed if the church is to effectively continue reaching the uncommitted into the twenty-first century.

231

What is the magnitude of secularization, as you see it? How is it affecting the Christian community?

In the United States alone, the proportion of secularized (non-religious) people is growing at an alarming rate. In the 1950s, only five percent of all Americans could be classified as secularized. Today, that number is 38 percent. In addition, 40 percent are nominally religious, meaning they may attend church on occasion, but are becoming increasingly secular. Of the remaining 22 percent who are considered evangelicals, only half of those are actively pursuing their faith. The other 11 percent are "passive" evangelicals who are slowly shifting into the nominally religious category.

Between Europe and North America, the church is losing 2,765,000 people per year to nominalism and unbelief—that's 7,600 people a day! In Europe we see the grand churches with their beautiful architecture, but they are empty. Take England, for example, which once was a leader in world evangelism. Today, fewer than two percent of its people attend church.

In the Navigator ministry, we used to see five hundred to seven hundred converts a year in the Netherlands, working within the framework of the Dutch Reformed Church. Within a decade, that target has virtually disappeared.

Why is secularization such an obstacle to evangelism?

The distance between the Christian world view and the non-Christian world view is just enormous. As time passes the greater it becomes. The mainstreams of society are increasingly characterized by secularization. It's a moving target, but we can look at the symptoms—divorce, abortion, government officials who, in the name of progress, lie with a clear conscience, the $120 billion pornography industry, proliferation of drugs.

While in Brazil I realized I was dealing with people for whom Biblical answers meant nothing. I found that to have an impact on the people I encountered, I had to drop my normal identity and methods. I had to return to the primary source, the Bible. The challenge became not talking directly about Jesus Christ, but discussing the question, "What is truth?", and trying to point to Him in the process.

Judging from your statistics, it sounds like the modern-day church is losing the spiritual battle. Is that the case?

The Navigators, working in virtually every country of the world, have found we are reaping the "prepared" people who already understand Biblical concepts and are ready to respond. But those are in a vanishing minority. It's like pitching a tent on an ice flow in hot water.

The problem is that we—the church and the parachurch—think we're making progress, since we're expending so much energy and our programs are so prolific. Actually, we're losing ground. With all of our activities and large budgets, we think we're knocking them dead, but basically, it's just a lot of smoke. We have reached the point where we have to do more than find the prepared and reap them; just stepping up the pace on old success patterns is not going to cut it. It's hard to predict, but if nothing changes in our approach to personal evangelism, by the turn of the century I'm afraid the United States will be a pagan nation, just as is the case in Europe today.

You are a strong proponent of "lifestyle evangelism" in your books. Do you think that is the answer to stemming the tide of secularization?

First of all, in America we generally have an attitude that everything legitimate in terms of Jesus Christ has to go on within the confines of the church building. We're going to have to widen our circle and redefine how the church structures itself. Circumstances will define how that is done.

We have to come to a Biblical understanding of evangelism. Much of our effort is spent in the *proclamation* of the gospel, but the Bible also teaches the *affirmation* of the gospel, which I believe is summarized best in Colossians 4:5–6: "Be wise in the way you act toward outsiders; make the most of every opportunity. Let your conversation be always full of grace, seasoned with salt, so that you may know how to answer everyone." To me, that means to create a context, an environment by the way we live, that attracts people to Christ. But it also means that as people see the incarnation of the gospel in our lives, we need to be alert to opportunities around us to speak out for Him.

In Brazil I realized that evangelism is a process, one which involved an ongoing examination of the Bible. Our job is not to prove the Bible is true or to convince a non-believer that he is wrong. That's the job of the Holy Spirit. All God asks of us is to help people to understand what is written, and let the Holy Spirit convince them that it's true.

Effective evangelism in a secularized society takes time and lots of hard work. It took months for students I was working with in Brazil to come to Christ, but once one did make that decision, it really stuck! I've led a lot of people to make decisions for the Lord after one or two conversations, but I have yet to see a single person go on. But when I have taken the time to make sure the person met the person of Jesus Christ, helped him understand what was involved, and guided him in studying the Scriptures, I haven't had a case where the person hasn't gone on with the Lord.

Soon after your first book, *Evangelism As a Lifestyle,* was published, "lifestyle evangelism" became a Christian buzzword of sorts. What were your thoughts then?

First of all, I had already realized that lifestyle evangelism was not a new concept, but one that was deeply rooted in the Scriptures. There is always some apprehension when you present something that even seems new. But when Rebecca Pippert's book, *Out of the Salt Shaker and Into the World,* and Joe Aldrich's book, *Lifestyle Evangelism,* were published within the next six months, it was reassuring. When God is saying something, He's not going to say it just through one guy.

For me, lifestyle evangelism had been like one of those "Aha!" experiences we have as Christians discovering spiritual truth. I traced evangelism in the book of Acts and, without exception, discovered that when the gospel was simply declared it was to a people with a certain amount of religious tradition and heritage. Those people had already been prepared. So I saw our task in reaching the secularized world as one of cultivating and sowing, so that the "soil" of human hearts is adequately prepared for the gospel message.

What do you think of traditional forms of evangelism — crusades, door-to-door witnessing, revivals?

I thank God for whatever is there, whenever the gospel is preached, but we've got to have the freedom, the "space," to go to the majority of people who will no longer respond to those kinds of approaches. For people who do not have a church background, it's not enough to just explain the "Christian contract" and ask them to "vote" by repeating the sinner's prayer. They may vote, but usually the whole person is not behind that commitment. Our goal should be to move a person one step closer toward Jesus Christ.

A person is ready to submit to Christ only when he understands that his basic problem is living in rebellion against God. That means coming out with your hands up, being willing to cease being your own god. Most of the time that can't be accomplished at one church service, even if a person is willing to attend, or by being witnessed to by a stranger. We have to bring the church to the world, living a quality of life before them "so that no one will malign the word of God," as it says in Titus 2:5.

In contrast with what we might call "confrontational evangelism," then, what skills are needed in lifestyle evangelism?

We need to learn how to establish friendships with the uncommitted. That calls for learning how to relate to people from a non-Christian mindset and taking a little initiative. We need to make them feel comfortable, to be at ease around us. After I have given a seminar on evangelism, I often find that the main problem many Christians have is they don't know any non-Christians. In many cases, they turned off their unsaved friends with their aggressive evangelistic techniques early on and felt that was a sign of being a good Christian. Unfortunately, it's not. We are not to be *of* the world, but we are told that we have to be *in* it.

Secondly, we need to find bridges of interest — common ground and mutual concern — with non-Christians we work with and those we have as neighbors.

What is the "prognosis" for evangelism in the next few years, in your opinion? Do you envision church leaders embracing these changes?

I see some really encouraging signs. I have a number of pastor friends who are doing some very innovative things to reach secularized people with the gospel. They realize the need to go to all the world rather than invite all the world to come to them. We still have a long, long way to go, but there is no reason for pessimism. More and more people are becoming committed to this. I know God is. He'll teach us and lead us. I feel that if we build a little trail, others will turn it into a highway. The key is, as Aleksandr Solzhenitsyn wrote, to learn how to implement change without tearing up the fabric of society in the process.

. . . and you will be my witnesses in Jerusalem, and in all Judea and Samaria, and to the ends of the earth.

Acts 1:8

48

TWO KINDS OF CHRISTIANS?

Ted DeMoss

I seldom meet a Christian who can clearly verbalize his purpose for life. Christians I talk with may express vague goals such as being a good parent, a loving husband or wife, a solid church member or other things that are good to do. Very few, however, have ever thought through and defined a purpose for their lives.

We are all different, with an assortment of gifts and talents, but we find a very worthy purpose statement included in Acts 1:8. In that verse, Jesus Christ said, "But you will receive power when the Holy Spirit comes on you; and you will be my witnesses in Jerusalem, and in all Judea and Samaria, and to the ends of the earth." Interestingly, those were the last words Jesus said to His followers before He ascended to heaven.

It's interesting to look a little closer at that passage. Using the "who," "what" and "where" form of analysis, we find that the *who* is all believers; *what* is to be His witnesses; and *where* is, put simply, everywhere. The problem we often run into is the misconception that "witnessing" consists of inviting people to church so that the preachers can tell them how to become Christians.

Not long ago I conducted a seminar for more than one hundred men, sharing with them some of the experiences I have had telling businessmen about Christ. After a while a man in the back of the room stood up and commented, "I don't know where you find people interested in the gospel. I can't find them anywhere." I asked where he looked for them. He replied that in his desk at his office he had a list of more than fifty men he had invited to his church, but none had ever come!

Nowhere in the Bible are we commanded to bring non-Christians into the church to get saved. In fact, there is not one instance in the Bible of anyone who ever got converted in a church or synagogue. For instance, in Luke 19, our Lord did not ask Zaccheus to meet Him at the synagogue on the Sabbath. Instead, he went to Zaccheus' home. The misconception is that the pagan is supposed to come and hear; the Biblical mandate for the believer is to go and tell.

If we are to be salt and light in our world, we need to go where the lost are. That might mean inviting them into your home for dinner, going next door to visit with them, playing miniature golf together, or doing something else with them. The Holy Spirit will start working in their lives as they watch our lives and try to figure out why we are different.

As we seek to formulate a purpose for our lives in light of Acts 1:8, we need to consider what is perhaps the greatest trick Satan has ever perpetrated on believers. That trick is the belief that there are two kinds of Christians—full-time workers and the rest of us. I accepted that myth for a number of years myself, thinking my job was just to put my money in the offering plate so the preacher could get the good news out. There is no support for that in the Bible.

Somewhere along the line, "church work" has become confused with the work of the church. By church work I mean activities such as selection of a new organ, choosing the color of the carpet for the sanctuary, or serving on the committee to plan the next congregational banquet. All are good things to do, but they have little to do with the work of the church, which is to reach the lost for Christ and help to nurture them into mature, reproducing Christians.

Jesus did not die so we could be harnessed to church work—we all do that automatically. Our Lord died to pay the debt for our sins, so that by repenting we might receive the gift of eternal life. The work of the church, then, is to introduce others to Christ and give them an opportunity to also receive this wonderful gift.

In Acts 5:42 we discover that "Day after day, in the temple courts and from house to house, they never stopped teaching and proclaiming the good news that Jesus is the Christ." These were not pastors or graduates from a seminary, but the followers of our Lord who each day, whether in the temple or in individual homes, shared their love and commitment to Jesus Christ.

As Christian businessmen, we are obligated before God to work diligently, honestly, and ethically, but most of all He desires for us to tell others about Him. I'm a businessman, and I've found that other business people will listen to me more easily than they will listen to my preacher, even though he is a gifted speaker and a highly intelligent individual. Why is this? It's simple, really. People see me not as a paid representative, but rather as a satisfied customer. That, in my opinion, is our purpose — to be beggars telling other beggars where to find bread.

*. . . and you will be my witnesses in Jerusalem, and
in all Judea and Samaria, and to the ends of the
earth.*

Acts 1:8

49

THE TWENTY-FIRST CENTURY GOSPEL
(What shape must evangelism take?)

Leighton Ford

Through the rest of this century and beyond, we will be evangelizing in an increasingly secularized and pluralistic America. We will
have to face increasing ignorance of the Bible, as Dr. George Gallup's
studies have so well shown.

Further, as theologian David Wells has written, there have been three
ligaments in the joints which have held civilization together — authority,
tradition, and power. In the face of forward-looking technology, tradition
has lost its grip and secularization is deaf to any higher voice.

"Tradition goes and authority goes. So what is left in our Western
societies?" he asks. "We have multiple centers of power, but very little
tradition and no authority." So our cultural and moral religious life becomes more and more like the food court in a modern shopping mall,
with something for every taste.

We could respond to this in two fatal ways. One would be to down-
play the uniqueness of Jesus as our only Savior. James Davidson
Hunter, in his book, *Evangelicalism: The Coming Generation*, has already professed to see this happening among younger evangelicals.

241

In a pluralistic age, conversation between those of different view-points calls for politeness in our discourse. Hunter has described an "evangelical civility" which accentuates the positive parts of the gospel ("let Jesus in and find purpose, meaning, and fulfillment"), but soft-pedals the harder parts (sin, repentance, cross-bearing, judgment, hell).

We who are evangelicals have to speak the name of Jesus with love, with conviction, and without apology. He is *the* Way. But we must also learn to speak with humility and sensitivity. We are not the moral majority who thank God that we are not as others. We are transgressors who pray, "God, be merciful to me, a sinner."

It is me, not my brother, who stands in the need of prayer. Yet having received the gift of salvation at great cost to Him, we must proclaim that grace — not impose it or coerce it — but offer it as a free gift.

Surprises in Heaven

George Whitefield, the great English revivalist, once said that when we get to heaven there will be three surprises. We will be surprised at those who are there we thought wouldn't be there. We will be surprised at those who aren't there that we thought would be. And, most of all, we will be surprised that we are there — by God's grace! If that note and tone of humility would be more often in our evangelism, maybe more would listen.

The other fatal mistake would be to create and retreat into our "life-style enclaves," holding fast to our orthodoxy and evangelizing only those who are like ourselves. Jim Petersen of The Navigators has pointed out that the evangelical student groups on the typical campus scramble each fall to get the most interested and likely freshmen recruits, but seem to make little impact in reaching beyond that first wave.

Evangelicals in the last decade have tended to adopt a defensive mentality to withstand the onslaughts of "secular humanism" as a social and philosophical movement. But not nearly as many evangelicals are asking the question, "How are we going to penetrate their world and win secular humanists to Christ?" Will evangelicals be content merely to be an orthodox holding operation or will we see the very genius of our calling to be that of a missionary movement?

It seems to me that we will need an evangelism that is both *narrow* and *wide*. When Jesus was asked if there are few that are saved, He responded by putting together two metaphors, that of a narrow door which would not always be open and that of a universal feast which draws an amazing cross-section of people from the East and the West.

It seems that Jesus is saying to us that we are to be as narrow as He is, holding that there is only one door. Jesus is that door and is the Savior, as no one else is. But we also are to open the door wide to all the different cultural traditions, so that we have a church which is rigorously committed to Jesus and His Word, and warmly and richly renewed by all kinds of people.

Frank Tillapaugh, pastor of Bear Valley Baptist Church in Denver, sees himself as the "vision caster" and "cheerleader" of lay ministers in his congregation who lead the various evangelistic helping and serving groups. This is typical of what I call the "second reformation." The first reformation put the Scriptures — the *Word* of God — in the hands of ordinary believers. The second reformation is putting the ministry — the *work* of God — in the hands of ordinary believers.

In much of the world, as in Nepal, for example, the work of the ministry is the work of all of God's people. Lay evangelists carry the gospel from person to person and from group to group. Some have estimated that by the close of this century, 83 percent of the unreached people groups of the world, that is, those who do not have a viable witnessing community among them, will be open only to Christian workers within their own national borders or to lay "tentmaker" witnesses. One has only to think of those areas which are largely closed to traditional missionaries, such as China, India, and most Muslim countries, to realize this truth.

In much of the world, the gospel is mainly spread by ordinary Christians who live and "gossip the gospel" in the neighborhoods, marketplace, and leisure areas. In the German Democratic Republic, some of the most effective evangelism is done through informal camping weekends where a group of Christian couples will take their nonchurched friends for an outing and look for opportunities to casually engage them in conversations about their life and faith.

Not long ago, a consultation sponsored by the Lausanne Congress on World Evangelization brought together representatives of forty lay "affinity" groups—ranging from the Christian Medical Society to the Hardhats for Christ—to encourage each other and learn from one another in their vocationally centered ministries.

Will our congregations of the future be far-seeing enough to realize that much of the work of the church is done not within the four walls, but in the worlds of work, home, and leisure where Christians are scattered? Will pastors be secure enough to trust and enable and let go of the lay Christians to carry out that task?

Things may get increasingly difficult in evangelism in the years ahead. So we will need young men and women who have learned to take a long view, who are not just quick starters, but are also good finishers. Some of our leaders are calling for the completion of world evangelism by A.D. 2000, or at least to see half the population of the world following Jesus by His 2,000th birthday. I welcome the thought of using the new millennium as an incentive, while I refuse to see the year 2000 as any kind of millennial magic number.

What will happen if we get to the year 2000 and we *haven't* won the world? What will we do then? For myself, I would like to be part of raising up a generation of finishers, young men and women whom we won't puff up for their immediate success or drop at their first failure, but in whom we will seek to instill the vision and strength to preach the gospel of the Kingdom with creativity, integrity and excellence to the glory of God, until Christ comes or until the end of their generation— whichever comes first.

When my wife's mother, Mrs. Morrow Graham, died at the age of eighty-seven, one of the last things she did was to pull Jeanie closer, pat her on the shoulder and say, "Daughter, pass it on to every generation." She was speaking of love, faith, and hope.

Mrs. Graham had already passed that faith on to her son, Billy. He passed it on to our son, Sandy, who accepted Christ when he was very little, through Billy's preaching. Sandy ran his race for Christ until he died in heart surgery at the age of twenty-one. By God's grace, I have determined to run my race for Christ—all the way—and to pass on the baton. May we all run that race together!

This chapter is an excerpt from an address Dr. Ford gave at the Consultation on Evangelicals and American Public Life, Philadelphia, Pennsylvania, in November, 1988. Used by permission.

*. . . and you will be my witnesses in Jerusalem, and
in all Judea and Samaria, and to the ends of the
earth.*

Acts 1:8

50

GENTLE PERSUASION
(Being good news so that you can share the Good News)

An Interview with Dr. Joseph C. Aldrich

Witnessing. For many people, it has become synonymous with "bad news" — for non-Christians, because they resent people trying to force their religious beliefs on them, and for Christians, because of their own uneasiness in trying to tell others what they believe and why. And yet Jesus clearly told His followers that "you shall be my witnesses" (Acts 1:8, RSV). How are we to share the Good News without being bad news?

Dr. Joseph Aldrich, president of Multnomah School of the Bible in Portland, Oregon, is probably best-known for his best-selling book, *Lifestyle Evangelism* (Multnomah Press). In that book, he explains that evangelism is not an isolated event, but a process.

He calls his newly published sequel to that book, *Gentle Persuasion*, a "user-friendly book on lifestyle evangelism." In it, Aldrich builds on his earlier concepts, drawing from Biblical principles to offer practical and creative ways for effectively communicating the gospel message to men and women who initially seem resistant to the truths of Jesus Christ.

I'm not sure that "lifestyle evangelism," although often discussed, is commonly understood. Define what that term means to you.

Successful evangelism is a three-phase process of cultivation, sowing and harvesting. Cultivation is an appeal to the heart through the building of a relationship. Sowing is an appeal to the mind through the communication of revelation. Reaping is an appeal to the will in anticipation of a response. Most churches today focus most of their efforts on the last stage, but reaping isn't all there is to evangelism. In fact, reaping isn't even the hard labor. Any farmer knows that. It takes one day to harvest what you've cultivated and nurtured for months.

But isn't evangelism a matter of presenting the gospel of Christ and giving people an opportunity to respond?

We cannot presuppose a Protestant ethic or Christian world view anymore when we're dealing with what you might call "pre-Christians." Secularism is here to stay, and we have such an eclectic spirit today that sectarian beliefs are almost automatically rejected. One of the reasons the New Age Movement is so appealing is that it allows the individual to make his own reality and develop his own world view. So as society moves away from the basic presuppositions of the Bible, changes are required in the way evangelism is done.

Are you saying, then, that confrontational evangelism has become outdated?

No, because wherever we go we will find some people whom God has already prepared for that form of evangelism. But although Jesus told us "the fields are white unto harvest," different crops ripen at different times. And studies have shown that only about 10 percent of Christians are gifted in the area of confrontational evangelism. Even at a progressive church like Coral Ridge Presbyterian, which pioneered "Evangelism Explosion," less than four percent of its members are actively involved in the program. So I say "amen" for those four percent, but my concern is for the other 96 percent.

Lifestyle evangelism is not a method; it's a way of living that uses methods that are appropriate for a particular time, place, and people. The key to lifestyle evangelism is that we're to go out as servants, not as "spiritual bwanas" with pith helmets. People hear the music of the gospel and see its light when Christians serve. If we read the Bible carefully, we see that we are to be towel wearers and basin bearers. As the Apostle Paul wrote in 1 Corinthians 9:19, " . . . I make myself a slave to everyone, to win as many as possible."

Evangelistic servants? I thought we were called to be spokesmen.

Certainly there must be telling (our part) and listening (their part), but Jesus invites the world to look at the "light." "Let your light shine before men, that they may see your good deeds and praise your Father in heaven" (Matthew 5:16). Jesus also commanded us to be salt in Matthew 5:13. But salt requires contact to work, and in evangelism, that means interfacing of lives must take place.

Okay, you're saying we have to cultivate relationships — friendships — with non-Christians. But isn't there a danger of never moving beyond "cultivation" into more aggressive evangelism?

Yes, there is that danger, but since most Christians right now are doing nothing in evangelism, I would rather see them at least involved in cultivating Christ-honoring friendships with unsaved friends, neighbors, and co-workers. It's true that we can become complacent, adopting the permanent excuse of "I'm not a reaper, so I'm just to cultivate." That's why the real burden for the lost has to be there, not an artificial guilt placed on us by the church. We need to continually remind ourselves that people without Christ are on their way to hell, being separated from God for all eternity.

Never in the Bible are we commanded to evangelize our neighbors; we are told to love them. Not long ago, I met a radiant Christian from India who was having great success in leading Hindus and Moslems to Christ. Every Sunday, he and his wife host thirty to fifty students for dinner. That's a key part of his strategy, since food and comraderie break down barriers. I asked him if they talk about Christ at those meals. "No, it is impossible to talk openly about Jesus Christ," he replied. "Then how are you able to see so many come to Christ?" His answer was simple: "I love them until they ask me why!"

Your book, *Lifestyle Evangelism,* in which you discuss your ideas in great detail, was published in 1981. Have you gained any new insights into this process since then?

Yes, particularly as I have studied Christ's sending out of the twelve in Matthew 10 and His sending out of the seventy-two in Luke 10. First of all, He taught His disciples the importance of developing dependence on the people with whom they were to minister. You'll notice Jesus told them to stay in their homes, not to check into the local Marriott.

The second is the idea of seeking out what I call a "prequalified audience." The disciples were instructed to search diligently for three things: a worthy man, a worthy home, and a man of peace. Those people are the easiest to reach, since they are already living in agreement with basic Biblical principles. And when people welcome you into their homes and respond to you socially, they are much more likely to respond to Christ. So once someone invites you to become a recipient of his hospitality, stick close. That is a tremendous clue for determining which people God wants you to minister to.

The third concept is that of *oikos,* which is a Greek word meaning household, or an extended family and network of friends. Biblical examples include Lydia and Cornelius. When they became saved, so did their entire households. In our relationships with non-Christians, we should look for *oikos,* a network of common, special interests such as vocations or hobbies. There usually is a strategic person or couple in each group, and when these people trust the Lord, the gospel will flow through them to the other members in their web of relationships.

So the goal of lifestyle evangelism is not to get someone to "pray the prayer" or walk an aisle, but to make a sincere, well-considered commitment to Christ?

We want full-term babies, not spiritual abortions. Whenever we see Jesus "witnessing," we see His sensitivity to the spiritual readiness of those He addressed. We are challenged to *disciple* all nations, not *decision* them. And the beauty of a lifestyle evangelism approach to an individual or group of people is that it provides a built-in follow-up matrix, since you already have a friendship established.

As any good salesman will tell you, people want to buy—they don't want to be sold. People usually buy a product not because they understand the product, but because they believe you understand them. In the same way, people trust Christ because they trust His messengers. We should pray every day for the salvation of people God has brought into *our* lives and look for opportunities to get involved in *theirs.*

The Facts About Evangelism

How can statistics influence our approach to and understanding of personal evangelism? Dr. Joseph C. Aldrich cites the following facts:

- More than 80 percent of those who trust Christ and remain members of a local church are led to the Lord by a friend. Furthermore, they have had over five (5.9) exposures to the gospel before their conversion.
- More than 70 percent of those who "trust Christ" and drop out of church are led to the Lord by a stranger. These converts average a little over two exposures (2.16) to the gospel before conversion.
- Seventy percent of those who remain as members of a local church were led to Christ by someone who viewed evangelism as a non-manipulative dialogue. Almost 90 percent of those who "drop out" were led to Christ by someone who perceived evangelism as a manipulative dialogue.
- More than 90 percent of those who remain within the fellowship of the church following conversion were dissatisfied with their non-religious lifestyle before anyone proclaimed the gospel to them. More than 75 percent of those who "drop out" of the fellowship following conversion showed no significant level of dissatisfaction before conversion.

From the book, *Gentle Persuasion,* by Joseph C. Aldrich, © 1988. Published by Multnomah Press, Portland, Oregon. Used by permission.

PART THREE

HIS FAMILY WORLD

Husbands, love your wives, just as Christ loved the
church and gave himself up for her.

Ephesians 5:25

51

WHAT A WOMEN ADMIRES
MOST IN A MAN

Gary Smalley

We live in a world that sends us confusing signals about what women find attractive about men. Everything from car commercials to razor blade ads tell us we're supposed to be hot, yet cool; rugged, yet romantic; self-sufficient, yet sympathetic; tough, yet understanding.

When we try to follow this crazy, mixed-up pattern for "manliness," we often end up frustrated and discouraged, hurting people in our lives who mean the most to us, especially our wives. Fortunately, there's a much simpler and saner answer to the question, "What do women most admire in a man?" We find it in a very reliable source: the Bible.

Honoring someone means attaching high value to them. We are willing to say to that person, "I treasure you, and I'm willing to do what it takes to always communicate how much you mean to me."

Avenue to Admiration

One aspect of honor that gains the respect and admiration of our wives is our willingness to be open to correction. Being humble enough to listen thoughtfully and carefully to their insights is a powerful way of saying, "You're important to me; I value you and your insight greatly."

One woman I know, Lynn, had tried for ten years to explain to her husband, Larry, how badly two of his habits made her feel, but he never made the effort to understand. His first problem was preferring his relatives over hers. Whenever they were around his family, Larry expected Lynn to adapt her schedule to fit theirs. It didn't matter what she had planned or how she felt. To make matters worse, Larry always sided with his family and defended them during arguments.

After countless attempts to help her husband understand, Lynn, in a flood of emotion, hit upon the right combination of words to help Larry understand how she felt about how he favored his parents over hers.

"Oh, so that's why you don't like my relatives," he said. "Now I see — when we're with my relatives, I always choose their feelings over yours. You feel second-rate. That makes sense, now." Lynn was thrilled: one problem down, one to go.

Larry's second problem was making more commitments than he was able to fulfill. His intentions were noble enough; he wanted to make people happy. But the reality of too many promises unfulfilled had brought Lynn (and some of his friends) to a point of real frustration.

Despite the progress he had made with the in-laws issue, Larry remained blind to his overcommitment problem. Although Lynn tried to tell him, he finally had to recognize it through a very painful experience with his friends.

Friendly Confrontation

Several of them called him and asked to meet with him. They confronted him about his habit of overcommitting himself. Firmly, yet lovingly, they each described how his inability to say "no" had caused them to suffer and was causing them to feel resentful. Embarrassed and humiliated, all Larry could do was think, "If only I had listened to Lynn."

When Larry finally was able to see the extent of this particular weakness, he was able to consciously initiate changes that gained the appreciation and respect of his friends, along with the love and admiration of his wife which became more deeply rooted than ever before.

Finally ready to listen and respond, he built a much closer relationship with all of those around him and worked at discarding those habits that were restricting him from being a more godly man.

Proverbs 13:18 says, "Poverty and shame will come to him who neglects discipline, but he who regards reproof will be honored," (NAS). As men, we must be humble enough to admit that we don't know everything, that we can make mistakes, and that we can always gain more knowledge and understanding. Our inability to do that can create unlimited stress in any relationship, particularly a marriage.

Although a man may fear that responding to his wife's suggestions might "open the flood gates" to her trying to take over control in the marriage, I've observed that just the opposite is true. When a woman sees her husband's willingness to accept correction — a mark of someone who wants to gain wisdom — she is more willing to follow his leadership in the home because she values him, and trusts him, more highly.

Adapted from *If Only He Knew* by Gary Smalley. Copyright 1979 by Gary T. Smalley. Revised edition copyright 1982 by the Zondervan Corporation. Used by permission.

*Husbands, love your wives, just as Christ loved the
church and gave himself up for her.*

Ephesians 5:25

52

MARRIAGE REKINDLED
(Pat and Jill Williams discovered that being Christians does not guarantee a successful and joyous marriage)

An Interview with Pat Williams

I s it possible for a husband and wife to share a strong commitment to Jesus Christ, appear to have the "perfect marriage" and yet watch their relationship succumb to a slow and agonizing death? Pat and Jill Williams can attest it is more than possible — it happened to them.

Pat is the highly successful general manager of the Orlando Magic basketball team and a gifted public speaker. Jill is a former beauty queen and a gifted entertainer. Despite their deep Christian faith, their marriage "died" on December 19, 1982. In fact, it was only determination to keep the vows made before God that prevented divorce from following.

The story, to the praise and glory of God, has a happy ending. Pat, totally immersed in his work and his speaking ministry, finally realized how years of inattention to Jill's needs had left her empty and devastated. What has followed is a total rethinking of priorities by Pat and an intense dedication to love his wife "as Christ loved the church." Today, the Williams' marriage — and family — are stronger than ever before, rebuilt in strict obedience to guidelines established in God's Word. They have six children — Jimmy, Bobby, Karyn, Andrea, Sarah, and Michael.

This nearly tragic story which has resulted in triumph is chronicled candidly by Pat and Jill in their book, *Rekindled*, published in 1985. In less than six months, the book was in its sixth printing, had sold more than 70,000 copies, and was the Fleming Revell publishing company's bestseller of the year. Through their willingness to reveal intimate details of their sorrows and struggles, Pat and Jill offer renewed hope to couples with troubled marriages.

In the following interview, he openly tells about the despair he experienced and how the Lord has turned "my mourning into dancing . . . and girded me with gladness" (Psalm 30:11, NAS).

How would you summarize the basic problems in your marriage leading up to December 19, 1982, the day you now refer to as "D-Day"?

I was totally unprepared for what happened that day. Jill had been in and out of moods, and for ten years I had heard her complaints. Personally, things were going well for me at work and spiritually. My public ministry was very broad-based, I listened to Charles Swindoll and John MacArthur every morning on the radio, our children were doing well in school, the 76ers were on the verge of winning the NBA championship, and my life seemed well in place.

My priorities in life, frankly, were my vocation, my hobbies and leisure activities, and then my family. But if you had asked me then, I would have said my relationship with God was number one, then my wife, my children, and my work number four. But Jill knew better. She felt like an outsider — for all intents and purposes, I had left her out of my life. My work consumed me. The day before we got married, for example, I had to make two major trades while I was still with the Chicago Bulls. I squeezed our marriage in on a Saturday, then we left for a honeymoon. A week later I was back at work, eager to get on with the season.

How did you discover something was wrong?

On Sunday, December 19, I noticed she was in a dark mood. I tried to draw out what was bothering her, but couldn't. Finally that afternoon I sat down with her and insisted she tell me what was wrong. When Jill finally spoke, it was with no emotion and no expression. She had no thought-out speech. She simply told me she hated our marriage. After ten years of faking it, she did not care anymore and was giving up. She wasn't going anywhere—as a Christian she was not going to file for divorce—but she had nothing left to give. At that moment, Jill died emotionally.

I was stunned—absolutely flabbergasted. Here I was, a man who thought life was all together, confronted with such a staggering situation. As the days went on, Jill did not change. She did not smile. She acted—and was—empty, dead inside, a walking corpse. My first reaction was a combination of devastation and embarrassment. I even wondered, "What if anybody finds out about this?" I desperately needed counseling, somebody to talk to, but I was too ashamed to talk with anyone.

At that point, two miraculous events occurred very rapidly in my life. I realized I had failed the Lord as a Christian husband, and I prayed that He would crush and break me. I asked him to rebuild our marriage from scratch, properly. I also asked God to give me some practical, specific help. That evening I found a book, *Love Life for Every Married Couple* by Dr. Ed Wheat, lying not six inches from me on a bedside table. It had been there where Jill had placed it, lying cover down, for eight months. I picked it up, and when I read strong endorsements by Dr. James Dobson and Chuck Swindoll, big hitters in my mind, I plunged into the book.

Through Dr. Wheat's book, for the first time I studied the practical application of Biblical principles in a marriage relationship. I was reading out of panic and desperation, but I suddenly realized how important Jill was in my life—and what an enormous job I had to do. I began to apply what Dr. Wheat said in his book, although I had no idea what the outcome would be. I was clinging to God as tightly as I ever had in my life. I had one word of hope: The book said as long as one person cares enough to save a marriage, that is enough.

What were the principles you began to apply?

In his book, Dr. Wheat talks about the B-E-S-T principle. That stands for Blessing, Edifying, Sharing, and Touching. I began to carry that out with vigor. I'm the type of person that when something comes into my life that is important, it becomes a fanatical obsession with me. I've done that with Bible study, scripture memorization, running, eating health foods, even studying the Civil War. At that point, I realized I was locked into the most important project I ever would be involved in—saving our marriage. And with God's help, I was determined to build the best marriage possible.

Could you explain the B-E-S-T principles and how they helped to rebuild your marriage?

The "blessing" principle revolves around the tongue: speaking well of your mate, responding with good words, and learning when to be silent. It also involves doing kind things, showing appreciation verbally, and praying for God's blessing in your partner's life.

"Edifying" means to build up your mate through personal encouraging, verbal praising and compliments, and never criticizing. I learned Ephesians 4:29 should be a cardinal verse in every home, "Let no unwholesome word proceed from your mouth, but only such a word as is good for edification. . ." (NAS). I am now convinced that no wife was ever intended to receive criticism from her husband—in retrospect, I realize I had gotten very good at doing just that. I had learned how to carve and slice.

In "sharing," the key is sharing time, activities, interests, concerns, ideas, your innermost thoughts, your spiritual walk, and your family objectives and goals. It means giving of yourself, listening to your mate with undivided attention. It's the toughest thing in the world for most men to share of themselves and be intimate, but women long for it.

"Touching," Dr. What pointed out, is most critical of all. No matter how much you bless, edify and share, it's worthless if you fail to master touching. A tender touch tells us we're cared for, it calms fears, soothes pain, brings comfort, and gives emotional security. I discovered Jill had a deep need for the warmth, reassurance, and intimacy of non-sexual touching.

How long was it before Jill began to respond to your efforts to love her?

It came very, very slowly—but surely. There were signs of encouragement within weeks, and they continued over the following months. I applied B-E-S-T in massive doses, but my problem was I wanted to rectify the problem in hours and have it all solved. It wasn't something that could be resolved quickly, even though Jill eventually wanted to restore our relationship as much as I did. As I committed my attention to meeting her needs, I realized what she needed was not a quick fix but a lifetime commitment, dedication to demonstrate my love for her on a daily basis.

You began writing *Rekindled* at Charles Swindoll's suggestion in February 1983. How did you feel about that idea, since your marital crisis had occurred only a few months earlier? Was Jill ready by then to tell the story?

We were rebuilding our relationiship then—we were right in the middle of it. I had seen lots of good signs, but I still realized how tenuous things remained. For Jill, her fear at that point was that it would all disappear. She was not at all certain the change was permanent, and dreaded the thought of waking up one morning with everything reverted to the way it was before.

How would you describe your relationship with Jill now? Do you feel the crisis is behind you—that the basic issue has been resolved?

When we started to write the book, we knew we were going to be extremely vulnerable, transparent, stark naked before the world, and susceptible to Satan's darts. The problems that afflicted our marriage are similar to those faced by a recovered alcoholic or drug addict. There is the danger of losing ground if you don't keep working at it. It's a daily battle, keeping priorities in their proper order. There is still much work to do in our marriage, and it's important to do it well.

I've learned I don't have to stay up until 2 A.M. watching every basketball game on TV, and I don't have to do everything here at the office three different ways. I've learned to delegate, and I feel I have become a better administrator—my staff feels more fulfilled. I've also learned the importance of time alone with Jill. When I'm with her, I need to make sure a newspaper or TV program doesn't come between us.

Pat, you have six children now. In fact, you have added three children since your marital crisis occurred—two little girls you adopted from South Korea and your youngest son, Michael. How have they affected your commitment to a strong, godly marriage?

The children actually have bonded us closer together. For ten years Jill had desired to adopt Asian children. Adopting Andrea and Sarah built a tremendous bond, and we view Michael as a special gift from God, as a key part of our rekindling process.

Do you think too much is expected of Christians in positions of prominence, whether it be sports, business, or other areas?

We expect our Christian leaders to be infallible. When they do fail, we tend to scorn them. It's such a delicate area. Now, any time I am asked to speak, I realize that I am just one step from failing. That's the problem with throwing young Christians up before the world—they are so vulnerable and open to Satan's attacks.

If you could talk individually to each man reading this article, what would you advise them?

Men need to understand that what their wives are saying, their pockets of complaints, are real. My tendency was to ignore them, responding just enough so my wife would get off my back. If you are to avert a crisis like Jill and I went through and instead, build a marriage relationship that honors God, you must talk to your wife and listen to her. Court her, date her, hold her hand. And seal it all off with an abundance of non-sexual touching, for the rest of your lives.

*Husbands, love your wives, just as Christ loved the
church and gave himself up for her.*

Ephesians 5:25

53

STAYING ON TARGET
(Goal-setting as a family affair)

Philip and Susy Downer

I t was at a spiritual enrichment conference in 1980 in Colorado
Springs, Colorado, where my wife, Susy, and I first learned about the
importance of setting goals in every area of our lives. Until then we had
never considered drawing up a purpose statement for our life together,
and goals had been something we related to our jobs, but not our personal lives.

But at the encouragement of Bruce Cook, the speaker, we went off
together in a beautiful mountain setting and spent half a day praying
about what purpose God had for us. Susy and I agreed that our purpose
was "to glorify the Lord in all areas of our lives." That, however, was
just a start. The next step was to formulate some specific goals for carrying out that purpose.

We learned there are three things a person can do in relation to
goal-setting: first, he can set no goals, and therefore will never reach
any. Second, he can set the wrong goals and meet them, but end up in
the wrong place. And third, he can seek to set the goals God would
want, thus seeking to fulfill God's purpose for his life.

As we worked through our goals, Susy and I recognized there were
a number of specific areas we needed to address. Those included our

263

relationships with the Lord, each other, our children, our jobs, and our personal ministry.

There were several immediate benefits as we worked through this process for the first time. For one, although we knew that God desired for us to establish a personal ministry where we worked, using the training we had gained through the Christian Business Men's Committee, we had not fully concentrated on using our home as a focal point for presenting the truths of Jesus Christ to friends and business associates.

At the same time, we saw the importance of making a distinction between cultivating our personal relationships with God and building a ministry as a couple. It's so easy for the two to begin blending together.

Goal-setting became important as well in planning for a family. At the time of the conference, Susy and I did not yet have children. We had been married almost ten years and had maintained two careers for five years, enjoying the freedom to travel wherever we chose, but we wanted very much to start a family. Our goal, we determined, was to have four children, but that goal actually was surpassed. Our first, Abigail, was born in 1981. She was followed by Paul, in 1982, and Matthew, in 1984. Then God gave us twins, Anna and Joshua, on Valentine's Day of this year, giving us a total of five.

As we proceeded in our goal-setting, we developed a financial strategy making it possible for Susy to resign from her job as assistant corporate secretary and senior attorney with Delta Air Lines and become a full-time mother and homemaker. We developed a two-and-one-half year plan which successfully resulted in her resigning from Delta in mid-1985.

Our plan included establishing and staying on a family budget. We had tried budgets before, but had not followed them consistently. Our second major goal was to get out of debt, which was a major factor in setting Susy's "retirement" timetable. By the end of the two-and-a-half years, she would qualify for the first phase in an incentive compensation plan, and we would apply that additional income toward our remaining debts.

We did not succeed in becoming debt-free by the time Susy left Delta, but we had made substantial progress toward that goal. Since then, we have maintained that objective. One significant step we have taken was the hiring of a consultant, Ronald Blue & Co., to review our finances, suggest any changes, and hold us accountable to our financial commitments. That has proved very helpful in keeping on track.

Susy and I have found ourselves to be a good team in goal-setting. I tend to be a visionary, eager to set long-term goals. Susy's focus tends to be more short-term. Combined, we have been able to achieve a good balance, setting goals that are both immediate and more future-oriented.

Goal-setting, we've discovered, greatly simplifies decision-making. For instance, one of our major goals continually is to share the gospel with our neighbors. Therefore, if our options are to go to church for a special event or to attend a neighborhood party, the decision is clear cut for us. The party probably will not be as much fun, and certainly not as edifying as being in church, but we understand that one of the ministries God has given us is with our neighbors. Without such a clear goal it would be easy to do what is most enjoyable, even it if isn't God's best for us.

One of my goals is to be a major influence in the lives of our children. Since my law practice often requires spending long hours at work, I try to be sensitive to the limited amount of time I have with the children. For that reason, I decided not to watch TV, dedicating that time instead to our sons and daughters. I also plan one regular one-on-one "date" every month with each of our older three children.

Four years ago, Susy and I decided a major goal should be that we spend more time with one another. With the addition of children and the frequent competition of our jobs, we saw that it was becoming harder and harder for us to really talk. We set a goal of scheduling a date together every Saturday night. That required having to find babysitters for each weekend and setting aside money for that purpose. Often we found that was our only opportunity to discuss important things, rather than giving each other a quick "report" during the week. Our dates also are good times for reviewing our goals and making course corrections when needed.

We try to do comprehensive annual reviews of our goals, but in the last several years we have had major mid-year decisions which necessitated examining our goals more frequently. For instance, not long ago we debated whether to buy a new house a few blocks away. A big part of making that decision centered around how it fit with our goals and overall purpose before God.

Practical factors all pointed toward moving, since the new house was considerably larger. When we bought our first house, we did not plan on adding five children. The house we were looking at offered a much larger, fenced-in yard for the children to play in and was located on a much quieter street.

But then we looked at the spiritual considerations. One negative was the impact on our financial stewardship, since the monthly mortgage payments would be higher. Since the house is beautifully constructed and of historical significance in downtown Atlanta, we also weighed our motives for wanting the house. We were concerned with appearing to overemphasize material things. That brought us back to our purpose. The uniqueness of the house, we realized, would enable the Lord to draw new people into our home to hear His gospel (our purpose), including many, we hoped, who had declined earlier invitations. The house could also accommodate larger functions, such as outreach dinners and Bible studies.

After praying and consulting with trusted Christian friends, we decided to buy the house. We hoped that the risk of offending some fellow believers by the appearance of the house would be outweighed by the increased opportunities to present the truths of Jesus Christ to those who don't yet know Him.

Susy and I have used the same approach in making other major decisions. It provides an interesting way of checking whether we are continuing to be within what we understand to be God's will for our lives. We still try to do an annual review, since that is a good time for updating or revising our goals.

We are convinced of the value of the goal-setting process. Studies have shown that a high percentage of written goals are accomplished, while resolutions or general wish-type goals are rarely achieved. Most importantly, they help us in getting a clearer picture of where we are in our relationship with the Lord.

*Husbands, love your wives, just as Christ loved the
church and gave himself up for her.*

Ephesians 5:25

54

FATHERS, FAMILIES, AND THE FUTURE

Gary Smalley

Some months ago, I had an opportunity to spend an evening with a family in Tampa, Florida. Tired after a long day of speaking, I looked forward to a night of relaxation and fellowship with the family. Their beautiful home seemed the perfect place for the peace and quiet I needed.

The next morning, however, I discovered this home was anything but peaceful. The wife had suffered from years of neglect by her husband, leaving her exhausted, disillusioned, and angry. Incredibly, I was there the very day she had planned to pack her belongings, take the kids, and leave her husband for good.

On the Brink of Tragedy

As I sat at the kitchen table, listening to her pour out her heart, I felt like I was watching the wreck of the Exxon tanker, Valdez. Disharmony and heartache were steering this stunning family onto the rocks of tragedy. Day after day, the poison of a ruptured marriage had poured into their lives, covering the one-time beauty of a loving family with the sludge of

267

strife and bitterness. The children had been cut off from spiritual truth, and the wife had grown numb to the pain she had endured for years.

This need for a loving husband and father who knew how to nurture and care for his family isn't the cry of just one lonely wife. Today, millions of families across the United States yearn for a loving leader who, when it comes to family relationships, knows what to do and how it should be done.

As I look ahead to the 1990s and the twenty-first century, I am convinced that more than ever, if we want our nation to be healed, men must have *a practical plan for building families that honor God and our families.*

All Champions Require a Plan

When my good friend, Norm Evans, first joined a National Football League team, it was mired in last place. The team's owner knew a change was needed, so he hired a new head coach. He had already changed coaches several times, but that had not changed the team's fortunes. Chances were, the young replacement would be history himself within a year or two.

As it turned out, this particular coach was destined to go into NFL history — but not as a failure. Today, he has been in the league longer than any other pro coach. The reason is simple: He built his team into a champion by following a clear plan of action.

The year before the coach arrived, the team had three wins and ten losses. Morale was down, motivation was low, and the players' efforts on the field were lackluster. Norm remembers how players would stand on the sideline, wondering how they would lose the game that day.

When the new coach arrived, he wasted no time. His first official act was to call a team meeting — it was a meeting the players never forgot. He walked into the room, folded his arms, and stood silently in front of them for what seemed like hours. After a few minutes, he looked each player in the eye and said in a clear, convincing voice, "Men, you're going to be champions of the NFL."

An awkward silence filled the room. Several of the veterans hung their heads to keep their smiles from breaking into laughter. "Sure coach

. . . ," they thought. "Anything you say. . . ." Many of them were thinking, "Who's this guy kidding? We've always been losers in this league. Champions? We're not even challengers!" But then the coach explained why he knew the team would be successful—he presented a clear plan of action.

"First," he said, "we're going to give you a great game plan that works each week. I'll guarantee that you'll know more about the person you're playing against than anyone, except his wife. *Second*, you're going to *practice* that plan over and over until it becomes a natural part of you. If you're willing to do that, you're going to win."

Team Transformed

Bit by bit, the wisdom of his strategy unfolded the next season. The players learned a specific plan, then practiced it again and again until they gained a confidence in themselves and in each other that they had never had before. Now they stood on the sidelines wondering how they were going to *win* games, not lose them. In only one year, they were a different football team.

They reversed their record that next season, winning ten games and losing only three. Then the next two seasons, in 1972 and 1973, the Miami Dolphins, under head coach Don Shula, won the Super Bowl as the best team in pro football.

"That's a great story if you're a football team," you may say, "but the only similarity our marriage has to an NFL team is that we're always taking cheap shots at each other!" Can a *plan* make that much of a difference in a marriage relationship—or even with our children? It did for the desperate wife in Tampa.

She didn't know much about the pro team in nearby Miami when we sat down that morning, but she still had something in common with them. For years, she and her husband had let circumstances and emotions of the moment call all the plays and control their relationship. Their lives were on the brink of a last-place finish as a result. And like the football team, their lives began to turn around once they began following and consistently practicing a clear plan of action.

What Is This 'Family Plan'?

To keep our relationships off the rocks, we need to follow two essential steps: We must first gain the *knowledge* of a workable plan, and then develop the *skills* needed to make that knowledge function in our relationships. The more we learn and practice what we have learned, the more adept we'll become at carving out intimate relationships within our homes.

The place to find the knowledge and skills we need is in the Bible. Here are just a few of the indispensible principles God establishes in His Word:

- *Honor is at the heart of all healthy relationships — and genuine love is a decision, not a feeling.* (See Romans 12:10, 1 Peter 3:1–2, 7)

Contrary to popular belief, love is actually a reflection of how much we decide to "honor" another person because at its heart, genuine love is a decision, not a feeling.

- *Recognizing the incredible worth of a woman.* (See Genesis 2:18–25)

As men, it's absolutely essential to understand that God has designed our wives with very unique talents that make them an invaluable resource in our homes.

- *Learning how to energize our mates in sixty seconds.* (See Ephesians 4:29)

To be successful in our homes, we must learn the skill of knowing when to step in when our loved ones are hurting or discouraged. By learning how tenderness, kindness, forgiveness, and a gentle touch can energize those we love, we can build security and strength in our homes.

- *Keeping a major destroyer of relationships out of our homes.* (See Ephesians 4:26–27)

There is a killer loose in many homes today that can take the life out of a relationship. It's crucial that we learn how to keep the destructive "tape worm" of anger out of relationships, and how to reopen the spirit of a loved one whose spirit may be closed to you.

- *Learning the art of tapping into the unfailing power source behind a great marriage.* (See Philippians 4:13, 19)

So many of us are expecting the "gifts" of life—including our spouse and children—to be the "source" of our life and happiness. Husbands, wives, and children can make great friends, but they make lousy gods. Learning to depend on Jesus Christ as the only consistent source of love, peace, and joy is the only way we will have the spiritual and emotional stamina to withstand the storms of life—and the stresses of the 1990s.

- *Turning trials in our homes into lasting benefits for our lives.* (See Hebrews 12:9–11)

In every relationship, there are roadblocks that seem to stand so high they block out any hope of ever getting past them to intimacy and oneness. Yet, the problems we face can benefit our lives and provide a consistent source of deeper love and sensitivity that we can pass on to others.

It's unnerving to realize that the twentieth century is winding down and the twenty-first century—bursting with the new, unexpected, and unpredictable—is almost upon us. Most of us don't have a plan for next week, let alone a plan for the next century!

I hope you're different, that you will work at learning and practicing a plan that is based on the Scriptures and grounded in God's love. The key is to fall more deeply in love with God and His Word. In doing so, you'll get the knowledge and skills needed to reflect His love to your family. I have no doubt that the Bible and the truths it contains comprise the greatest key to your family's heart.

Adapted from *Love Is a Decision* by Gary T. Smalley with John Trent, Ph.D. Published by Word, Incorporated, 1989. Used by permission.

Fathers, do not exasperate your children; instead, bring them up in the training and instruction of the Lord.

Ephesians 6:4

55

FAMILY TIES
(Making your children top priority)

Tony Eager

The Bible tells us that "If anyone is in Christ, he is a new creation; the old has gone, the new has come!" (2 Corinthians 5:17). From the time I became a Christian in 1976, that has proved true for me in many ways, especially in the area of being a father.

Until that time, I wanted to be a good father, but was unsure of how to go about it. "What should I teach my two daughters?" "What life philosophy do I want to pass on to them?" Those had been questions that troubled me. In the midst of a successful career with an advertising agency, I had been influenced by factors such as pride, worry, greed, and envy. Even before I committed my life to Jesus Christ, I knew those were not qualities I wanted my children to emulate.

As a Christian reading the Bible for the first time, I discovered God offered sound, practical answers to problems of everyday life, including inflated egos, continual anxiety, and preoccupation with "things." Most important, I learned, were my relationships with God, my family, and people I associated with each day. Although my wife, Jan, had been a Christian since high school, the Bible told me that God had entrusted me with the primary responsibility for spiritual leadership in our home. That was a responsibility I did not take lightly.

About the same time I became a Christian, I left the advertising business and moved into commercial real estate. It was difficult at first, trying to become established in a totally new vocation, but that career step helped draw me closer to God at a key point in my Christian growth. The uncertainties of the future reinforced how vitally dependent I am on God to meet my daily needs.

A secondary benefit, which I have appreciated more and more, is scheduled flexibility. No longer faced with a lengthy commute into downtown Chicago, I am able to begin most days with my family, eating breakfast and leading a devotional time that has become important in our home. We read a brief portion of Scripture, comment on what we've read, and pray together. In the morning, we ask for "pleases" — areas of concern in which we are asking for God's help, such as a test at school or an important business meeting — and then at the dinner table we share our "thank you's," reporting on how God answered those prayers.

My daughters are now eighteen and fifteen, and although they are following the normal path toward independence as they move into adulthood, we remain a close-knit family that truly enjoys being together. I believe that is largely due to activities we have maintained focusing on our relationship with God. The following are several that have meant a lot to us.

Date night: Each Monday night is a very special one for us, because I set the evening aside for a date with either my wife or one of my daughters. (Jan and I go out every other Monday.) The two of us go out to dinner and talk with each other about what is on our hearts. In a neutral, peaceful environment, we can look back and discuss the past week. This is a particularly good time for the girls to express concerns or complaints openly.

We've been doing this for ten years, and it has become a foundational time for all of us. Since it has proven to be such a great opportunity for one-on-one communications, we consider Monday nights "sacred." Very seldom does anything interfere with that schedule. I've found if you don't dedicate that kind of time exclusively, something will arise to change your plans.

Goal bowl: About three years ago, we began thinking about where the girls would be going to college. Katrina was a junior in high school, and we saw value in planning ahead. We scheduled a vacation trip to visit some college campuses. Since our excursion was based on a goal for the future, I suggested that we examine what the Bible said about goal-setting. Each day we looked at some Scripture passages relating to goals, such as Colossians 3:17, "And whatever you do, whether in word or deed, do it all in the name of the Lord Jesus, giving thanks to God the Father through him." We would discuss these passages and record our thoughts in personal notebooks.

At the conclusion of our trip, I suggested that we each review what we had studied and pray about what God had for each of us as life goals. We then scheduled a time at a local restaurant to talk about our conclusions. The result was that each of us adopted life goals, ones we could use whenever we were weighing important decisions. Kristin, for example, determined that God's goal for her was, "To be more like God and live for Him," based on Ephesians 5:1 which says, "Be imitators of God, therefore, as dearly loved children."

It seemed like a good idea to put our thoughts into concrete form — actually, ceramic. I had a friend produce custom-made ceramic cereal bowls bearing our individual names, key Scripture verses, and personal goals. These quickly became known as our "goal bowls," and served as continual reminders of our need to spend each day in pursuits that honor God.

When Katrina left for college last fall, she left her goal bowl behind. I thought maybe she had decided she was too old for it, but after the Thanksgiving holidays, she wanted to take the bowl back to school.

Praise notebooks: When Katrina and Kristin were younger, we gave each of them spiral-bound, pocket-sized notebooks in which Jan and I periodically wrote words of praise. When they did something praiseworthy, we would compliment them, recounting what they did and how we felt about it. Then we would place the notebooks in conspicuous places, such as on their pillows, so they would easily find them.

Today our daughters have positive self-images, and I believe it is in part because we tried hard to "accentuate the positive," as the old song says. As a parent, it is so easy to keep saying "No, no, no," but we have found it very helpful to regularly and promptly reinforce the good things our children have done.

Floating history lessons: I have always enjoyed sailing, and we are fortunate to have a twenty-six-foot sloop which we use every summer for family vacations. A number of years ago, we decided to use our trips as firsthand opportunities to learn about the spiritual heritage of the United States.

Jan obtained a series of books which deal with the Christian foundations of some of our American leaders, such as Robert E. Lee, George Washington, Christopher Columbus, Francis Scott Key, and Abraham Lincoln. While sailing to such places as the Bahamas, Jamestown, Virginia, and the Chesapeake Bay, the Potomac River, and Plymouth Harbor on the coast of Massachusetts, we have not only gained valuable history lessons but also learned about the spiritual motivations that prompted the historic events in those areas.

We have also used those trips to study some of Jesus Christ's character traits during morning devotionals, challenging one another to then demonstrate those qualities during the day. Since sailing can present you with some rough experiences, ranging from high winds and storms to hot days without a hint of a breeze, it is not always easy to remain Christlike. More than once, the girls have reminded me when I exhibited a decided lack of patience. And we've all gained some valuable insights into unconditional love.

Looking for a college: As Katrina approached high school graduation, Jan and I discussed whether she should go to a Christian or secular college. We prayed about it, did a lot of soul searching, read God's Word, and sought the advice of other Christians we respected. Since Katrina had attended a public high school and had proven herself able to withstand temptations and non-Christian peer pressure, we felt she could do well in a secular university environment. However, we recognized that even the strongest Christian will not thrive in a vacuum.

For that reason, we decided that if we found a secular school that Katrina liked which also offered some strong Christian groups that she could identify with, be accountable to and "retreat" to, we would agree to send her there. Before personally "inspecting" any campuses, we contacted the Campus Crusade office in Arrowhead Springs, California, asking for names of their staff people at the universities we planned to visit. Knowing you cannot get a true spiritual barometer of a school from reading catalogs, taking campus tours, or even meeting with administrative people, we wanted to meet personally with staff from Campus Crusade, Inter-Varsity, the Navigators, and other campus Christian organizations and get their assessments of the spiritual environment at each school.

Through this process we were able to eliminate a number of schools very quickly. Katrina finally settled on Vanderbilt University in Nashville, Tennessee. The school is very "Greek" oriented, but we found there were three sororities with strong Christian involvement. Katrina has been able to pledge one which has fifteen or sixteen Christian members and where Bible studies are conducted regularly. She is enjoying the university and feels she has made the right choice. Without the pre-screening we did, however, leaving home to attend a secular college could have been very difficult and traumatic for Katrina. Since we did take the time, we feel she will have a great opportunity to be "salt and light" as the New Testament tells us, serving as a good, loving Christian witness in a world that desperately needs it.

Being an effective, consistent Christian father has been challenging and a lot of work, but very rewarding. You can't beat the compensation. So often I fail to live up to the very standards I profess, but Christ has made all the difference in my relationship with my wife and daughters.

Fathers, do not exasperate your children; instead, bring them up in the training and instruction of the Lord.

Ephesians 6:4

56

FENCES AND SNAKE PITS

Gary Smalley

W ho ever would have thought that ignoring a boundary would nearly cost us our lives? Certainly not my friend and I. But that is exactly what happened.

As boys growing up in Washington state, Jim and I had often heard his mother say, "Don't go near that fenced area around Boulder Flats." Boulder Flats had been the bed of our local river until a major flood had changed the course of the waterway. Now it was just several acres of various sized river rocks that had been fenced in by the park service. Coming from a home where there were no boundaries, I felt that fences were only something designed to disrupt my life, not protect it. Therefore, I placed little value in Jim's mother's warning.

One beautiful late summer morning, Jim and I were hiking through the woods nearby. With lunch time nearing, we (or more accurately, I) decided we should take a shortcut home—right through Boulder Flats. For ten-year-old boys, hunger can make a shortcut very appealing!

Pulling apart the weathered barbed wires and ignoring the "Keep Out" signs, I let Jim through and then he held the wires so I could crawl inside the fence. Large rocks were scattered all across the old river bed, and we happily scrambled from one rock to another. We figured we would be home within minutes.

We had hopped onto a rock about halfway across when suddenly the quiet morning air was punctured by the hissing and piercing sounds of rattlesnakes. Our failure to heed the warning had put us unwittingly in the midst of a sprawling snake pit!

Small baby snakes and grown snakes, as thick as a fist, lay coiled or slithering around and under the rocks. There were dozens of them, and we were surrounded. We clung desperately to our rock, crying for help at the tops of our voices and trying not to lose our footing.

The day passed, but no help came. Everyone else was wise enough to avoid Boulder Flats. We stood on that rock for what seemed like forever, thinking of what to do. Finally, we decided that if we were to escape from the snakes, our only alternative was to proceed to the far side. Several pieces of driftwood lay nearby, remnants of a time when water had coursed freely through this terrain. We grabbed two long pieces of wood and began a terrifying journey across the riverbed.

I can never adequately express the horror of the next hour. As we summoned all our courage and jumped from one large rock to another, we knew that if we slipped and fell to the ground, the snakes would strike before we could climb back to safety. At times, we used the sticks to beat the rattlers from their perches on the rocks. At one point, we needed to employ the driftwood in lifting baby rattlesnakes and throwing them out of the way.

Alternately crying, praying, hoping, and losing hope, we carefully made our way across Boulder Flats. Finally, after an hour that took a lifetime to pass, we leaped from the last rock onto the sand and ran to safety. Later, after hearing our story, the Park Service took men and a small bulldozer to the Flats, capturing or killing more than 300 snakes — some of them trophy-length!

Even today, I shudder to think how ignoring a boundary nearly cost my life.

That incredible afternoon taught me a valuable lesson: boundaries are imperative. Signs need to be posted, and warnings must be given. In a family, parents can — and should — put up healthy, loving boundaries to help their children avoid the "Boulder Flats experience." Such experiences can result from the unrest that comes from lying, the perils of impure relationships, or the damage of uncontrolled anger. Parents who provide and maintain protective boundaries demonstrate the value they place on their children. They bestow their children with "the Gift of Honor."

Boundaries help children know they are loved. Clear limits or protective boundaries provide a person with feelings of security and safety. God tells His children He loves them by setting protective boundaries around them and then disciplining them if they wander outside the fence of His Word. "My son, do not regard lightly the discipline of the Lord. For those whom the LORD loves he disciplines," (Hebrews 12:5–6, NAS). Discipline is God's way of encouraging us to return within the protection of His divine fences.

If we are to demonstrate genuine, sacrificial love, we must be committed to seeking the best interests of another. In that sense, love and the establishment of boundaries are inseparable. We will warn our children of potential dangers, as Jim's mother had years ago. Parents must take time to put up the protective boundaries, just as the Park Service had done in fencing in Boulder Flats. By setting up loving limits, we demonstrate God's limitless love.

Adapted from *The Gift of Honor* by Gary T. Smalley and John Trent, Ph.D. Published by Thomas Nelson Publishers, 1987. Used by permission.

*Fathers, do not exasperate your children; instead,
bring them up in the training and instruction of the
Lord.*

Ephesians 6:4

57

WHEN BAD THINGS HAPPEN TO GOOD FAMILIES

L. Donald Barr

Your son has epilepsy," the physician calmly and professionally informed me and my wife, Martha. The words struck like a battering ram, sending our emotions into a spiral of fear, frustration, and uncertainty.

Earlier that day, Martha had gone to check on our two-year-old son, Blake, while he was taking a nap. She found him lying on his bed, trembling uncontrollably. Panicking, she called me at work, and we rushed him to the hospital.

That was nineteen years ago. Since then, hardly a day has gone by in which Blake hasn't had a seizure. His eyes become glassy and dilated, and his body becomes rigid. Often he loses his balance and falls unless there is someone nearby to hold him up. The episodes rarely last more than a minute or two, but Martha and I try not to leave him for very long, concerned that he could fall and seriously injure himself.

It's been difficult for all of us. Blake's older brother, Brooks, was a normal, healthy, athletic boy. In high school he played on the basketball and baseball teams. Blake also loves sports and would have liked to follow in his footsteps. But he can't: one of the things that triggers his seizures is overexertion, so the doctors have advised us not to let Blake play competitive athletics. Although he's twenty-one years old, he also is not able to drive since the seizures are totally unpredictable.

Blake is a very astute, bright fellow — really a deep thinker. Unfortunately, the medication he takes to control his seizures also slows his mental responses, so he's always had trouble in a traditional school setting, although he is currently attending Richland Community College and doing fairly well.

Not long before we discovered Blake's epilepsy, I accepted a management consulting position with Coopers & Lybrand. Like many business executives, my career advancement has sometimes meant relocating to a new city. When a child has health problems, the difficult process of moving your family becomes even harder. Once, not long after I had been transferred by the firm to Philadelphia, Blake got an ear infection that triggered a series of seizures five minutes apart that continued for three days and nights. Since I had not yet had time to establish any close relationships at work, and Martha had left all her friends and family in Dallas, we had only each other — and God — to carry us through the traumatic time.

My job has also required extensive travel, and that has presented an additional challenge in being the kind of father I need to be. I've worked to maintain a sense of balance, trying to set aside weekends to be with the boys and make special celebrations — such as birthdays, anniversaries, and other occasions — a top, non-negotiable priority. I try to arrange my work schedule so I will be free for those times, even if it means leaving the office in the middle of the afternoon and then returning later that evening.

Over the years, we have tried not to slight Brooks, even though Blake's problems sometimes required us to spend more time with him. Martha and I have tried to treat the boys as equals, do special things with each of them. I've had private conversations with Brooks, making sure he understood when his brother needed more of our attention. He has been remarkably understanding. Almost from the time he was born, he was an independent sort, and I believe that has been to his benefit. I can't say that our family situation hasn't affected Brooks in some way, but he's twenty-three now and has given us every reason to be proud of him.

Even though I committed my life to Jesus Christ as a boy and understand God's love, accepting Blake's epilepsy has been hard. I asked questions like, "Why me?" or "God, what are you trying to teach us?" At times Martha and I have felt angry toward God, at the point of despair. We've entertained self-pity, thinking, "Lord, we're good people and we're trying to live for you. Why won't you heal Blake?" It's been a hard process coming to realize—and accepting—that there is nothing we can do about Blake's condition and that we need to accept God's will for him. The teaching from Philippians 4:6–7 to "be anxious for nothing," (NAS) committing our concerns to God and receiving His peace in return, has not been an easy principle to carry out.

Only in recent years have Martha and I reached a turning point. Proverbs 3:5 tells us "do not lean on your own understanding," (NAS), and that's exactly what we have come to accept. Trusting in God means that He doesn't have to answer our "why" questions; we just need to believe that He knows what is best.

Today, I can be truly thankful for Blake's epilepsy, realizing it has drawn our entire family closer—to the Lord and to each other. I also see how God has blessed us equally with Brooks and Blake; each is very special in his own way.

Despite the trials, I would still have to say fatherhood has been—and continues to be—fun. If you asked my wife how many children she has, she'd probably tell you three—ages twenty-one, twenty-three, and forty-seven. We enjoy doing things together as a family, including extended vacations. The boys like to horse around as any other brothers, and we are all very close.

It's been a joy having Blake. There are not many fathers who have such a sensitive, loving son. And he's an excellent companion; we have a great time going to ball games together. If he has a seizure while we're out, so what? We are able to regard that as part of life, at least for us.

Recently we have learned about a surgeon in Dallas who specializes in cases like Blake's. He has had a marvelous success rate in curing certain severe cases of epilepsy, and Blake could be a candidate for surgery within the next few months. My wish, of course, would be for him to be completely healed. But if he is not, I know one thing for certain: Blake will still be Blake . . . and God will still be God. And I will love them both.

*Fathers, do not exasperate your children; instead,
bring them up in the training and instruction of the
Lord.*

Ephesians 6:4

58

*SHOOTOUT
AT THE NOT-SO O.K. CORRAL*

An Interview with Dr. Ross Campbell

If you are like most parents, you have probably asked yourself at one
time or another, "How can I really know what my son (or daughter)
is thinking? I don't think I understand him at all." In an increasingly
complex society, with pressures and temptations that were virtually un-
known only a generation ago, a pleasant journey from childhood to
adulthood is not at all certain. Parents fear for the future of their youngsters, yet are puzzled over how to best influence their lives.

In light of this common concern, Christian psychiatrist D. Ross
Campbell wrote *How To Really Know Your Child*, in which he asserts
that to help a child develop into a strong Christian adult, the parent must
understand the child's unique personality traits, responding with a positive, affirming approach to parental leadership.

Today is a particularly challenging time for fathers, according to Dr.
Campbell, and requires a special blend of time, energy, wisdom, and
understanding. For the busy businessman, burdened with multiple commitments and responsibilities, the paternal challenge may be acute, but
not impossible.

Dr. Campbell heads Southeastern Counseling Center in suburban
Chattanooga, Tennesee, overseeing a staff of twelve people who counsel

more than one hundred men, women and children daily. He also is an associate professor in the departments of pediatrics and psychiatry at the University of Tennessee College of Medicine.

A best-selling author and seminar speaker, he has authored four other books, including *How To Really Love Your Child* and *How To Really Love Your Teenager*. His expertise in parent-child relationships is not secondhand. He and his wife, Pat, have four children, ranging in age from sixteen to twenty-seven, and he has observed in his own home the effectiveness of the principles he endorses.

In the following interview, Dr. Campbell discusses parenting, particularly the role of the father in the modern family.

In your experience, how significant is the role of the father in a child's development? What are the consequences of the man who does not — or cannot — fulfill his responsibilities as a parent?

The father plays a critical role in a child's life. He has a strong influence in the development of a child's personality, sexual identity, and respect for authority. In fact, research has shown that children lacking a father's influence frequently have problems in responding properly to authority and in forming a healthy conscience.

I see the results of this everyday in my counseling practice. And it's not just in cases of divorce; it can happen in intact families if the father is gone on business all the time, or is at home but not doing his job as a dad.

The other side of the coin is that if a father really wants to, he can do a lot for his children in any circumstance, even if job requirements limit the time he is at home. A lot of it depends on the personality of the child.

In your book, *How To Really Know Your Child,* you state that a child's basic personality must be taken into account if a parent is to be truly effective. How does personality make a difference?

While defining specific personality types is very complex, I have found that in terms of raising children, it is helpful to place them into one of two categories: the 25 percent of all children who are basically pro-authority, and the 75 percent who tend to be antiauthority.

The "25 percenters" want to be under authority and are eager to please those in authority over them. Their primary self-esteem comes from the approval of those in authority. In their minds, whether it is true or not, the father is the greater authority figure in their lives—thus the approval of their fathers is so critical.

The 75 percenters, however, would rather do it themselves. They like to do their own thinking, make their own decisions, and control their own destinies. This is not hostility, but they would like as little interference in their lives as possible. At the same time, it is the father whose approval helps to build into them a respect for authority, especially as adolescents and teenagers.

How does this difference in attitudes toward authority affect spiritual development?

Three of my four children have been 75 percenters, and I can say nothing has been more rewarding than having one of them go through a *normal* rebellion period, between the ages of thirtenn and fifteen, and still respect me and continue to have respect for other people in authority, such as law enforcement officers and teachers.

If children develop a proper respect for authority, they will be natural leaders and a tremendous influence in the church, reflecting a strong conscience and good moral character. Unfortunately, few 75 percenters actually become Christians. One reason is because they don't respect their father, even if they are Christians.

Another reason 75 percenters reject Christianity is the way we are raising our kids. There is too much harshness; too much authoritarianism demonstrated by parents. We don't see a negative reaction from the 25 percenters, because they want to be under authority. We would almost have to kick them out of church.

In your book, you note that while the "authoritarian" type of discipline seeks to keep a child totally under control, it actually produces the opposite result since the 75 percenter will eventually rebel and reject his parents' values. How does that approach differ from what you call the "authoritative" type of discipline?

This method is based on deep, genuine, unconditional love. The child knows his parents are sincerely concerned for his well-being. He also feels his parents are appropriate, worthwhile, worthy models. Proverbs

22:6 says we are to "train a child in the way he should go, and when he is old he will not turn from it." That implies setting a right example as well as setting and enforcing rules. He receives direction and correction, but his parents don't have the mistaken notion that they can discipline him into becoming a Christian.

A third important element of the authoritative approach is teaching a child to handle his anger maturely. If we treat a child with harshness, not realizing how brutal we can be, the child will naturally rebel against authority. However, if the child is corrected with love, compassion, and respect, by the time he has passed through the "teen rebellion" years, he will be able to handle anger maturely, without an antiauthority bent. And when it is time for him to select his own value system, he will choose that of his parents and be open to God's Word.

This is so critical. It is so dangerous to misuse our authority as parents. What is more important than for our children to become Christians? I can think of nothing that would be more devastating than for one of my children to choose not to become a Christian.

In your view, has the attitude of men toward fathering changed substantially in recent years?

Yes, but it's a case of the good news and the bad news. A lot more fathers are taking on some of the traditional "mothering" roles, and that is encouraging. But look at the divorce rate—it's hard to be optimistic and hopeful about fathers becoming more involved when we see how broken homes are killing our society.

There are not many things that make me furious, but one of them is the myth that children are resilient and can adapt from a divorce. They are *not* resilient; they are very fragile. There is no way we can say that a divorce will not affect a child adversely.

Every day I see cases in which fathers have failed with their children. Without an involved father to teach a healthy respect for proper authority, an antiauthority attitude is fostered. This can result in promiscuous sex, running away, taking drugs, and teen suicide. Today we are concerned about the rise of homosexuality. I've never seen or heard of a homosexual—and I've counseled many of them—who had an affectionate father. Each had a harsh, critical father. An absent or inadequate father can certainly be a large contributor toward the development of a homosexual child.

Earlier you mentioned that even fathers who must travel frequently on business can succeed. What steps must they take?

Like many fathers, I've found that I'm too busy and constantly need to cut back on commitments outside the home. It's easy to do things with your children when you are in a good, restful, loving mood and everything seems to be going your way. Unfortunately, most days are not like that. You arrive home exhausted, still thinking about something bad that happened during the day. It's easy to take things too personally, too seriously. The last thing on our minds is giving our kids what they need.

At these times, I try to remind myself of the difference between *behavior* and *verbal* response. Even if I'm in the worst mood, behavior is simple. What our children need most is eye contact, physical contact, and focused attention. As I wrote in *How To Really Love Your Child*, these physical acts demonstrate our love. Even if I don't feel like doing them, I can make myself go through the motions. That sounds sterile, but children are so insightful. Seeing us get out of the TV chair and put down the paper to give them the attention they need, they know we are making a fantastic sacrifice because we love them.

Sometimes I respond strictly on a selfish note, recognizing that I am not only helping my children but also saving myself incalculable heartache in the future. If children are poorly raised, when they reach adolescence they can make their parents' lives a living hell on earth. However, seeing your child do well will bring unbelievable joy, more than you could have ever hoped.

These acts of love, of course, presume that the father is available to his children. With the demand on your time — counseling, writing, speaking, serving on a medical school staff — how have you managed to set aside time for your children?

I have made a practice of adhering closely to my appointment book. I *allot* time to be at home with the kids and include it in my schedule. When children are small, time with them can be shorter, but must be frequent. As they get older, longer periods of time are needed, perhaps even an entire weekend.

Often I need to plan ahead. During the past two months, for example, I've allotted time with my son, Dale, to help him get ready for baseball season. I did the same for his older brother, David. When Dale was playing basketball, I would schedule my appointments around his games so I could go to them and encourage him. That meant I would go back to work afterward and work later into the evening.

Then being a good father requires some conscious, specific decision-making?

A father has to be clear about his priorities: How important is it to him to be a good father? There is a definite price to be paid, either now, in terms of time, or later, in having to deal with problems. Going to a psychiatrist or counselor can be very expensive, but heartache is even more costly.

I believe that if a man plans carefully, he'll be able to give his child what is needed without missing out businesswise. He may have to sacrifice some here or there, but I've known many men who have done both successfully. If, however, a job required so much commitment that it prohibited a man from adequately caring for his children, I would question whether that job was worth it.

Are there any other recommendations you can offer on successful fathering?

I believe it was Dr. Howard Hendricks who wrote that the best thing a man can do for his children is to love their mother. After all, mothers are usually around the kids more than their fathers, and research has shown that a depressed mother can be worse than having no mother at all.

We must not become so focused on our children that we forget to fill our wives' emotional tanks. It's amazing, but if a husband gives his wife a half-pound of love, she can then produce one thousand pounds of love—what a huge increase in the investment! If husbands take the time to keep their wives happy, their jobs as fathers will be much easier.

*"Anyone who looks at a woman lustfully has already
committed adultery with her in his heart."*

Matthew 5:28

59

THE SEXUAL SNARE
(Why so many Christians are falling into immorality)

An Interview with Lois Mowday

L ois Mowday was abruptly thrust into the world of single adults ten years ago after her husband, Jack, was killed in a hot-air balloon accident. The ride, which had been a birthday gift to Jack from Lois and their two daughters, ended in tragedy when the balloon struck a power line, resulting in an explosion. Lois and the children could only watch in helplessness.

The story of the accident, along with Lois' account of the amazing peace she felt at the moment, knowing that her husband had been instantly ushered into the presence of his Lord, became the much-discussed topic of magazine articles and a movie.

Suddenly single again in the aftermath of the accident, Lois was startled to discover how much the singles environment had changed during her thirteen years of marriage, even within the Christian community.

Her book, *The Snare* (NavPress, 1988), was her response to a naiveté within the Body of Christ which seemed to assume that sexual purity was an automatic part of Christian life. That attitude has actually encouraged immorality among Christians, she says, because it ignores the factors that contribute to sexual sin, not only among highly visible

Christian leaders, but also among the typical God-fearing men and women who fill the churches each Sunday.

Lois discusses the apparently intensifying problem within the church — and suggests possible remedies.

What were your observations upon re-entering the single adult environment after the death of your husband?

Ten years ago, nobody was saying anything about immorality within the Christian community, but it was there. I saw that any lifestyle you would like to engage in was available, although you might have to lie to maintain it.

After Jack died, I went to work with a Christian organization in public relations. A friend of mine told me that I would have to change my behavior. I was too outgoing, she said, and people might misunderstand the "signals" I was sending. I soon saw what she meant, that being single and available had a way of attracting a lot of attention — not all of it wholesome.

As Christians, we have high standards for living — and we have the indwelling power of God. So why is immorality such a problem among Christians?

It's partly a factor of ignorance, an unawareness that Christians can be tempted just like anyone else. We also tend to equate immorality with physical action, unaware of the dangers of emotional involvement that can eventually lead to physical involvement.

The common assumption is that most affairs are impulsive acts of passion between virtual strangers. But in your book, you state that sexual infidelity most often results through a process, a friendship that gradually deepens in intimacy.

That's right, particularly in the Christian community. Two people don't realize that an emotional entanglement can be just as binding and seductive as physical attraction.

A typical scenario is that of two people working together. The job requires that they spend a lot of time together and share some common interests. They both believe they are on "safe" ground, but because of needs unmet in both of their lives, the professional relationship develops more personal aspects. Over time, an emotional attachment occurs, and if not acknowledged and properly dealt with, a physical relationship can follow.

That is not to say that it is necessarily wrong for a man and woman to have lunch together, or to work late when the job demands it. But there can be a lot of denial about what is really going on, rationalization to create excuses for spending time together.

So you're saying that in many cases, people are drawn into adulterous affairs for reasons other than for sexual gratification?

Actually, there are many things people seek — acceptance, a better self-image, intimacy, the feeling of being needed, comfort in a time of loss, companionship. There is an excitement about participating in an illicit relationship, particularly if one's life seems routine or boring. The sexual involvement may actually be only a means to an end.

You indicate that the business environment is especially conducive to immoral relationships. Why?

Because of the amount of time people spend together in business, there is more potential for this to develop. There are more women in the workplace than ever before, particularly at management levels, and men and women are traveling together a lot more.

The office atmosphere is charged with factors that heighten emotional response: energy, motion, excitement, stress, competition, weariness. People in similar situations under similar pressures are drawn together for reinforcement. If unprepared, adulterous relationships can develop rapidly as a result.

When I wrote my book, I initially directed it toward Christian wives at home, because I felt they needed to be aware of the dangers their husbands were facing, working with women who possibly were better educated, always dressed attractively, and had common career interests — and anxieties. I've talked to too many homemakers who naively said, "I don't think any woman would be interested in my husband," only to learn just the opposite.

Why is it that sexual sin seems to be the unforgivable sin? A Christian leader might be dishonest or unethical, and easily forgiven, but sexual sin seems to incur greater judgment.

I think it's because adultery nullifies trust and destroys respect and integrity. Fornication defrauds and reduces people to objects of use, not love. In most cases, once the trust in the marriage relationship is broken, it can never be completely restored. Others perceive it as much closer to home, more personal than other forms of sin. And sex is the closest analogy to our mystical relationship with Christ.

Some people reading this interview may be in the midst of an immoral relationship, or may be trying to get out of one. What advice would you give?

Most important, they need to recognize that they have a choice, even if they don't feel like they do. And the only Biblical choice is to end immoral relationships. I've never known of such a relationship to end gradually, turning into just a friendship. In fact, sometimes physical distance has to happen, even if it means changing jobs — or even churches.

What about the person who is not living immorally, but recognizes that with the right person, in the right time and place, such a thing could happen? What steps should be taken to avoid what you term "sexual entanglement"?

We need to be very honest with ourselves about our weaknesses. People may tell themselves, "Flattery doesn't affect me" or "I'm not really attracted to that person," when that is not really true.

For instance, I'm a person who is attracted to people in power positions, individuals who are articulate and have charismatic personalities. I learned that I needed to be careful not to get into verbal games with that type of man. There is nothing wrong with having a conversation with a person like that, but I know it can be a turn-on and result in an unhealthy attraction. The best step, I've discovered, is to avoid the temptation before it presents itself.

It's also important to be accountable, preferably with someone of your own sex, although a couple can be helpful to an individual. We need to give people permission to ask difficult questions. If we are unwilling to be accountable, we need to ask why.

Would you advise that male-female relationships outside marriage should be strictly avoided?

No, because they can be very healthy and godly. I have benefited from some myself. But there have to be some limits, and there needs to be a conscious effort to avoid provocative conversations and surroundings.

I'm not big on drawing up a list of don'ts, because you can be following them and still be on the way to trouble. The most important thing is to be honest — with yourself, the other person, and certainly with God. If we play around with our motives, tease a little, meet needs or have needs met with unavailable people, pretty soon we will fall all the way off the road of obedience into total immoral involvement and disobedience. As I state in the book, the most challenging difficulty is being able to see the sin involved even when there is an absence of physical contact.

"Anyone who looks at a woman lustfully has already committed adultery with her in his heart."

Matthew 5:28

60

BURNING MEMORIES

Ken Korkow

M y wife, Liz, and I had dated for six years and after I returned from Vietnam in 1974, got married. Unfortunately, Liz did not get what she had expected, because I was a different man from the one she had known prior to Vietnam.

In spite of the rough environment in which I grew up in South Dakota, which included the rodeo and truck drivers, I had been, as the old saying goes, "Pure as the driven snow." My mother had raised a good boy. But my wartime service had changed me, and when I returned home my motto was, "Make Kenny happy." I was committed to serving God, but I was god.

So it wasn't long after we got married in 1968 that I started cheating on my wife. In 1972 I informed Liz it was about time we got divorced, telling her I had some women on the side who were meeting my needs better. I didn't say that to hurt her; I just didn't care about anyone but me.

Liz was devastated by my infidelity, but she was committed to our marriage and was not willing to get a divorce. She told me she would do anything necessary for us to stay together. Somehow, her love for me touched my stone heart and gradually I tried to do better. When I became a Christian in 1978, those changes became dramatic. I stopped committing adultery and reading pornographic magazines, but even with those external changes, I was dismayed to discover I couldn't kick the old mental images and memories.

I felt a lot of guilt, but those still-precious memories would not go away. It was amazing, because generally my memory is poor, but I had total recall of those old, sinful relationships. Being a new Christian, eager to learn about and please God, that really wiped me out. Finally, while I was attending a CBMC retreat, a friend from Minneapolis gave me some help. He pointed me to Hebrews 12:1–2, which says, ". . . let us throw off everything that hinders and the sin that so easily entangles, and let us run with perseverence the race marked out for us. Let us fix our eyes on Jesus, the author and perfecter of our faith. . . ."

My friend explained that when I dealt with temptation, I should make a mental image of Christ on the cross. That was unusual for me, because I envision an empty cross since I serve a risen Savior. But he said in times of temptation, I should visualize Christ on the cross. With my mind fixed on the Lord, there wouldn't be room for other thoughts.

I tried that, and it did work about 10 percent of the time. But the other 90 percent was so frustrating. Those thoughts from the past would surface at the worst times, even while I was sitting in church! It was terribly defeating, and I began to think there was no hope for this.

Then I happened to read a magazine article by a man who wrote that he had discovered a way to conquer lust. He explained he would imagine Jesus Christ driving a moving van, coming to his door, and asking permission to take old memories away from his house. The writer said he would mentally place a picture frame around each memory, watch Christ put them into the van, and then drive off. That eliminated his problem.

That was too simple for me. Being a "sharp" businessman, I always looked for loopholes in any deal. I realized that if I chose to resurrect old memories, all I'd have to do would be to have the moving van come back around the block and unload. But the man's illustration did give me an idea.

One cold morning, long before any of my family was up, I went to my office in our house. Taking out a yellow legal pad, I wrote down every name and memory that I wanted to get rid of. They came quickly and easily, like old friends. They were true love-hate relationships.

When I was done, I combined the idea from the magazine article with the advice of my friend in Minneapolis. I pictured Christ on the cross, with all the blood and pain He went through, and below His left hand I imagined the fiery furnace of Shadrach, Meshach, and Abednego from the book of Daniel. As I mentally went down my list, I put a picture frame around each memory, placed it in Jesus' left hand, and watched Him drop it into the fire. When I was all done, I put a match to the list I had written down and burned it in the fireplace.

Admittedly, it seems too simple, but for me it worked. I don't know why, except that before, I had been trying to avoid sin's power myself and this time I turned it over to the Lord.

Afterward an occasional memory would return and I'd think, "Did I deal with that?" If not, I would handle it the same way I had the others, but if I had, I would just say, "Satan, through the blood of Jesus I've dealt with that" and instantly it would be over. God has an amazing power to make changes when they are critical to our well-being.

Once the old memories were taken care of, I realized I could form new memories. It's a case of "if you don't want to be eaten by a bear, you stay out of bear country." Understanding I am susceptible to sexual lust, I know I have no business being at a swimming pool with dark glasses on. I also try to avoid being other places where I might be tempted.

Being in the world, I know there's no way I can always avoid being around women who might catch my attention. But although I can't stop birds of the air from flying over my head, I can stop them from building a nest in my hair! In 1 Corinthians 10:13 we are told, "No temptation has seized you except what is common to man. And God is faithful; he will not let you be tempted beyond what you can bear. But when you are tempted, he will also provide a way out so that you can stand up under it."

It's reassuring to me knowing that when I'm tempted, I'm not unique and God will provide a way of escaping it if I'm willing to look for it.

I get ambushed occasionally and confront a sexual temptation that I had not realized was there. The key is to be mentally prepared for any circumstance, and that means spending time with God in His Word and prayer. The question becomes, am I focused on Christ and abiding in Him? You can't do that simply by going to church one hour a week. The better I know the Lord, and the more time I spend with Him, the more successful I'll be in dealing with temptations when they come.

"Anyone who looks at a woman lustfully has already committed adultery with her in his heart."

Matthew 5:28

61

BEHIND CLOSED DOORS

Ted DeMoss

etween 3 and 4 A.M., the man was awakened from a sound sleep by a persistent knock at the door of his hotel room. He lay still for a few moments, unsure whether he had been dreaming, or if there had been a knock either at his door or the one across the hall. Seconds later, the knock was repeated. He groggily stumbled toward the door and asked, "Who is it?"

A woman on the other side of the door replied, "Open the door and you'll see who it is." The door was chained, so the man briefly considered peeking out the door to see who was there. He decided not to, but continued the conversation through the closed door. "What do you want?", he asked. The woman responded that she believed he might like a companion for the rest of the night.

Startled by her statement, the man was again tempted to open the door a crack—even though he had no intention of letting her in. He was curious to see what a woman would look like who would come to his door at that hour of the morning, offering herself. Instead, he told her if she did not get away from the door, he would call the front desk. She quickly left, and he returned to bed.

Later that morning, as he was checking out, he reported the incident. The motel management was distressed that he had not notified the desk at the time of the incident, since the local police had been looking for that woman for several months. The businessman learned that the woman, who had been nicknamed "The Nighttime Bandit," actually offered nothing, but would rob unsuspecting men at gunpoint when they opened their motel room doors.

In fact, police speculated she had robbed many more men than were reported, due to the circumstances. A man would have a great deal of difficulty explaining why he would let someone like that into his room, especially if he was a married man away from home.

The CBMC member to whom this incident happened related it to me. He has frequently spoken throughout the United States and overseas, telling what Jesus Christ has meant in his life. This account, obviously, fits in well. He recognized the truth of 1 Corinthians 10:13, that his temptation was no different than what other men have faced and that God would enable him to gain victory by giving him a way out, in this case by not giving the woman a way in.

I have often talked with men individually about how I handle sexual temptation. The verse I've often used is Job 31:1, "I have made a covenant with my eyes; why then should I look upon a young woman?" (NJKV). Like my friend in the motel room, I, too, would have been tempted—leaving the door still chained with no intention of opening it—to take a look at what a woman with such boldness would look like, presuming that she was a prostitute, not a robber. However, because I have committed Job 31:1 to my heart, I am confident the Holy Spirit would have reminded me of that verse, therefore giving me a way out and a reason for not opening the door, even with the chain still fastened.

Another verse to rely on is found in 2 Timothy 2:22, "Flee also youthful lusts: but follow righteousness, faith, charity, peace, with them that call on the Lord out of a pure heart," (KJV). And in James 4:7, we are reminded that if we resist the devil, he will flee from us. The verse after that, by contrast, assures us that if we draw near to God, He will draw near to us.

I'm reminded of the story I heard years ago of another motel scene, with a considerably different outcome. One night a married man went to a motel and called a phone number he had used before, arranging for a prostitute to be sent to his room immediately. Within minutes there was a knock at his door. When he opened the door to welcome his "guest," the young woman standing there was his daughter.

This man had no idea his daughter was a prostitute, nor had he ever anticipated a confrontation like that one. Unlike any other time in his life, that unbelievable moment convicted the man of his sinfulness before God. After some soul-searching, he committed his life to Jesus Christ, as did the daughter, his wife, and other members of the family. Having three daughters and now two granddaughters myself, I can imagine how heartrending an encounter like that would be. Thank God, He still used it to His glory.

Relying upon God's grace, we must equip ourselves to stand up against all temptations, and especially sexual temptation. We must never forget the warning of 1 Corinthians 10:12: "Let him who thinks he stands take heed lest he fall," (NJKV).

"Anyone who looks at a woman lustfully has already committed adultery with her in his heart."

Matthew 5:28

—————————————————— *62*

BUILDING AN AFFAIR-PROOF MARRIAGE

An Interview with Dr. Willard F. Harley, Jr.

The extramarital affair: If we based our thinking on television soap operas, we would have to believe that everyone is involved in one. And judging from the activities of some of the people we know, we could reach the same conclusion.

One study of six thousand business executives indicated that only one in every five married men participates in an extramarital affair, either on an occasional or regular basis. However, the same study reported that as incomes increased, so did the likelihood of affairs, with 32 percent of the men in the fifty-thousand-dollar-a-year or higher income bracket responding that they had been involved in affairs. On the opposite side of the coin, it is not unusual for a hard-driving, career-oriented businessman to discover that his wife has become romantically involved with another man, often someone he knows well.

Is there no hope for marriage today? Is it, as some authorities claim, an institution destined for extinction? Dr. Willard F. Harley, Jr., a licensed clinical psychologist who has counseled more than three thousand couples with troubled marriages, explains there is hope in his bestseller, *His Needs, Her Needs: Building an Affair-proof Marriage* (published by Fleming H. Revell Co.).

Dr. Harley, what would be a typical scenario for an affair today?

It would be of a man who has worked with his secretary for more than three years. They do a lot of work together, she is impressed by him, and he goes to bat for her and gives her raises. She's a good secretary and encourages him. They have lunch together and occasionally work late on special projects. Once in a while they have to go to another city together on business and go sightseeing — totally innocent and just as good friends.

The man notices the secretary is exceptionally talented and pretty, and she communicates the love and attention he wishes his wife would give him. On one particular occasion, impulsively, he says he thinks he is falling in love with her. She replies that he means a great deal to her, too. They have not yet become physically involved, but soon they hug, at first casually and then tenderly.

One day when they are alone, they make love, even though it had not been planned. It is the best experience of their lives. They feel guilty and promise never to do that again, but a few weeks later they again have sex together, passionately, and it becomes more frequent. They try to conceal the affair, but eventually the wife becomes alarmed and then discovers the truth.

It's amazing how insidious it all is. It's not a case of a guy consciously saying, "My marriage has been so bad for so many years, it's time to find somebody else." It's more a matter of an important need going unmet, then someone stepping in to fill that vacuum.

Generally, affairs occur between people with long-standing relationships — people who work together, or good friends. It's not the girl spotted wearing a bikini on the beach, and often the women involved are not bombshells in appearance, just what we would consider decent, nice people.

Today we hear a lot about commitment in marriage, a dedication to the relationship that transcends personal feelings and desires. Yet in your book, you place virtually no emphasis on that concept. Why?

I have discovered that methods of successful married life are not based upon commitment. In fact, I've concluded that commitment has little to do with it. As Christians, we know it is God's will that we have a good marriage, but the issue is—how do we do it? Among the thousands of couples I have counseled, it seems that commitment has very little impact upon decision-making within a marriage.

That is because we misunderstand the concept of commitment. It's not a simple matter of me saying to my wife, "I commit myself to you, Joyce," but rather "I will do my best to take care of you and to meet your needs." The goal of our commitment in marriage should be that our spouse would never want to have an affair.

What led to the development of your ideas on how to build an "affair-proof" marriage?

Actually, I was not very successful in marriage counseling until the early 1970s. I had done extensive reading and research in the use of behavior modification in marriage counseling, and saw the positive results that was having. I began taking a similar approach myself, and since then have had a success rate of 90 to 95 percent.

In working with a tremendous number of people, from very diverse backgrounds—urban, rural, retarded, brilliant, Christian, non-Christian— I found that the primary needs that men have and women have are almost universal, and methods for saving a marriage (focusing on these needs) hold up across cultures and ethnic groups.

Specifically, what are these needs?

First of all, I define a need as what people enjoy tremendously when someone does that for them. I've discovered that in women, the primary needs are: affection, conversation, honesty and openness (a solid basis of trust), financial support (enough money to live comfortably), and family commitment (her husband must be a good father).

Among men, the five basic needs are: sexual fulfillment, recreational companionship (having his wife join him in leisure activities), an attractive spouse (she tries to always look her best), domestic support (he finds peace and quiet at home), and admiration. There may be individual exceptions, but my studies have shown that for women and men, these five areas of need cause the greatest discomfort when they are not being met—and give the greatest pleasure when they are.

Failure to have any of these marital needs met creates a vacuum of major proportions. And when a vacuum exists, it seeks to suck in whatever (or whoever) is readily available to fill it. However, if a husband and wife are doing a great job of meeting each other's needs, they should not have any major marital problems. When a person finds the five major needs being met, I've never had him (or her) express a need to work on something else.

It's interesting that although you cited affection as a basic female need, you did not list sex, while for men you included sex — and not affection. Why is that?

Women have a more natural tendency to build long-standing relationships, an orientation toward families, regardless of culture. That's why even when wives are abused, it's difficult for them to shake marriage relationships. Men hardly ever demonstrate that kind of loyalty. A man's needs are more superficial, while a woman's are deeper and more philosophical, more constructive. For that reason, sex to man often is simply a case of meeting a strong biological drive, while for a woman, sex fits within the context of a complete relationship. She has a need to feel close and cared for.

How do these facts relate to improving marital harmony?

Let's say that a woman feels a need for more affection. Her husband must develop a style and approach to meet that need. If affection does not come naturally for him, it can be learned. To make a marriage really work, it's not enough to hit four out of five. You've got to bat one thousand.

Suppose a husband senses a need for admiration and cannot get that from his wife. Admiration is a real key; it's a big deal for men. If he happens to find someone who will give him that admiration, that vacuum will be filled. And it's interesting how quickly men get involved sexually with a woman who meets a basic need, even if their other needs — including sexual — are already being met by their wives.

You discuss the concept of the "Love Bank" in your book, stating that it also plays a major role in the building and maintaining of

relationships between men and women, regardless of whether they are married. What is this "Love Bank"?

Basically, we like people we associate good feelings with. We tend to draw a distinction between our attraction to someone — how much we like them — and our caring for a person, which is more of a philosophical matter. In building a good marriage, you want your spouse to be attracted to you, so you do things that make her feel good. The result is that each time you do something that pleases her, especially in meeting one of her basic needs, you gain a Love Bank deposit in your name. Over time, you can build a sizeable account.

However, if a person is annoying, irritating, and critical of you, those actions debit his or her account in your Love Bank. That's why it is so common to find people who are married to spouses they dislike. And when you have an intense dislike for someone, even if that person does something you normally would like, you *still* don't like it! The Love Bank accounts are not transacted consciously, but they are a neat little way of conceptualizing how we develop feelings toward others.

You recommend that a husband and wife spend fifteen hours a week together, excluding sleeping and eating. Is that realistic?

Actually, I recommend that only for solid marriages. In trying to get people's marriages back together, I prescribe more time. That seems like a lot, but if we evaluate the amount of time people spend courting, they spend at least fifteen hours together — and in the process they are making sizable deposits into one another's Love Banks. Everybody is horrified at the thought of devoting fifteen hours exclusively to a spouse, but I point out that if anything were to happen to that spouse, it would require at least that much time to develop a new relationship.

What it comes down to is evaluating the array of things you could do, then focusing on those that you like in common. To do a lot of things separately, truthfully, is a waste of time. Busy people cannot afford to do something that serves only one function. For instance, in recreation you should find activities that will build the marriage, promote personal health, and provide the enjoyment you need, all at the same time.

What can we, as Christians, do to help one another avoid affairs and foster good, God-honoring marriages?

It's gratifying that the people who are reading my book the most are in the business of helping other people resolve their own human problems. Each chapter has little ideas that you can expand and tailor to your own situation. Basically, we all need to know how to form good habits. That does not come from good intentions, but by doing something over and over again.

Christians are especially good at putting up a front, and sometimes their problems are worse because the truth isn't known. We need to establish some kind of accountability with one another. If we can learn about our spouses' needs and concentrate on meeting them, the problem will solve itself.

His Needs/Her Needs

Dr. Willard F. Harley, Jr. says men and women almost universally have five primary needs that must be met to assure a prospering, affair-proof marriage. Those needs are:

Men	Women
1. Sexual fulfillment	1. Affection
2. Recreational companionship	2. Conversation
3. An attractive spouse	3. Honesty and openness
4. Domestic support	4. Financial support
5. Admiration	5. Family commitment

---

*Do not get drunk on wine. . . . Instead, be filled with
the Spirit.*

Ephesians 5:18

63

WE DIDN'T THINK
IT COULD HAPPEN TO US

Stephen Carley

L ooking back, it seems hard to believe, but for six years of our
marriage, I had no idea that my wife, Nancy, was abusing prescription drugs. After our first two babies had been born, she seemed to
have a rough time, so I was prepared for that by the time our third child
was due. But after Grace was born, Nancy's problems grew much
worse.

A series of horrifying events convinced me that my wife was struggling with much more than a high level of stress. One night, I could not
find Nancy anywhere in the house, so I looked outside. I found her
behind some bushes near our front door. She was lying in the dirt, trying
to bury herself.

Thinking she was going through a nervous breakdown, we began
consulting with what I would term today a "medicating psychiatrist." He
prescribed a series of mood-altering drugs for her—antidepressants and
tranquilizers. Unfortunately, these only intensified her condition.

On another occasion, I returned home to find Nancy lying on the
floor in the living room unconscious. On the floor next to her was a
revolver, cocked and loaded. I had Nancy admitted to a psychiatric hospital, where they placed her in a locked ward with people who had at-

tempted suicide. She was released after ten days, but I still did not comprehend the drug problem that so dominated her life.

A third incident convinced me that what a friend had been trying to tell me was true—Nancy did have a chemical addiction. I had come home from work and again could not find her. After looking throughout the house, I found her in the basement, lying under a pile of old rugs, with a jug of wine under her arm.

In retrospect, it seems so obvious, but I had refused to believe Nancy could have a drug or alcohol problem, even when I periodically found empty wine bottles around the house. Being an attorney, I finally admitted that the evidence was indisputable.

During that period, which went on for six months, I didn't know what to do. Since Nancy was incapable of caring for the children, I would get up, dress and feed them, and take them to a day care center on my way to the office. I lost more than twenty pounds because of worry, stress, and added responsibilities. It was shattering to see Nancy trying to be so sweet as we left each morning, but knowing she would go back into the house to spend another day of misery, alone, and without hope.

After the incident in the basement, I took Nancy to a chemical abuse treatment center which offered a special program for health care specialists, including doctors, nurses, pharmacists, and dentists. At the center, we discovered the extent of Nancy's problem. The psychiatrist had put her on five different medications, and all those had accomplished was to deepen her dependency.

It was hard for me to relate to her problem. Even though I had had difficulties with alcohol myself much earlier, I had never been closely involved before with anyone having any form of drug dependency. But watching her, I could see how helpless she was. It became obvious that she was fighting a deadly foe that was more powerful than she was or I was. She seemed like a person with both legs broken, lying in the middle of a busy highway, unable to move out of the way of the cars whizzing by.

Nancy originally was to be in the hospital for one month and then be released to a halfway house for three months. The strain on both of us was intense. I didn't know if she could overcome her problem, and Nancy was near the point of despair, wanting so badly to get her life straightened out. After two months in the program, she "escaped," and I found her at home with all her things unpacked. Reluctantly, I consented to let her stay, but we both were fearful about what was going to happen.

I'm so thankful for the support I received from Christian friends during that time. They not only encouraged me and prayed with me, but they also assisted in caring for the children, making hospital visits, and keeping our house in order. It was the greatest crisis point in our lives, and I must admit, I had some doubts that things would ever be right again. It was an agonizing time for us all.

However, it also was a time for me to experience the grace and power of Jesus Christ. I'm convinced that if I had not been a Christian, I would have given up and left. For so many people in that situation, all they can see is a sinking ship, and the most logical thing is to abandon it. Even during moments of hopelessness, I trusted Christ to see me through it. Disaster was the only alternative.

When Nancy and I went to church one Sunday in May of 1984, I had no way of knowing something special would happen. Nancy had been out of the treatment center for several months, but she was struggling as much as ever. However, having been a Christian for five years, I knew that God is faithful and clung to that hope. In Jeremiah 29:11, He says, "For I know the plans I have for you, . . . plans for welfare and not for calamity, to give you a future and a hope," (NAS).

I did not realize how much the sermon that morning had touched Nancy; we weren't communicating much in those days. However, the message had been so powerful, I was determined to go back again that night. At the close of the message, when my friend, Phil, tapped Nancy on the shoulder and said he wanted to talk with her, all I could do was pray, crying out to God to take control of my wife's life.

When she decided to talk with a counselor about her relationship with God, I rejoiced, sensing that He was answering our prayers. That night, Nancy did turn her life over to Jesus Christ. As Christians, we use the term "saved," meaning we have been spared the penalty of sin, which is death — eternal separation from God. In Nancy's case, she also was saved from the compulsion to use and abuse drugs which had controlled her life.

Today, my life with Nancy is wonderful beyond any of my expectations. Freed from the grip of drug abuse, she is the loving, caring wife and mother I had always wanted. God has restored our marriage and our family life in such a way that it is better now than ever, even before Nancy's problem with addiction began.

Nancy is wary of taking any medication, even when she is ill, knowing that physiologically she is still an addict, although a recovering one. But she truly is a new person, as 2 Corinthians 5:17 promises—a new, beautiful creation of God.

*Do not get drunk on wine. . . . Instead, be filled with
the Spirit.*

Ephesians 5:18

64

TO THE RESCUE

Whipple S. Newell, Jr.

F riendship cannot be fully appreciated until it is most needed. Bob
Wilson and I had met in Houston in the early 1960s, while we
were both building prospering careers in commercial real estate with
American General Investment Corporation. Not only were our careers
on a roll, but we also became friends since we shared other common
interests: money, drinking, gambling, and pretty women.

Over the next twenty years, we kept in contact, even though we
made decisions to affiliate with different companies and eventually, to
establish our own businesses. For a long time, we remained like the
proverbial "peas in the pod." But it wasn't until 1985 that I discovered
just how important Bob's friendship would be for me.

It's amazing how much failure can be concealed in a life of external
success. During those two intervening decades, I experienced five un-
successful marriages. When I married one of my wives a second time,
she became known as "Mrs. Re-Newell." The reasons for my marital
failures were simple: While I was making a name for myself in the real
estate industry, I was making a fool of myself with alcohol. And morally, my life was a shambles.

My father, who had been my idol, died an alcoholic. All I wanted
out of life was to be just like him; unfortunately, I succeeded. I had all
the trappings of success as the world defines it—membership in a fancy

country club, living in a large mansion, and even a South Texas quail lease. I had everything a man could want materially, and seemed on my way to acquiring more.

Enslaved to Alcohol

I had even formed my own company in 1970, Southwest Business Properties, but it's hard to be your own man when you're a slave to alcohol. Drinking virtually dominated my life, to the point where I ceased to care what happened to my business. Financial problems were inevitable, and physical problems soon followed.

The fourth woman I married was wealthy, and since I was in no condition to support myself, I moved to her home in Gilchrist, Texas in 1981. But my personal decline continued. My life during the early 1980s was totally vacant, without any direction or purpose. In the spring of 1984, a Veterans Administration hospital became "home" for sixty days, which saved me from drinking myself to death, but my life remained a mess.

Fresh from another ruined marriage, I decided to move back to Houston. I could not return to real estate, so I tried driving a truck for a delivery service until I was fired for not being able to learn a map of Houston quickly enough. An attempt at being a maintenance man for a storage firm also failed, and I spent seven months unemployed before my old friend Bob Wilson reached out to me like a lifeguard to a drowning man.

Attention Welcomed

I felt so completely lost at that juncture of my life, and gratefully responded to any attention that was paid to me. His kindness was like throwing a piece of meat or a bone to a starving dog.

Bob found some temporary work for me and then, in the summer of 1986, he took a chance and gave me a job with RW Management Company as property manager. That was his gracious title for maintenance man and rent collector. Working with Bob this time, however, I could see there was something different about him. It was evident that his life had undergone tremendous changes.

Something I Hadn't Found

He had become a Christian several years earlier, and told me about having a personal relationship with God by committing his life to Jesus Christ. I didn't really understand what he meant, but as I watched him and got to know some of his friends, I recognized a sense of peace and joy in their lives that I had never found in a bottle.

I thought back to the previous Christmas Day, 1985, when I had been all alone, without a job and down to my last dollar. Feeling my life was near its end, I had pleaded with God to help me. Bob Wilson was part of God's response to my feeble, helpless prayer.

Bob began taking me to Christian Business Men's Committee meetings, and one of his friends, Joe Calvert, invited me to meet with him and discuss the Bible through a program called "Operation Timothy." Not long after we began meeting, I said a much more specific prayer, confessing my sins to God and asking Jesus Christ to take control of my life.

Today, I'm still an alcoholic, although I no longer drink. The chains of slavery have disappeared. I'm a completely different person, and I understand why Jesus said, "unless you are born again, you cannot enter the kingdom of heaven." That's exactly how I feel — reborn.

Memories of the worst years, 1984 and 1985, are becoming dimmer and dimmer. I enjoy life now more than I ever thought possible; each day is a new lease on life for me. A year ago, I got married again. Mary and I met in a Bible study group and for the first time, I can confidently say, "This one is for keeps."

I'm rebuilding my relationship with my two daughters, Helen and Elizabeth, and my son, Whipple III. As Bob pointed out, if I had died a couple of years ago, none of them would have shed any tears for me, but I feel that I'm regaining their love and respect. One day I was talking with Elizabeth, my middle child, and I told her, "You know that we have not gotten along in the past. I'd like to in the future." It thrilled me to hear her say, "So would I, Dad."

I used to look back over my life and fill up with regret and remorse. But the Bible tells us to forget what lies behind and press toward the future, so I prayed, "Lord, please let me move ahead and grow, shutting the door on the past." Sometimes the troubling memories return, but I've learned that although I'm not proud of my past, there is nothing I can do about it now. And through the favor of God that I could never deserve, He's teaching me that today and tomorrow are all that matter.

Someone asked not long ago if I had become a Christian through a catastrophic event or in a more gradual way. Much of my life before I accepted Christ as my Savior and Lord was a catastrophe, but I guess my commitment came in a more progressive way as I slowly learned more about Him through reading the Bible and talking with Bob, Joe, and other Christian men.

Recently, I learned about another friend who has meant a lot in my life spiritually. I had gotten to know Clifford Ray in 1984 while I was in Gilchrist, and he assisted me in some of my most helpless moments. I didn't know he was a Christian—and at that point, I wouldn't have cared anyway—but he faithfully continued praying for me through 1985. "I was about to give up on you, Whip," he told me, "but my wife talked me out of it. So I just kept praying until I heard you had given your heart to Christ."

I beat the odds—overcoming alcoholism and becoming a Christian at the age of fifty. But I know I didn't do it alone. The staff at the VA hospital saved my life physically, and then Christ came in to fill my life spiritually.

In the book of Proverbs, it says "there is a friend who sticks closer than a brother." I'm thankful for a few true friends who cared enough to pray for me and throw me a rope when I was about to go under for the third time. Most of all, I'm thankful that they pointed me to the best Friend anyone could ever have.

*Do not get drunk on wine. . . . Instead, be filled with
the Spirit.*

Ephesians 5:18

65

CODEPENDENTS
(How addiction affects the entire family)

Jim Dickerson

C hemical dependency is typically regarded as an individual problem, but in most cases, the disease afflicts the addict's entire family, as I learned from research — and personal experience.

In fact, the term "codependency" has been coined to describe persons who derive their sense of well-being from a chemical-dependent
loved one and are strongly influenced by that individual's behavior.

My first wife came from a family of alcoholics. She, too, became
chemically dependent, although not on alcohol, since she understood
how dangerous it was. Instead, she developed another form of addictive
behavior — anorexia nervosa, a disease in which the victim virtually
starves herself, binging on food and then quickly purging it, stubbornly
convinced of a nonexistent weight problem.

She and I experienced strong conflict in our marriage, primarily because her compulsive behavior contrasted sharply with my reserved personality, one of rarely doing anything to excess. My wife was looking to
me to meet her needs, to be the kind of indulgent, nurturing person that
her mother had been. Because I could not do that, a wall grew between
us, and our marriage eventually fell apart.

My second wife, Judy, also came from an alcoholic background and
had been married twice before. Although she did not become addicted to

alcohol herself, her codependency led her to marry men from similar environments. The first was a passive individual who had trouble holding a job, while the second was an alcoholic.

The fact that Judy and I were attracted and decided to marry I can attribute only to the grace of God, since our personalities are not at all alike. A "normie" like me is usually too calm and unexciting for someone with a codependent personality. In our case, we both had become Christians before we met, and the bond of Jesus Christ has served as a cement that is stronger than our differences.

When Judy was younger, she struggled with and overcame a drinking problem, but she still has to fight a food compulsion. Through the support of Christian friends and Overeaters Anonymous, which operates according to principles similar to Alcoholics Anonymous, she has been able to maintain her normal weight for more than four years.

Her three children also have exhibited various forms of compulsive behavior resulting from their codependency, but Judy and I have learned that the right kind of counseling and support groups, which approach alcoholism or other addictive behavior as a family illness, can provide a solution, particularly if that answer is Christ-centered.

It is phenomenal how strong an influence the addicted person has upon the remainder of his family. An alcoholic, for example, generally becomes a *controller*, manipulating other family members. The spouse unwittingly becomes the *enabler*, trying to hang on and hold the family together.

Depending on the size of the family, children will fit into other roles. The *family hero*, for example, is a self-starter, working diligently to overcome the situation. That person is a good candidate to become a workaholic. The *scapegoat* is a family member who always seems to be doing things wrong, creating a series of problems as he desperately seeks to please the ones whose love he needs.

The family may have someone filling a *lost child* role, one who seems to remain on the periphery and constantly questions his self-worth. This individual is likely to run away or at least live away as soon as possible, trying to escape. And then there is the *family mascot*, who is always trying to make jokes and distract other family members from the real problem.

All of these, in their own way, are striving subconsciously to maintain family unity in spite of the monumental problems presented by the alcoholic. For that reason, in counseling and seeking to help anyone who is chemically dependent, it is essential to understand that the entire family must be helped. Without that, the consequences of codependency may be perpetuated from generation to generation.

Do not get drunk on wine. . . . Instead, be filled with the Spirit.

Ephesians 5:18

───────────────────────────── *66*

WILL YOUR KIDS JUST SAY NO?

An Interview with Dr. John Q. Baucom

D rug abuse. Everyone seems to be talking about it, but is anything really being accomplished? Are we winning the war against drugs or just celebrating victories in a few minor skirmishes? Why is it such a problem anyway?

Dr. John Q. Baucom, author of *Help Your Children Say No to Drugs* (Pyranee Books, 1987), has been a drug abuse counselor since 1974 and presents some provocative views on the subject. A licensed family therapist, Baucom found himself in the national spotlight in 1985 after conducting a symposium to combat an alarming problem of teenage suicide in Chattanooga, Tennessee. In February of that year, Chattanooga had one of the highest suicide rates in the country, but by year-end, that rate had dropped to among the lowest in U.S. metropolitan areas.

The author of two other books, *Fatal Choice: The Teenage Suicide Crisis* (Moody Press) and *Bonding and Breaking Free* (Zondervan), Baucom and his wife, Bennie, cohost a twice weekly call-in radio talk show dealing with human relationships.

How widespread is drug abuse among children?

Research has shown that 92 percent of all teenagers will experiment with alcohol and drugs before age eighteen. It's a statistical reality that drug abuse is now at epidemic proportions. I believe President Reagan is correct in calling it "Public Enemy No. 1." As New York City Police Commissioner Benjamin Ward has said, "The crime problem *is* the drug problem."

USA Today not long ago reported that cocaine and marijuana use among teens is going down, but that study was limited to high schools in Northeastern urban areas, surveying juniors in high school. What about teens who are not seventeen-year-old high school juniors from the Northeast? The research also did not take into account the large numbers of teenagers who drop out of high school entirely each year. Their drug habits need to be considered for any study to be valid. Contrary to the *USA Today* report, the National Institute of Mental Health states that drug use is increasing in *all* age brackets.

What is causing the drug abuse "epidemic"?

With adults, it's primarily loneliness; with children, drugs are a salve for fractured, scalded emotions—a way to deal with pain. Many kids today are experiencing a sense of aimlessness, and drugs provide what appears to be relief.

We have read about the deaths of prominent entertainers and athletes due to drugs. When a Len Bias dies of cocaine, we presume people will get the message. Why does the problem persist?

Because we live in a drug-oriented society. Even on the Mayflower, historians tell us that there was more distilled alcohol—forty two tons of beer and ten thousand tons of wine—than drinking water—only four tons. Drug use has become an American tradition. Alcohol is seen as a prestigious, ritualistic beverage. It's commonly used for various celebrations, serves as a rite of passage into manhood, and is even used in certain religious settings.

On a typical Sunday afternoon in the fall or winter, we watch a professional football game in which former athletes argue over whether their favorite beer tastes great or is less filling. And there is Spuds Mac-Kenzie. Here we have man's best friend—"the party animal"—with three gorgeous women, pushing alcohol at halftime of man's favorite game. We also have Alex the dog, again, man's best friend, promoting a well-known beer, along with rock stars like Phil Collins and Eric Clapton. Sandwiched in between all these commercials we have an occasional, fifteen second public service announcement with some athlete telling us, "Don't do drugs."

Sadly, the commercials are extremely well-produced. They are indirect, dramatic, humorous, and entertaining. And most never actually say, "Drink beer." They're subtle, intended to raise our curiosity to find out if drinking beer is really as much fun as it seems to be. By comparison, the public service announcements are extremely direct and poorly done. Any parent knows that when you tell a child, "Don't do *that!*", it only makes him want to do it more.

Are you saying that the "Just Say No" campaign isn't working?

Exactly. In the six-and-a-half years since the campaign was started, alcohol use among high school students has tripled. To me, that slogan is insulting. The word "just" makes it sound so easy. Many of us can't even say no to a donut, let alone drugs.

The one positive effect of Mrs. Reagan's campaign has been to get the nation's attention, but so far it's only resulted in an attitude of laissez faire acceptance. Rather than getting involved in the fight against drugs with any degree of enthusiasm, we would rather ignore it and hope it goes away.

Is an anti-drug media blitz a waste of time, then?

No, but we can't fight the media unless we play the media's game. One drug-related death, no matter who it is, will not make a difference. We have to make our anti-drug messages entertaining, attractive, and non-intimidating. Even when God told Adam and Eve not to eat from one tree in the Garden of Eden, that didn't stop them.

Is drug abuse less of a problem in Christian homes?

A common presumption is that this kind of thing doesn't happen in Christian families, but that's wrong. A Christian environment does not give automatic immunity to drug abuse, suicide, or stress. Faith and belief in God can provide a child with strength, but the example set by the parents is so important. It's impossible for a child to believe in a God he *can't* see if he can't believe in a father and mother that he *can* see. Studies indicate that fathers spend an average of seven to eleven minutes per week with each child, even in Christian homes.

Some time ago, I was speaking on a nighttime Christian radio talk show. Most of the listeners, obviously, were Christians. Of the twenty calls we received in those two hours, six were from parents whose children had attempted suicide; two of them had died. On another talk show in California, a caller told about his son who had been president of his high school class, captain of the football team, and leader of the church youth group—an all-American type. He was found hanging in his room with a suicide note nearby. Being a Christian is not necessarily an antidote to this kind of poison.

You mention "believing in a father and mother." What is the extent of parental influence in this whole problem?

The influence can be great in positive or negative respects. Studies have shown that if a mother uses tranquilizers or other prescription medicine regularly, more than four times a week, children are twelve times more likely to become problem users of opiates. If a father consumes alcohol three or more times per week, his children are fifteen times more likely to become alcoholics.

If a child sees a parent getting nervous and having to take a pill or a drink to relax, it is natural for the child to conclude that to be okay, to be healthy, he will also have to take a substance from a pill, a bottle or a glass. It's an exceedingly dangerous pattern for children to see—even something as innocuous as Rolaids. Youngsters learn that relief is not spelled p-r-a-y-e-r, but by something you put in your mouth.

You term tobacco and alcohol as "gateway" or "stepping stone" drugs. What do you mean by that?

Research has shown that 99 percent of all cocaine and heroine addicts started out smoking tobacco or drinking alcohol. That does not mean that 99 percent of all people who smoke or drink alcohol will one day shoot heroine or snort cocaine, but those are often stepping stones to harder drugs.

Take an example from my own life. I served in Vietnam in the 1960s, but I never smoked marijuana or took drugs. The *only* reason was because I didn't know how to smoke a cigarette. If I had been handed a "reefer"—a marijuana cigarette—I would not have known what to do with it. And I would have been embarrassed to try and smoke one, fearful that I would cough and gag, making a fool of myself. If I had been smoking tobacco cigarettes, I probably would have tried the other, since at that time I had no personal convictions that I shouldn't. The easiest way to deal with drug abuse is not to start, in any form.

Most parents want to know, "How can I tell if my child is a candidate for drug abuse?", or "How can I tell if my child is taking drugs?" What advice can you give them?

In the back of my book, I include a questionnaire which analyzes both child and parental attitudes and behavior that might encourage drug abuse. But basically, if a parent is spending sufficient time with a child, he will recognize the symptoms. I'm not talking about dilated pupils or red eyes, but behavioral changes—a marked shift in attitudes, new friends and peer group, a radical change in performance at school and at home. If we're doing a good job with our kids, we'll recognize when something is wrong.

Also, every drug abuser I have ever worked with has left evidence—things such as marijuana residue, "roach clips," a mirror with a white, filmy residue, a small straw, or a razor blade. If there is a combination of two or three things that warrant concern and they persist for several weeks, then it would be a good idea to determine the cause of the problem.

What is the link between drug abuse and teenage suicide?

You may recall the news reports a few years ago about four teens in Bergenfield, New Jersey, who took their lives about the same time. They all had high levels of cocaine and alcohol in their bodies at the time. Alcohol and/or drugs are involved in more than 90 percent of all adolescent suicides. We can't say that drug abuse is the cause of suicide, but it may be. At least we know there is a positive correlation.

Where do you see God fitting into this whole picture?

Not long ago, a Jewish researcher did a study of Christian homes. Statistics showed indisputably that children have a much better chance of not becoming problem users of drugs if they go to church a certain number of times before they reach the age of ten. In his conclusion, the researcher cited the effects of socialization and the extended family that church participation offers, but I feel there is a direct spiritual relationship.

Kids raised in a Christlike environment will have a much better opportunity for many things in life, not the least of which are high self-esteem, understanding, and forgiveness. And of course, for those who already are victims of drug abuse, God offers the power to overcome that affliction.

What would you like to tell Christian business and professional men specifically regarding drug abuse and their children?

First, that fathers need to take a more active role in child-rearing in this country. In our society, fathers are absent for many reasons — death, divorce, separation, travel — things kids can adjust to and cope with. But when a father is physically present but psychologically absent, a child can't handle that. That is the ultimate rejection. The message the child gets is, "I'm not worthy of his attention."

And secondly, I would encourage them not only to spend time with their children, but to have intense interaction. I'm referring to *real* time, involving sight, hearing, smell, and touch — the kind of intense, caring interaction that stimulates all of the senses. This might include skiing, walking in the woods, hiking, camping out, or just riding together in the car.

Children need a father's full attention, love, energy, and focus. More than anything else, the complaint I receive from teenagers about their parents is that they don't get those things. Chances are, if they receive that level of attention, they won't need to turn to drugs.

PART FOUR

HIS FINANCIAL WORLD

*"So if you have not been trustworthy in handling
worldly wealth, who will trust you with true riches?"*
Luke 16:11

67

TAKING STOCK OF THE FUTURE
(Tremendous uncertainty, confusion, and fear cloud the 1990s financial picture)

Ronald W. Blue

Many times I am asked what the future holds — for our economy, a particular investment, interest rates, the stock market, and other financial variables. When someone seeks advice from me on a particular stock, I always (tongue in cheek) ask the question, "Well, is it going to go up or is it going to go down?"

Obviously, if the price is going up, you should either buy it or hold it, and if it is going to go down, you should sell it or not buy at all. The point is that no one knows for sure which way anything is going to go in financial matters. Many of us can make educated guesses and give our opinions, but when you are dealing with the future, regardless of the area, it is always a guess or an opinion.

The 1990s are receiving a lot of attention, particularly concerning whether anything needs to change from a personal planning standpoint, simply because in just ten years we will enter the twenty-first century. I can only give predictions and opinions — not facts — about what will happen in the 1990s. I can advise, however, on how to do personal planning for the next decade, *regardless* of the economic changes that may occur. First we need to go back to 1980 and see what the situation was then.

By looking at the last ten years, we should get some idea of what to expect in the next ten years.

In 1980, the three biggest financial concerns that families faced were inflation, taxes, and high interest rates. Inflation was running in double digits, taxes were as high as 77 percent, and home mortgage interest rates were at 13.16 percent, as of July 1980. The best investment over the previous five years had been gold, which had a 254 percent return over that period, even after paying taxes on the gain. The Dow Jones average on July 21, 1980 was 923.

Predictions for the 1980s by almost everyone, Christian and non-Christian, were that inflation was going to continue rising, perhaps even approaching triple-digit levels by the middle of the decade. By 1985, many speculated, we almost certainly were going to have some type of economic crash or depression, and by 1990 the dollar would be worthless.

The reality for the 1980s was that inflation dropped back dramatically to below 5 percent per year, taxes were reduced to the lowest rates in over fifty years, and interest rates came back down to late 1960 levels. We have had the longest period of economic growth in our country, and while the dollar has depreciated in value on a worldwide basis, it certainly has not become worthless.

As the world looks at the United States in 1989, more money is flowing into this country from outside investors than into any other country in the world, which says that the rest of the world looks at our economy and says it is one of the strongest in the world.

On the other hand, if you look at what happened in the investment world during the 1980s, you see that every investment area crashed during that period. The stock market experienced a crash in 1987, silver crashed, numismatic coins performed poorly, art and collectibles did not perform very well, and on and on. That is not to say that these have been bad investments over a ten year period; it's just that at some time during the 1980s, all investments crashed in value.

As we sit on the threshold of the 1990s, the biggest concerns, I think, are the Federal budget and balance of payments on a national level, and consumer debt and housing prices on a personal level. As we look ahead, I believe Solomon said it best, "What goes around comes around" (Ron Blue paraphrase). In other words, as we look into the

1990s there is tremendous uncertainty, confusion and fear, just as we had in 1980. No one can do a better job of predicting the 1990s than we did the 1980s.

Notwithstanding this fact, my *opinion* is that during the 90s we will see taxes go up, inflation continue, interest rates continue to reflect inflation, our economy will become even more global, and over-consumerism will continue.

On a positive note, I believe, from my experience in speaking and counseling with Christians all over the United States, that Christians during the 1990s will give more, save more, and spend more wisely. I believe this is because with continuing and increasing economic uncertainty, we are forced to turn back to the only truth that there is, the Word of God. The Bible is very clear about how to experience continued financial success in the light of changing and uncertain economic times.

Keys to Personal Financial Success

There are five Biblical keys to financial success, whether we have inflation, deflation, economic collapse, or even a political upheaval:

- To understand that God owns it all, and therefore we are only managers of His resources.
- Always spend less than you earn, so that you are never over-consuming.
- Avoid excessive use of debt; as a matter of fact, if you can avoid debt totally, you are always better off.
- Maintain liquid reserves to meet any unexpected financial changes and emergencies.
- Always have written long-term goals so that you know in what direction you are heading.

These five keys to financial success will work regardless of what happens in our economy and around the world. When followed, they also will provide real inner security regarding personal finances because the focus will be on God and doing what is right based on His system of truth. That is the only way to have real continuing security, financial or otherwise, as we move into the 1990s and the twenty-first century.

"So if you have not been trustworthy in handling
worldly wealth, who will trust you with true riches?"
Luke 16:11

68

MIDDLE CLASS SQUEEZE

Russell D. Crosson

W hy do middle income families struggle so much financially? That seemed to be a major topic of discussion during the recent presidential campaign. Americans in the twenty thousand to fifty thousand dollar income range often feel "squeezed" and experience a difficult time in managing their finances.

In analyzing this phenomenon, one general cause becomes obvious: *Those in the middle income range do not want to stay in the middle income range!*

Many people have not learned to be content with their level of income. This is true at any level, but especially for those in the middle income brackets. Middle income families today have had their expectations elevated by feeling they need to live at the level at which their parents are currently living after thirty or forty years of work! The problem with being middle income is that one can't have all the trappings and signs of success that go with upper income.

Four specific problems which contribute to the "middle income squeeze" are apparent:

Outgo Exceeds Income

First of all, middle income Americans tend to elevate their lifestyles beyond their income levels early in their lives, thereby accumulating debt early (that is, they spend twenty-two thousand dollars while earning twenty thousand dollars). Easy credit makes this possible. Then, even if income goes up to forty thousand or fifty thousand dollars, they remain strapped for living expenses because they have to repay several thousand dollars in consumer debt accumulated while living beyond their means.

One of the biggest traps for the middle-income American is an inability to limit expenses until the income goes up. Expecting to live like Mom and Dad or "keeping up with the Joneses" early on can have devastating consequences. Debt will always sentence one to a lower ("squeezed") lifestyle in the future.

The Second Income

A second problem is assuming that the answer to this squeeze is more income. To generate more income, the typical decision is to put the wife to work. But usually, when the wife goes to work the couple spends as if they are taking home the total additional salary.

Many times I have asked a working wife what she earns, and she answers fifteen or twenty thousand dollars. She does not think in terms of after-tax and after-expense dollars. Then, when she spends the fifteen or twenty thousand dollars and has not made provision for additional taxes and expenses, the family goes into debt to pay those taxes — and the vicious debt cycle starts all over. Despite added income, debt still straps their living ability.

The Dream House Nightmare

The third specific problem contributing to excessive living expenses is buying too much house too early. It is the American dream to own a home, but today, many couples are not willing to wait until their "dream" fits their income. The best advice is, if you can't afford it, rent for a few years.

Several years ago, I compared the cost of renting to that of buying a home. If a person does not live in a home for at least two or three years, renting is just as good as buying in most situations, in terms of how it affects cash flow. It is imprudent stewardship to purchase a home by spending more than he is making.

We need to buy homes that fit our incomes and not accept the world's lure to "let our income grow into it." That stretch puts us in a position where any emergency resumes the squeeze cycle.

Haphazard Spending

The fourth problem that plagues middle income Americans is failing to plan to control living expenses. When income is lower, the need for a detailed, workable budget is critical to insure that they live within their means and not go into debt. (Of course, those with larger incomes need to plan, too.) A simple truth I have observed is that without a plan, people in any income level will spend more than they earn.

To avoid this financial struggle, middle income families must be committed to living within their means. The Bible has this word of encouragement: "And my God shall supply all your needs according to His riches in glory in Christ Jesus" (Philippians 4:19, NAS).

In other words, God is in the business of meeting our needs. Christians who find themselves in the middle income level must take Him at His word and live within their means, realizing He will indeed meet their *needs* — if not all of their *wants*. Living within an income will lead to financial freedom and, very possibly, a higher lifestyle in the future.

*"So if you have not been trustworthy in handling
worldly wealth, who will trust you with true riches?"*
Luke 16:11

_____ *69*

STRAIGHT TALK ABOUT INVESTING
(One man's "bull" can be another man's "bear")

Horace Holley

The man I was talking with was very discouraged. A young professional in the early stages of his career at age twenty-six, he was plagued by ever-present budget pressures. He was particularly concerned with the very slow growth of personal savings and an inability to afford replacing his aging automobile.

His living expenses were not excessive. Even in a time when so-called "yuppies" are so obsessed with materialistic status, this young man was a financial conservative in every way. He had no debts and was determined to be a good steward of the resources God had given him to manage.

As we talked, the reason for his budgetary stress became clear. His company had a retirement program that provided matching funds for a portion of his own contributions. Intrigued by the immediate return generated by his employer's contributions, as well as receiving deferral of taxes on the portion he put into the fund, he had signed up for the maximum allowable deduction.

He saw the plan as a great "investment," and from a purely numerical point of view, he was correct. His problem, however, was a misunderstanding of financial priorities.

Funds placed in a tax-deferred retirement plan are not available, without paying a penalty, until age fifty-nine-and-a-half. For this twenty-six-year-old, it would be thirty-three years before the funds became available without paying a significant penalty—along with taxes due. In the meantime, he would have to meet living expenses, finance automobile and home purchases, and plan for marriage and children.

Was investing for retirement wrong for him? No. But he had failed to take into account short-range financial objectives that should be considered before investing for long-range purposes. His investment strategy was simply to gain employer contributions and save on taxes, not to meet prioritized financial goals. For the Christian, investing should always be done according to a plan for achieving goals God has for that particular individual.

One basic principle for sound investing is that *it should always be done from surplus funds*. But what is a surplus? That's what you have when taxes have been paid, you are debt-free (home mortgage debt excluded), living expenses are being met, you have given all that you believe God would have you give to various charitable causes, and there is still money left over.

The first priority for the surplus is to build an adequate savings—three to six months of living expenses in the event of an emergency—and to set aside regularly into a fund for depreciating items, such as the next car, appliance replacement, and major repairs. Once this critical foundation is established, you are then ready to consider investing to achieve long-range goals.

At this point, however, it is helpful to pause and evaluate yourself in terms of two major problems that can accompany a financial surplus—greed and pride. To avoid these pitfalls, you should evaluate your *investment attitude* and *investment temperament*.

One way to check *investment attitude* is to ask yourself, "What am I doing—and why am I doing it?" This question helps to detect the most dangerous of wrong financial attitudes: "get-rich-quick." A symptom of this attitude is getting into something you know nothing about and investing funds (or time) you cannot afford to invest, with the idea that you will make money quickly and then get out of it, living happily ever after. These often are investments that are sold on emotional appeal rather than economic substance. You usually invest in the sizzle instead of the steak.

Newspapers frequently carry articles about investors trying to recover losses from an investment opportunity that was just too good to be true. Unfortunately, Christians are not immune from such traps, and most who try to get rich quick only get poor quicker. Proverbs 23:4, 5 offers this caution: "Do not weary yourself to gain wealth, cease from your consideration of it. When you set your eyes on it, it is gone. For wealth certainly makes itself wings, like an eagle that flies toward the heavens," (NAS).

Most people tend to operate at extremes. In fact, Dr. Howard Hendricks says the only person he ever saw in balance was the one going through the middle as he moved from one extreme to the other. For that reason, God has provided an invaluable resource for performing an investment attitude checkup—He calls them husbands and wives. In God's plan, one of the purposes of the spouse is to neutralize our tendency toward extremes, provided we share our plans with our partners and intend to benefit from the balance they can provide.

Often I have counseled with men suffering from business or investment losses who admitted they did not seek counsel from their wives because they "don't understand anything about business or investments." But even if a wife does not understand the technical details of a situation, she usually understands her husband and will be uniquely able to discern his underlying attitude or motivation—particularly when his proposed actions put her home and family in jeopardy.

A friend of mine is a great salesman for a very technical product. Once, I made a sales call with him and was amazed at his ability to explain complex concepts to non-technical people. His secret, he explained, was to never make a sales presentation until he had first presented the product to his wife and she understood what he was talking about. Applying that principle to investments, if you can't adequately explain an investment opportunity to your wife, she may not be the only one who doesn't understand.

What about your *investment temperament?* Stated another way, how well do you handle risk? Do you understand market volatility? Investors got a hands-on lesson on October 19, 1987, when the Dow Jones Index plummeted more than five hundred points in one day. Many investors that day discovered they could not handle the losses they faced. As I received calls that afternoon and during the days that followed, I was surprised to see how some men who had appeared to be so spiritually sound became distraught when their material wealth was threatened.

One professional investment manager offers this advice: If he wakes up at night thinking about a certain investment, he sells it immediately the next morning. He values the peace in his life that only God can give and will allow nothing to compete with that peace.

Many times I ask people I am counseling how they feel about having their funds invested in specific stocks or mutual funds. If they express any doubt, I suggest that they switch to an insured certificate of deposit or other government instrument. Usually, they show relief that confirms such a move would be a good one for them. The rewards may not be as great, but the risk is minimal. I have not counseled anyone who would knowingly sacrifice inner peace for a hope of monetary reward.

If we are investing from a goal-oriented financial foundation and with the right attitude, it should be easy to observe another investment rule: *Do not invest what you cannot afford to lose.* No one plans to make a bad investment. Although it's good to think positive, consider the cost of a loss before calculating how much an investment may earn for you. If an investment is being made from "investment funds," the loss of that investment should not affect your daily living at all. For that reason, your home should not be considered an investment—it's your home. And you don't want to borrow against your home to fund an investment unless you are willing to accept the possible loss of the home. Don't borrow to invest; if you have to borrow money to invest, you can't afford to lose.

One final guideline for investments: *Stay with what you know.* If you don't understand what you are planning to invest in, stay out until you have had time to learn about it. Many investments are made based on what someone else did. A good friend tells you about his great investment; it sounds good, and it worked for him. A word to the wise: If you hurry, you can probably buy just in time to absorb the loss.

Don't be afraid to ask questions. Where did he get his information, and how much does he know about the investment? Is he a professional investment analyst? If he were a doctor, would you trust him to remove your appendix? I've learned that for every piece of good advice, there seems to be ten times as much bad advice. Make sure your investments fit your short-term and long-term goals, along with your ability to analyze and manage.

These principles may seem obvious, but it's usually the violation of the basics that causes so much heartache and loss. If you follow the principles I've covered, I'm not sure how much money you will make, but I'm sure you will minimize the risk of loss. And you'll have peace in the process!

*"So if you have not been trustworthy in handling
worldly wealth, who will trust you with true riches?"*
Luke 16:11

70

GOD OWNS HIS BUSINESS

An interview with Stanley Tam

Although he was an innovator in the reclamation of silver in the photographic process, Stanley Tam of Lima, Ohio, is best known for his commitment to Jesus Christ. A large sign adorning the home of United States Plastic Corporation proclaims "Christ Is the Answer," and Tam's widely read book, *God Owns My Business*, describes how he arrived at the conviction that he should legally make God the literal owner of his business.

Tam, who has traveled throughout the country and world to testify about his Christian faith, is one who is willing to "put his money where his mouth is." Although his business success could have made him a millionaire many times over, he and his wife, Juanita, draw only modest salaries from U.S. Plastics. All profits are channeled through the Stanita Foundation, with those funds designated for a variety of Christian ministries, primarily overseas missions.

In the following interview the seventy-five-year-old Tam talks about his determination to make Jesus Christ the central focus of his life and business.

Many Christians wrestle with the question of whether they should tithe, which is generally regarded as paying 10 percent of personal income to the Lord's work. Yet years ago, you reached

the conviction that God wanted you to give far more than that. How did that come about?

First of all, I must emphasize that I don't believe anyone should use me as an example. I must live Stanley Tam's life, being obedient to the directives I feel God gives me, and everyone else must live their own lives, being equally obedient to the priorities God asks of them.

For me, all I can say is that the Lord led me over a period of time to give increasing amounts of my income. I have always tithed, from the time I became a Christian at the age of eighteen. A few years later, I felt led to increase the amount of my giving to 15 percent, and then in 1940 I felt clearly directed by God to literally make Him my Senior Partner. That meant giving 51 percent of my earnings to His work. That still did not amount to a lot, since my company's gross sales only totaled twelve thousand dollars a year, and I was only drawing a salary of fourteen dollars a week.

How did you go about making God your senior partner in a literal sense?

From 1940 to 1952, I maintained a self-declared trust, recognizing it as a contract between me and God. Then in 1952, my wife and I established the Stanita Foundation (the name resulting from the combination of Stanley and Juanita) through which company profits would be channeled and directed to help fund missions around the world and in the United States.

A point came, though, when you recognized the Lord as more than your partner.

Yes, in the fall of 1954, I was speaking at a revival meeting in Medellin, Colombia when God confronted me in a supernatural way. At the close of my talk, people began responding in a magnificently spontaneous way, but the Lord began directly speaking to me through my thoughts. At that point, He let me know He wanted me to turn the business over to Him completely and become His employee. So, on January 15, 1955, I ceased being a stockholder in either of my companies, States Smelting and Refining Corporation or United States Plastic Corporation.

As you pointed out, God works differently in each of our lives, so we cannot presume that His plan for you is the same for each of us. But why do you think the Lord made such an unusual request?

I have always enjoyed making money, and God knew that. Had He left me undisturbed in this area, I could have become a proud, materialistic, self-centered spiritual misfit. In asking of me the submission of the greatest drive of my life, He removed a blighting influence and replaced it with an inner peace and satisfaction such as I could never have known otherwise.

Inner peace and satisfaction by giving away most of your company's profits — that certainly doesn't seem to fit in today's society.

It does if you recognize that a person's soul is the thing of greatest value in all the world. And if it is true that only spiritual things are eternal, it makes sense to use the profits of a business to win others to Christ.

Jesus told us in Matthew 6:20 to "lay up for yourselves treasures in heaven," (NAS) so really the only difference is where we are depositing our money. It is said that "you can't take it with you," and it's true — unless you send it on ahead. In 1952, I was in Korea to speak to a number of churches. During that time, the Lord impressed on me Psalm 2:8, "Ask of me, and I will make the nations your inheritance, and the ends of the earth your possession."

My prayer was to ask God that I would be used in His harvest field, and as my burden for lost souls has grown, so has my business, so I have been able to do more.

How much of a financial commitment are you making to God's work around the world?

In 1988, we committed about $1.5 million to foreign missions and to help fund Christian work in the United States through our foundation.

With the sign on the outside of your building proclaiming "Christ Is the Answer" and your commitment to devote business

proceeds to reaching people for the Lord, you don't seem to see a distinction between your Christian and secular pursuits.

We built our business on the promise in Matthew 6:33, "But seek first His kingdom and His righteousness; and all these things shall be added to you," (NAS). I don't think there is such a thing as a part-time Christian; we are all in full-time ministry. We each need to ask God to take our vocation and make it a ministry. And if we ask Him, He will do it.

You're 73 now. Do you have any goals that you have yet to achieve?

Mainly, I want to do more of the same. But I do have three goals I hope to reach before I die. I want to have talked to one million people about Christ during my lifetime. In forty-five years, I believe I have spoken to about six hundred thousand. I also want to see one year in which we are able to invest $2 million in foreign missions. The best we've been able to do so far is $1.7 million.

And third, I'm asking God to see three people a day commit their lives to Him through our various business mailings. We publish two catalogs and send out two million each year, along with about one hundred and twenty thousand product shipments. We always include literature that gives a clear presentation of the gospel message. Responses to our non-denominational Bible study course indicate that, each year, more than seven hundred people receive Christ as Savior and Lord through our communications.

To some, that may sound like counting spiritual scalps. I hope it doesn't, because I know that God's greater goal is that none should perish, and I just want to participate in that.

*"So if you have not been trustworthy in handling
worldly wealth, who will trust you with true riches?"*
Luke 16:11

71

MAKING THE PIECES FIT
(How to be sure your giving is
a worthwhile investment)

James E. Hindle, Jr.

The scriptural principle concerning giving is a paradox. God states
that He owns everything (see 1 Chronicles 29:11–12 and Colossians 1:16), yet He commands us to give to Him according to how He
has prospered us (see 1 Corinthians 16:2). We can conclude that if giving is not for God's benefit — since He owns it all anyway — it must be
for our benefit. How, then, is giving beneficial to us and what are some
practical guidelines?

Let's look at the guidelines first. In Old Testament times, God had a
requirement for giving called "tithing." In the New Testament, however,
the Lord indicates that Christian giving is voluntary and a test of sincer-
ity and love, in contrast to the law which was a divine requirement. God
has given His church the freedom to determine how much to give and
where to give.

The anchor passage in the New Testament which answers the questions about tithing — who, what, when, why, how, and where — is 1 Corinthians 16:1–2: "Now about the collection for God's people. Do what I
told the Galatian churches to do. On the first day of every week, each of
you should set aside a sum of money in keeping with his income, saving
it up, so that when I come no collections will have to be made."

- Who? Each of us.
- When? Regularly, on the first day of the week.
- What? Money or "first fruits."
- How? Based on ability, in keeping with income, as was planned.
- Why? God commands it.
- Where? Give to God's people.

Most Christians would not argue with the who, when, what, how, and why of giving, but many would disagree on the "where." In this article, giving is viewed as synonymous with eternal investing. The Bible has much to say about where our giving/eternal investing should go, but let's first look at the stages of giving/investing.

Giving/eternal investing stages can best be illustrated by two circles representing all charitable giving and all investing. Giving/investment habits vary significantly as our relationship with God matures. For instance, an unbeliever's giving and investment habits can best be pictured by the two circles below:

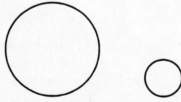

I have had many clients whose charitable giving was negligible, while their investing was substantial. Charitable giving to *any* cause was overshadowed by the need to pile up dollars for the uncertain future.

A second stage, when a person commits his life to Christ and realizes there is a divine command to return to God a portion of what he has received, can be seen as two circles where the dollar amount for giving may remain the same as prior to conversion, but now the dollars are being invested for eternal purposes, represented by the areas where the circles intersect.

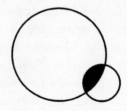

As a believer grows in his walk with God, giving/investing becomes greater in amount and higher in priority—the third stage. He personalizes Matt. 6:19–21, which says, "Do not store up for yourselves treasures on earth, where moth and rust destroy, and where thieves break in and steal. But store up for yourselves treasures in heaven, where moth and rust do not destroy, and where thieves do not break in and steal. *For where your treasure is, there your heart will be also*," (emphasis added). He sees that heart and treasure go together. The giving circle gets larger, and the area of intersection (eternal investing) also expands.

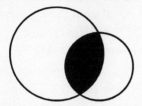

In the final stage, the mature believer, who has gone through the financial planning process and has structured his finances and provides for his family's basic needs, develops the attitude not of "How much do I give?" but "How little do I keep for myself so I can give more away?" This can be illustrated as follows:

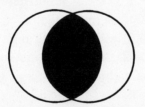

So *where* should our eternal investments be made? First, let's look at verses in Romans and 1 Corinthians. Romans 15:26–27 says, "For Macedonia and Achaia were pleased to make a contribution for the poor among the saints in Jerusalem. They were pleased to do it, and indeed they owe it to them. For if the Gentiles have shared in the Jews' spiritual blessings, they owe it to the Jews to share with them their material blessings." And 1 Corinthians 9:11–12 states,"If we have sown spiritual seed among you, is it too much if we reap a material harvest from you? If others have this right of support from you, shouldn't we have it all the more?" These verses tell us that if we *take* from a ministry by receiving spiritual blessings, then we *owe* our support to that ministry.

Let's compare our giving/investing with the evangelistic target in Acts 1:8 — "Jerusalem, and in all Judea and Samaria, and to the ends of the earth." In our walk with God, many ministries affect our lives and influence our growth. Most notably would be where we go to worship God — the local church. Obviously, one does not have to go to his local church to worship, but the local church provides a building for worship, utilities for comfort, a pastor who imparts lessons from God's Word which we can apply to our everyday lives, support for missionaries to reach out to the unsaved world, and fellowship and corporate prayer.

For many people, the local church represents the only ministry that moves them a step further down the road to spiritual maturity. Therefore, a majority of their giving/eternal investing should be aimed toward "repaying their debt" for blessings they have received. This is their "Jerusalem." Any ministry which benefits a person or family while challenging them to move toward getting to know God better is a candidate for being a "Jerusalem" ministry.

Other people are influenced spiritually not only by the local church but also by other ministries. These ministries enable them to advance further in their walk with God. These might include Christian education and Christian radio and TV. Other ministries may help people get to know God better, assist them in realigning priorities, being stretched spiritually (see Isaiah 54:2) and enlarging their territory (see 1 Chronicles 4:10), such as CBMC and the Navigators. These would be their "Judea and Samaria," ministries that benefit/affect to a lesser degree than "Jerusalem" ministries.

It may well be that one person's priorities for giving may not match another person's priority order. One may get more benefits from a ministry such as CBMC than he does from his local church. Under this system, a proper priority would be to eternally invest more in CBMC than the local church. Care must be taken, therefore, to ascertain which ministries affect a person and his family more than others.

Besides giving/investing to areas where we take spiritual benefits, we also should give to ministries that have been impressed on our hearts even if we receive no direct spiritual blessings. For example, we may be sensitive to a counseling ministry or a caring ministry for the poor. God not only gave us a heart with a God-shaped vacuum to be filled by

Christ, but when Christ came in He also gave us a new heart with a desire to care for others.

What about charitable organizations that are not Christian ministries — such as United Way, the Cancer Society, and Heart Fund? Our families may benefit from one or more of these organizations, so if we receive benefits, we should participate in their support. But those causes also receive the support of unbelievers who would not support Christian ministries, so our foremost priority should be supporting those organizations which further the cause of Christ.

In Acts 10:1–5, we see an excellent example of a man who understood the principle of giving/eternal investing. Cornelius gave generously to those in need and God rewarded him for it. As we likewise are generous in giving to those in need (which includes almost all Christian organizations), the Lord also will reward us.

The rich rule over the poor, and the borrower is servant to the lender.

Proverbs 22:7

72

WHEN THE BOOM WENT BUST

Richard T. Case

When it comes to handling finances, I was considered the expert. For years I had taught seminars on money management; I even wrote a book about it. How, then, did I suddenly find myself more than two hundred and fifty thousand dollars in debt and on the brink of bankruptcy?

My critical mistake was simple: As a teacher, I had proved to be my own worst pupil. Since becoming a Christian about sixteen years ago, I had found the Bible, more than any other book, to be the ultimate reference for proven financial principles. Repeatedly the Bible cautions against borrowing, warning against the pitfalls of becoming "surety" for unsecured debts. In my book I had written quite clearly, "Don't borrow for investments." Yet when presented with opportunities to invest in what seemed like fail-safe real estate projects, I fell victim to the "do-as-I-say-not-as-I-do" syndrome.

It was in 1982. While much of the nation was slowly recovering from the recession of the late 1970s, the economy in Dallas remained as strong as ever. Texas was a hot real estate market — it looked like nothing but gold.

I was doing full-time management consulting at the time and, while serving on the board of directors for one development company, I had watched the developer make a lot of money. It seemed so easy. Before long I was invited to join with some other investors in building a forty thousand square foot office building. The project was very profitable and, having done it once, I decided to get involved in real estate on a much more ambitious scale. With other investors, I set up limited partnerships to develop office buildings. Our goal was to sell them in the booming Texas market, making a large profit in the process.

I began to sign for a number of the loans, making myself personally liable for them, but to be honest, I didn't think I was compromising my Biblical standards. Even if the projects didn't do well, I rationalized, the asset value of the real estate would cover the loans. At worst I would break even. It never occurred to me that the Dallas economy could go bad, drastically reducing the real estate values.

In a sense, I felt I was pursuing my real estate ventures "for God." I planned to use a lot of the proceeds to help support Christian work and just presumed the Lord would reward my efforts. While I was "expanding" my career, I remained very active spiritually — reading my Bible every day, being involved in Christian Business Men's Committee activities, and teaching a Sunday school class. And I had bought into a popular theology that if you are spiritual, God will bless you materially.

After that first project, however, things began to turn sour. Our second venture was a loser almost from the beginning. At that point, my partners and I could have gotten out and avoided any big losses, but I was like the man at the gambling table who keeps at it, even though he's losing ground, expecting things to start going his way. I kept thinking, "I'm going to make it. The next project is really going to make some money."

The third real estate project, a thirty-two-thousand-square foot office building, did fairly well, and I was encouraged, but about the time I got involved in my fourth and fifth projects — a sixty-thousand-square foot office complex and a land deal where I had planned another development — the whole market in Dallas just went to pot. In 1985, within just a matter of months, the great demand for office space simply evaporated. At that point, it was far too late to turn back.

Eventually everything was lost. The two buildings that were profitable had to be sold at cost. My bank foreclosed on the second project, and we negotiated a settlement that left me owing one hundred thousand. The other two ventures also went to foreclosure, leaving me with substantial additional debts that are still being resolved with the banks.

The problems over the past three years have been the most painful of my life, but as God declared in Jeremiah 29:11, "I know the plans that I have for you, . . . plans for welfare and not for calamity, to give you a future and a hope," (NAS). I'm not sure how this situation will work out ultimately, but God has taught me some important things I could not have learned in one of my seminars.

First of all, Jesus taught that "you cannot serve both God and money" (Matthew 6:24), but I guess I was trying to prove that you can. I would have denied it at the time, but my primary motive for getting involved in real estate was greed. There's no other explanation for it—I simply wanted to get richer. I saw people all around me making lots of money, and I concluded that if God really loved me, He would help me to do the same. Basically, I was ignoring what the Scriptures teach about material wealth. The truth is, God loved me too much to let me succeed.

In the fall of 1984, before my projects began to collapse around me, I bought a new Mercedes. Since my office was only three miles from my house, I didn't buy the car because I needed comfortable, dependable transportation. I got it because it fit with the image of prosperity I wanted to present. One day I decided to reconsider that purchase. Over an eight-month period, I had driven the Mercedes four thousand miles. I calculated that, amortizing what I was paying for the car over a four-year period, it was costing me $2.75 per mile to drive—which is very expensive just to enjoy the smell of leather.

Pride was a second problem. Instead of being willing to admit I was having trouble and trying to get out soon enough to really cut my losses, I just hung on, trying to do more to work my way out of the hole. Unfortunately, the more I did, the deeper my hole got, not only for me but for the other investors as well. We all lost substantially.

Even though other people had invested heavily in my projects, I still had no real accountability to anyone. I did not have a group of guys, or even one person, who knew me well enough and cared enough for me to challenge what I was doing. Even when I recognized what I was doing was wrong, I shrugged it off. "God will forgive a little sin like this," I thought. In the Bible we find quite a few people who violated God's laws and still were blessed, so I presumed I could be another one.

God also has used this experience to reaffirm to me what is truly important in life. Our financial problems caused unbelievable emotional distress for my wife, Linda. She had been against my getting involved in real estate from the beginning, knowing (better than I did) that I couldn't be a good management consultant and real estate developer at the same time.

My children showed that they had a better perspective on material possessions than I did. When things began getting tight and we started losing some of the nice things we had acquired, they said, "We never wanted those things anyway, Daddy. We just want you." Even when Linda and I were at the point of despair, the kids' faith was strong and kept us going.

My daughter, Michelle, who is our creative writer, would slip notes under our bedroom door at night. She would write, "Daddy, God is with you." "Daddy, don't give up." "Daddy, don't worry about it. We love you."

Adversity generally has one of two effects on a family. It either pushes them apart, or pulls them closer together. It pulled us together, closer than ever. Linda and I spent countless hours together, reading the Bible and praying. She was a phenomenal source of support for me.

Even though we were going through a bottom point financially, that was not the case spiritually. God has used those circumstances to strip away the superficial things in my life, impressing upon me that what He really wants in my life is Him. As time passed, it became clear that the Lord wanted me to relax and let Him again take leadership in my life as I followed His scriptural principles.

That can be hard for someone with an entrepreneurial spirit. It's difficult to give up control, but the fact is, God *is* in control. He wants us to be patient—to wait on Him to do what is best in His timing.

Now when I read the Bible, I pay a lot closer attention since I'm keenly aware of the consequences for not following what it teaches. I've learned a lot the hard way; now I'm hoping to learn in an easier, less painful manner.

There are still some struggles, in addition to the financial obligations that remain. Even though I know God has forgiven me, it's hard to let myself off the hook. Sometimes I can't help thinking, "I'm not supposed to fail. I'm a Christian leader, a successful businessman. I've lost a lot of money, and I've angered some people who were counting on me."

But I've concluded that all God expects of me is to be His man for today — and not to fear the future. He has promised, "I will never leave you nor forsake you," and I can't think of any greater assurance than that. As a teacher and consultant, I've had to learn some tough lessons by enrolling in the so-called School of Hard Knocks, but I'm thankful for my "post-graduate study." Sometimes failure is a better instructor than success.

The rich rule over the poor, and the borrower is servant to the lender.

Proverbs 22:7

73

GETTING OUT AND STAYING OUT

An Interview with Larry Burkett

S ince establishing the Christian Financial Concepts ministry in 1976, Larry Burkett has become a recognized authority on personal and family financial planning. His syndicated radio program, *Money Matters,* is aired on seven hundred and fifty stations and heard daily by nearly one million people. That audience is expected to triple with the creation of a new, half-hour live call-in program to be broadcast weekdays from 3:30 to 4:00 P.M. EST on stations across America.

Burkett also is a popular seminar and conference speaker, and the author of more than ten books and practical workbooks on money management. The most recent book is, *Answers to Your Family's Financial Questions.* His column, "Your Money in Changing Times," has been a regular feature in CBMC publications since 1984.

In addition to a staff of approximately forty men and women at his Christian Financial Concepts headquarters in Gainesville, Georgia, Burkett directs six men who lead conferences on financial and business management around the United States. An estimated fifteen hundred lay people also have been trained by Burkett's organization to serve as financial counselors within their own churches. His videotapes and training materials are utilized by one hundred and fifty thousand people each year.

To make sure that we are discussing the same thing, please give us your definition of "debt."

That can be a difficult question, because today when we say "debt," it usually means anything you owe for, or that you borrowed money. That's not a good definition. A more accurate definition is an obligation beyond your value—that you owe more than you own.

The Bible does not use the word "debt." The word used in the Scriptures is "surety," which means that you have signed for an obligation without an absolutely certain way to pay for it. You have presumed upon the future. Legally, a debt means that you have borrowed beyond the asset value, and scripturally it means that you have taken on an obligation to pay without having collateralled it properly.

Does that mean, for example, that a home loan for less than the appraised value of the house would not be considered a debt?

Possibly so, but that depends on the economy that you are in. The troubled oil and farming areas would be good examples. People there lost their homes, but had deficiency agreements and were still paying on the houses because they were no longer worth what was owed on them. So the only true way to avoid any form of surety is if the note you have guarantees that the property is collateral and the lender cannot come back against you for any deficiency.

By the way, that is the most commonly violated Biblical principle on finances in America—people who borrow money and are surety for it. If there is a major economic setback, they can easily get wiped out.

What are some other specific principles that you teach about indebtedness?

First of all, let's use the term "borrowing." God's Word does not prohibit borrowing, but it gives great cautions. The *misuse* of credit is the problem in our society. There are three general Biblical principles about borrowing, and if we followed those we would never have a problem.

Number one, never do it needlessly. Second, never sign surety or personally endorse a note encumbering things that are already paid for to buy something else. The third principle is, never borrow long-term.

There is never any indebtedness shown in the Scriptures for God's people that should extend more than seven years.

Explain the dangers of long-term borrowing.

Even the most successful man in the world, if he continues to borrow and co-signs notes against all of his other collateral, will eventually hit a bad economy and lose everything. It's just a matter of time. We've built an economy around indebtedness — if you eventually exceed the amount you can borrow for a short period of time, what's the logical extension? To string it out for a longer period of time. Now we're up to forty year loans; eventually that's going to all stop. You can't do that forever.

The Bible taught that after every forty-ninth year there was to be a "year of jubilee," in which the whole economy recycled. Interestingly, that cycle is pretty much verified by the economy of the world. About every fifty to sixty years, there is a major rescinding of all indebtedness — we call it a depression. In America, we think we can beat the odds, but as the scare of October 19 showed us last year, it doesn't take very much to set our economy off.

What should a person do, then, if he already is committed to long-term debt, such as in building a business?

Obviously, most of us can't get out of debt this year in a business, but the question is, do you have a plan to *ever* get out of debt? If you're always in debt, you're going to be wiped out. The principle the Scriptures teach is this: you may have to go into debt during a bad cycle, but during a good cycle, pay off your debts and build a surplus. A proverb says, "I entered the dwelling of a wise man and therein I found precious oil, but I entered the dwelling of a fool and found the cupboards were bare."

I would advise any Christian businessman that if he is borrowing to get into a business, and probably he's going to, make a plan — a long-range goal — to get out of debt totally. He may not be able to do that in one year, or five years, or ten years, but he ought to have that as a goal. If he doesn't have that as a goal, he will just keep expanding on debt. We see it all the time — a business that could be debt-free borrows to be bigger, and then hits a downturn and loses everything, when it could have remained smaller and debt-free — and survived.

So the thing to do is decide, "If God gives me the ability, I'm going to be debt-free." To do that requires a commitment to freeing some surplus to pay off his debt. At some point you have to say, "That's enough. I'm not going to get any bigger or build another plant. I'm going to pay this one off." I know thousands of businessmen who don't owe anyone a dime. That even includes some car dealers, who buy every car on the lot with cash. A bad economy may not help them, but it won't wipe them out.

Looking at indebtedness — or borrowing — from an individual perspective, is there a basic pattern that takes place?

Consumer debt almost always begins with the purchase of a home, one that is more expensive than a family can afford. Usually a couple, in their first three years of marriage, try to duplicate what their parents took thirty years to accumulate.

The second — and over a lifetime, biggest — purchase is the automobile. Typically, young couples spend far too much for automobiles. They buy new cars because of creative financing.

But I think the thing that ultimately is going to sink our whole economy are loans equivalent to home equity loans. We changed the tax laws in 1986 and made all consumer loan interest non-deductible except home equity loans. I believe that was done purposely. We are so dependent upon borrowing that equity was the last big slug of credit available to the consumer, so the tax laws were changed making no other loans deductible to encourage people to borrow against their homes. The largest expansion in consumer credit ever in history was the amount of home equity loans taken out in 1987.

The difficulty with those loans is that there is a high origination and maintenance fee: One thousand to fifteen hundred to get the loan and five hundred to one thousand a year to keep it going. Secondly, there is a floating interest rate, no fixed rate mortgages on home equity loans. And third, it's a demand note payable in thirty days. So it's just like a ticking time bomb, for the bank as well as the consumer. What happens when the consumer reaches the point where it's impossible to borrow anymore? What do we do then?

You're presenting a bleak projection for the future of the economy.

I think so, long-term. Not short-term, but over the long run you cannot build a debt economy as we have without paying the price. No one else in history has ever done it.

What about credit cards? You recommend to people in debt that they destroy their credit cards, don't you?

The difficulty with credit cards normally lies with middle and low-income families, because they use credit cards to buy consumables — food, clothes, toys, vacations, those kinds of things — and with a credit card you can borrow far beyond any family's reasonable ability to pay back. The credit card company, on the bottom line, does not want the loan paid back. They want consumers to maintain the loan at the maximum rate and pay interest only. Twenty percent is a good rate of interest.

Now I know some people use a credit card as a substitute for cash. The people who use it with discipline will stay within their budget and pay it off every month. But families who go beyond their budget with a credit card end up buying something that's too expensive for them. When they do that, they don't avoid the decision that they couldn't afford it — they delay it.

What are some helpful guidelines for using credit cards?

I advise young couples that if they observe three rules for credit cards, they'll never have a problem with them. First, never buy anything on a credit card that's not in your budget for the month. Second, pay your credit cards off every month. And third, the first month you find that you can't pay your credit cards off, make a vow to God that you'll destroy them and never use them again. It's not the cards that are the problem, it's the fact that they encourage indulgences.

What is your advice to people who are in debt and desperate to get out?

Number one, they have to *get a realistic picture of what is costs them to live.* The way they can do that is by reviewing their checkbook for the

last year and dividing it into categories. I have prepared a little budget
guide that breaks down every spending category.

Sometimes people don't know where they stand because they use
cash, so I recommend to a couple that they use a diary for about thirty
days so they can keep track of miscellaneous spending, like eating out,
going to movies, things that ordinarily wouldn't appear in a checking
account.

You have to average in non-monthly things, like annual insurance
payments, clothing, and vacations. Once they write all that down and get
an accurate picture of what it costs them to live, the bottom line is
they're probably spending more than they make.

Then they have to face some realistic decisions. The first decision
is, *no more borrowing, no matter what.* That means getting rid of the
credit cards, no more family loans, no consolidation loans, no more borrowing from the church. They've got to decide, "I'm going to live on
what I make. If God doesn't provide it, I'll do without it."

The next step is to make a list of all their creditors, and look at their
budget realistically to *determine how much they can pay on their total
indebtedness each month.* Let's assume that they can only pay half of
what was promised—that's not unusual with the couples I have counseled with. They were robbing from one creditor to pay another creditor
each month. They need to write each one and say, "I'm sorry. I haven't
been honest with you. I can't pay what I promised to pay you. This is all
I have, here's my budget and a list of my creditors, and I ask you to
work with me." There are only two choices that a creditor has—either to
work with them or force them into bankruptcy.

Once they have made the commitment that says, "Okay, no more
borrowing. I'm not going to get further into debt, and I've been honest
and am going to pay my creditors what I can," then they need to *start
working on the smallest bill.* When additional money comes in—and
almost everybody during a year has what I call "windfall profit" of
some sort, and typically if you don't exert financial discipline, you just
spend that money—commit that money to repayment of debt.

They need *to stick to the plan for two-and-a-half years,* and anytime
they have surplus money, put it on the smallest bill until that is paid off,
and then put it on the next smallest bill. I've never counseled a family

that was in debt, except for a major investment or business that was lost, where they haven't been totally debt-free — except for their home — in two years. Now I get letters from families who have even paid their homes off, and they once were so far in debt they couldn't make it.

The rich rule over the poor, and the borrower is servant to the lender.

Proverbs 22:7

74

BREAKING THE LEVERAGE HABIT

Robert S. Dervaes

U ntil the late 1970s, if you had asked me to explain my philosophy of financial management, I could have summed it up with one word: leverage.

Through my economics courses at Carnegie Institute of Technology, and then in our family business, the A.R. Dervaes Company in Wilmington, Delaware, I became an astute practitioner of the Principle of OPM (Other People's Money). And it seemed to work. After three years with the Westinghouse Corporation, I joined my father's company in 1967. Over the next decade, we saw the business expand from seven to one hundred employees, primarily through credit and speculation on future profits.

I liked the principle so well I applied it to my personal finances as well. I invested in real estate, business developments, restaurants, and apartments, with each venture being highly leveraged. I also maintained an expensive lifestyle, buying a big home, nice cars and taking elaborate vacations. It was fun.

Unfortunately, the recession of the late 1970s showed me that those who live by leverage can also perish by leverage. The prime rate soared from around 8 percent to 21 1/2 percent, pushing the interest rate on our seven-figure business loan to 24 percent. Obviously, the consequences to

371

our family's company were disastrous. The business collapsed on its shaky underpinnings.

My personal finances suffered a similar reversal. It was quite a shock to suddenly realize my personal interest payments alone amounted to more than my salary. My indebtedness overall was in the middle six figures. The pressure I endured during that time was intense, but I'm thankful for it because it caused me to recognize a basic fact of life: *I was not in control.* That discovery eventually resulted in my encounter with the One who is in control: Jesus Christ.

After becoming a Christian in 1981, I began avidly reading the Bible. That literally turned my life around as I determined to follow its principles, particularly those related to money. Two things helped me to apply the Biblical teachings in my life: a "Business By the Book" seminar presented by Larry Burkett, which taught financial principles for operating a business, and becoming involved in a CBMC "Caleb" group — men who meet monthly to study the mind of God relative to finances.

In 1985, I prayed to God, committing to — with His help — become totally debt-free. That thought in itself was revolutionary, not only because of my own history but also because everything in our society seems keyed to the concept of borrowing. And at that point, at age forty-three, I calculated that I would not become free of debt until I was 110 years old if I continued to pay on my obligations at the current rate.

But I felt that was what God wanted me to do. Romans 13:8 says, "Let no debt remain outstanding, except the continuing debt to love one another. . . ." I decided that (1) I needed to establish a time frame, giving me a specific goal to work toward, and (2) that timetable should be well short of anything I could possibly accomplish on my own, so I would know that God had done it, not me. So I set a goal of being debt-free within ten years (quite a drop from almost seventy).

Interestingly, once I made that commitment, God began to turn my life around financially. Sales increased unexpectedly at Depsco Services Inc., an industrial machine shop I had acquired in Baltimore in 1980, while costs declined substantially — also unanticipated. In 1986 I accepted an opportunity to sell the company, which significantly reduced my indebtedness. Not long afterward, I was offered a job with Generic Business Solutions, selling computer systems to businesses. My income has allowed me to continue hammering away at that debt total.

Today, I'm still in debt, but the amount I owe has been reduced by more than 50 percent, less than three years after committing to become debt-free. I believe God will enable me to reach my goal well ahead of my ten-year timetable.

I'm not a proponent of the "God-wants-me-to-be-rich" prosperity theology, but I do believe that *when we are in debt, we limit the Lord's ability to work in and through our lives.* Obviously, when we owe money, that means we must give our money to the bankers rather than for the Lord's work. It also restricts our mobility if God wants us to go elsewhere, especially if the job would pay less.

As I have read the Bible, I have discovered a number of key truths. God wants our complete commitment. In 2 Chronicles 16:9 it says, "For the eyes of the LORD range throughout the earth to strengthen those whose hearts are *fully committed* to Him," (emphasis added).

In the Bible, God also says that if we trust Him in every area of our lives, He will meet all of our needs. In Matthew 6:33, Jesus Christ said, "But seek first his [God's] kingdom and his righteousness, and all these things [our needs] will be given to you as well." Philippians 4:19 promises, "And my God will meet all your needs according to his glorious riches in Christ Jesus." Those verses give me the assurance that, as I work to eliminate my debt, God will continue to provide the food, clothes and other needs I have.

As Psalm 37:4 says, "Delight yourself in the LORD and he will give you the desires of your heart."

The rich rule over the poor, and the borrower is servant to the lender.

Proverbs 22:7

75

PERSONAL FINANCES: A BLESSING OR A CURSE?

James E. Hindle, Jr.

W here does my money go? How do I pay off my credit card debt? How can I be a good steward when there is more month than there is money?

These are valid questions for Christians as well as people with secular perspectives. Business people who easily manage successful careers and businesses often have much less success in managing their personal resources. One reason for this is a failure to recognize the importance of careful planning. Proper management of personal finances does not happen by accident.

If we are to maintain an effective witness for Christ, it is critically important that we commit ourselves to sound management of personal resources. Time, talents, and money are among the personal resources God gives to us. Properly managed, they can allow us to be a lighthouse to the unsaved world. But if managed improperly, they can be used by Satan to dilute our personal testimonies and inhibit our spiritual growth.

There is no better place to find principles for mastering your finances than in the Bible. In fact, that must be the starting place for the Christian committed to representing God in the marketplace. Dr. Gary Inrig states in his book, *A Call To Excellence*, ". . . when a believer is called to the Lord Jesus Christ, he is also called to excellence, to be the best that he can be for his Savior. The God of excellence calls His people to live lives of excellence which reflect His character to this world . . . there is no room for mediocrity or apathy."

So where do we start? I would suggest some keen insights that are found in the Old Testament book of Haggai. As the Apostle Paul stated in 1 Corinthians 10:11, "These things happened to them [forefathers] as examples and were written down as warnings for us, on whom the fulfillment of the ages has come." We can learn much from the rebuke given to the returning exiles for their delay in rebuilding God's temple and their encouragement to get to work:

- The people needed *prodding*; they were apathetic. "This is what the LORD Almighty says: 'These people say, "The time has not yet come for the LORD's house to be built." ' " (Haggai 1:2)
- The people were told to *plan*. "Now this is what the LORD Almighty says: 'Give careful thought to your ways.' " (Haggai 1:5, 7)
- The people had wrong *priorities*. " 'You expected much, but see, it turned out to be little. What you brought home, I blew away. Why?' declares the LORD Almighty. 'Because of my house, which remains a ruin, while each of you is busy with his own house.' " (Haggai 1:9)
- The people were told to *prepare* (work). "So the LORD stirred up the spirit of Zerubbabel . . . and the spirit of the whole remnant of the people. They came and began to work on the house of the LORD Almighty, their God . . ." (Haggai 1:14)
- When people plan, they are *blessed*. ". . . Give careful thought: Is there yet any seed left in the barn? Until now, the vine and the fig tree, the pomegranate and the olive tree have not borne fruit. From this day on I will bless you." (Haggai 2:18–19)

The process of financial planning begins with data gathering and establishing goals. These are the two most difficult steps in the process.

Data gathering means determining annual income and expenses, as well as listing assets and liabilities. This is time consuming, especially since it usually requires digging through old financial records.

Establishing goals requires evaluating future financial needs and desires, both short-term and long-term, and ranking them in order of preferences. Goals could include planning for retirement, budgeting, savings for children's education, charitable giving, investing, reducing income tax burdens, insurance analysis, and getting out of debt. For the Christian, this also should be done in light of God's purposes for our lives—observing the Great Commandment and the Great Commission.

Let's be honest: When it comes to financial planning, many of us need to be prodded, like the people of Haggai's days. It's not a favorite topic for family discussion. For others, prodding is not the problem; it's realigning priorities to allow for proper planning. This often merits the assistance of a professional who can help in completing a comprehensive financial plan.

So let's admit it, financial planning may not be everyone's idea of fun. But remember God's promise to those who follow His steps from prodding to putting plans into action: "From this day on I will bless you." What better reason do we need to not be mediocre or apathetic?

ABOUT THE AUTHORS

A s of the time *The Complete Christian Businessman* went into production, the contributing authors of the book held the following positions:

- Gordon Adams is Executive Director of Vision Foundation, Inc. in Knoxville, Tennessee.
- Dr. Joseph Aldrich is President of Multnomah School of the Bible in Portland, Oregon.
- Eric Allen is a former Assistant Editor of *CONTACT* magazine and now a graduate student at the University of Georgia in Athens.
- L. Donald Barr is associated with Coopers and Lybrand, Certified Public Accountants in Dallas, Texas.
- John Q. Baucom is a licensed family therapist in Chattanooga, Tennessee.
- Ted Benna is Executive Vice President of the Johnson Companies in Langhorne, Pennsylvania.
- Ronald W. Blue is a CPA and Managing Partner of Ronald Blue and Co. a personal financial planning and management firm based in Atlanta, Georgia, and the author of several books.
- William D. Bontrager heads Shepherds for Peace, speaking on Biblical principles for resolving conflict, based in Ignacio, Colorado.
- Larry Burkett is President of Christian Financial Concepts, a financial counseling and management consulting ministry based in Gainesville, Georgia.
- Dr. Ross Campbell is the head of Southeastern Counseling Center in Chattanooga, Tennessee. He has authored several books.
- Stephen Carley has a private law practice in Atlanta, Georgia.

- Richard T. Case is Chief Operating Officer of Polymedica Industries, Inc. in Wheat Ridge, Colorado.
- Charles Colson is the founder and Chairman of Prison Fellowship Ministries, based in Washington, D.C.
- Jeffrey W. Comment is President and Chief Operating Officer of Helzberg Diamonds, based in Kansas City, Missouri.
- Joe Crawley is Director of AMR Information Services in Fort Worth, Texas.
- Russell D. Crosson is Chief Operating Officer of Ronald Blue and Co., in Atlanta, Georgia.
- Nevius Curtis is Chairman and Chief Executive Officer of Delmarva Power Company in Wilmington, Delaware.
- Fred DeFalco is head of Encouragement Enterprises in Boca Raton, Florida.
- Ted DeMoss is Past President and a member of the national board of directors of Christian Business Men's Committee of USA in Chattanooga, Tennessee.
- Robert S. Dervaes is Senior Vice President for Living Wealth, Inc., a Tampa, Florida corporation.
- Jim Dickerson directs Ashland Home Care Pharmacy in Ashland, Nebraska.
- Philip Downer is President of the Christian Business Men's Committee of USA in Chattanooga, Tennessee.
- Michael Drye has a private law practice in Asheville, North Carolina.
- Jim Dudleston is Managing Partner of The Advisory Group, Inc. in Phoenix, Arizona.
- Tony Eager is Associate Vice President of Coldwell Banker Commercial Real Estate Services in Lincolnshire, Illinois.
- LeRoy Eims is an author of numerous books and Assistant to the General Director of The Navigators in Colorado Springs, Colorado.
- Leighton Ford is President of Leighton Ford Ministries in Charlotte, North Carolina.
- Thomas S. Fortson, Jr., formerly Vice President of Human Resources for the Edwards Baking Co. in Atlanta, Georgia, is Dean of the Atlanta Consortium for Theological Studies, a division of Columbia Bible College and Seminary.
- Joe Glover is President of Learning Technologies in Dallas, Texas.

- Lorin Griset is affiliated with Griset and Coady, an insurance agency in Santa Ana, California.
- Dr. Willard F. Harley directs a network of mental health clinics and chemical dependency programs in Minnesota.
- Dr. Archibald Hart is Dean of the Graduate School of Psychology and a professor of psychology at Fuller Theological Seminary in Pasadena, California, and the author of several books.
- Jim Hartsook is Director of Human Resources for the Atlanta Group of Price Waterhouse in Atlanta, Georgia.
- William Hendricks is Vice President of Career Impact Ministries in Arlington, Texas. He has co-authored several books.
- Walt Henrichsen is an author, speaker, and associate with the Leadership Foundation in El Cajon, California.
- James F. Hind is a management consultant in Knoxville, Tennessee.
- James E. Hindle, Jr. is a partner in the accounting firm of Dulin, Ward, DeWald, Inc. in Fort Wayne, Indiana.
- Clyde Hawkins is President of ServiceMaster Associates, Inc. in Knoxville, Tennessee.
- Horace Holley is a financial counselor with the Christian Counseling Service of Atlanta, Georgia.
- André Iseli heads Iseli Nursery in suburban Portland, Oregon and is Chairman of the Board of Media America.
- Gayle Jackson is a management and data processing consultant with CSI in Atlanta, Georgia.
- Ken Korkow is a staff Metro Director in Omaha, Nebraska for Christian Business Men's Committee.
- Carl H. Lindner, III is a partner in American Financial Corporation and President of Great American Holding Corporation in Cincinnati, Ohio.
- Ken Lutters is Manager of Control and Analysis for Sun Refining and Marketing Co. in Philadelphia, Pennsylvania.
- Colonel Nimrod McNair is Chairman of the Executive Leadership Foundation in Atlanta, Georgia.
- Scott McReynolds is a mortgage banker in Orange, California.
- James McClure is a corporate executive who resides in Lutherville, Maryland.
- Bill Michael is owner of AM Concepts, a steel construction company in Hanover, Pennsylvania.

- Don Mitchell is Director of Quality Network and a member of the corporate training committee for General Motors in Detroit, Michigan.
- Lois Mowday-Rabey is a free-lance writer living in Colorado Springs, Colorado.
- Whipple S. Newell, Jr. is associated with RW Management Company in Houston, Texas.
- Bruce Neuharth is Dean and Director of Operation Training for Burger King University in Miami, Florida.
- Jim Petersen is a member of the executive staff with The Navigators in Colorado Springs, Colorado.
- Tim Philpot is a partner in the law firm of Anggelis, Philpot, Gordon and Simpson in Lexington, Kentucky.
- C. William Pollard is President and Chief Executive Officer of ServiceMaster, Inc. in Chicago, Illinois.
- Randy Schroeder is a banking executive in Houston, Texas.
- Dr. Win Ritchie is an optometrist in Mobile, Alabama.
- Doug Sherman is President of Career Impact Ministries in Arlington, Texas, and co-author of several books.
- Gary Smalley has written many books, is a seminar speaker and President of Today's Family in Phoenix, Arizona.
- Ken Smith is Director of Christian Stewardship Ministries in Fairfax, Virginia.
- Ted Sprague is President of the Atlanta Convention and Visitors Bureau in Atlanta, Georgia.
- Joni Eareckson Tada is an author, artist, speaker, and President of Joni and Friends, a ministry to the disabled in Agoura Hills, California.
- Stanley Tam heads United States Plastics Corporation in Lima, Ohio.
- Robert J. Tamasy is National Director of Publications for the Christian Business Men's Committee of USA in Chattanooga, Tennessee and Editor of *CONTACT* magazine.
- Denis Waitley is an author and seminar speaker from Rancho Santa Fe, California.
- William H. Walton is President of Walton Hotel Corporation in Germantown, Tennessee, and Chairman of the Board Emeritus and Senior Corporate Consultant for Park Inns International.

- Pat Williams is General Manager of the Orlando Magic, a professional basketball team in Orlando, Florida. He and his wife, Jill, have co-authored several books.

ABOUT CBMC

T he Christian Business Men's Committee, established in 1930, consists of more than thirteen thousand business and professional men across the United States. As members of local "committees" or teams in many of the country's cities and towns, they share the common purpose of:

- Presenting Jesus Christ as Savior and Lord to business and professional men (Colossians 1:28–29), and
- Developing Christian business and professional men to carry out the Great Commission (Matthew 28:19–20).

CONTACT magazine is published bimonthly by CBMC of USA, designed to help Christian business and professional men to carry out Christ's Great Commission more effectively in their personal and business lives.

For more information about the CBMC ministry, or to inquire about subscriptions to *CONTACT* magazine, write to: CBMC of USA, P.O. Box 3308, Chattanooga, Tennessee 37404, or call (615) 698–4444.

The typeface for the text of this book is *Times Roman.* In 1930, typographer Stanley Morison joined the staff of *The Times* (London) to supervise design of a typeface for the reformatting of this renowned English daily. Morison had overseen type-library reforms at Cambridge University Press in 1925, but this new task would prove a formidable challenge despite a decade of experience in paleography, calligraphy, and typography. *Times New Roman* was credited as coming from Morison's original pencil renderings in the first years of the 1930s, but the typeface went through numerous changes under the scrutiny of a critical committee of dissatisfied *Times* staffers and editors. The resulting typeface, *Times Roman,* has been called the most used, most successful typeface of this century. The design is of enduring value to English and American printers and publishers, who choose the typeface for its readability and economy when run on today's high-speed presses.

Substantive Editing:
Michael S. Hyatt

Copy Editing:
Darryl F. Winburne

Cover Design:
Steve Diggs & Friends
Nashville, Tennessee

Page Composition:
Xerox Ventura Publisher
Printware 720 IQ Laser Printer

Printing and Binding:
Maple-Vail Book Manufacturing Group,
York, Pennsylvania

Dust Jacket Printing:
Strine Printing Company
York, Pennsylvania